George Sand

and the Nineteenth-Century
Russian Love-Triangle Novels

George Sand
and the Nineteenth-Century Russian Love-Triangle Novels

Dawn D. Eidelman

Lewisburg
Bucknell University Press
London and Toronto: Associated University Presses

Associated University Presses
440 Forsgate Drive
Cranbury, NJ 08512

Associated University Presses
25 Sicilian Avenue
London WC1A 2QH, England

Associated University Presses
P.O. Box 338, Port Credit
Mississauga, Ontario
Canada L5G 4L8

The paper used in this publication meets the requirements
of the American National Standard for Permanence of Paper
for Printed Library Materials Z39.48-1984.

Library of Congress Cataloging-in-Publication Data

Eidelman, Dawn D., 1961–
    George Sand and the nineteenth-century Russian love-triangle
novels / Dawn D. Eidelman.
        p. cm.
    Includes bibliographical references and index.
    ISBN 0-8387-5269-1 (alk. paper)
    1. Russian fiction—19th century—History and criticism. 2. Love
in literature. 3. Women and literature. 4. Sand, George,
1804–1876—Influence. I. Title.
PG3098.L68E37   1994
891.73'309354—dc20   93-48926
                                                          CIP

PRINTED IN THE UNITED STATES OF AMERICA

Contents

List of References in the Text 7

A Note about Translations and Transliterations 9

1. Introduction: Toward an Erotics of Reading 13
2. Women and Fiction: Who is to Blame? 18
3. Jacques, the Enlightened Husband: Narrative
  Desire 29
   Polinka Saks—Alexsandr Druzhinin 38
   "Iakov Pasynkov"—Ivan Turgenev 42
   What is to be Done?—Nikolai Cherny–
    shevskii 48
4. Edmée, the New Woman: Desire for
  Androgyny 64
   Oblomov—Ivan Goncharov 73
   On the Eve—Ivan Turgenev 78
   Crime and Punishment and *The Brothers
    Karamazov*—Fëdor Dostoevskii 83
5. Horace, the Superfluous Rake: Triangulation
  of Desire 93
   Who is to Blame?—Alexandr Herzen 98
   A Common Story—Ivan Goncharov 111
   Rudin—Ivan Turgenev 118
6. The Woman Question: What is to be Done? 130

Notes 146
Select Bibliography 157
Index 171

List of References in the Text

References cited parenthetically throughout this book are to the following primary sources. They are listed here in order of appearance.

Jacques	Sand, George. *Jacques*. Paris: Perrotin, 1842.
Polinka Saks	Druzhinin, Aleksandr Vasil'evich. *Polinka Saks*. Moscow: Gosydarstvennoye Izdatyelstvo Hydozhestvennoy Literatury, 1955.
"Yakov Pasynkov"	Turgenev, Ivan. "Yakov Pasynkov." In *The Novels and Stories of Ivan Turgenieff*. New York: Charles Scribner's Sons, 1904.
What is to be Done?	Chernyshevsky, Nikolai. *What is to be Done?* Translated by N. Dole and S. S. Skidelsky. Introduction by Kathryn Fever. Ann Arbor, Mich.: Ardis, 1986.
Mauprat	Sand, George. *Mauprat*. Paris: Garnier-Flammarion, 1969.
Oblomov	Goncharov, Ivan. *Oblomov*. Translated by Natalie A. Duddington. Introduction by Nikolay Andreyev. New York: Macmillan, 1929.
On the Eve	Turgenev, Ivan. *On the Eve*. Translated by Stepan Apresyan. Moscow: Foreign Language Publishing House, 1958.
Crime and Punishment	Dostoevsky, Fyodor. *Crime and Punishment*. Translated by Sidney Monas. New York: Dell, 1968.
The Brothers Karamazov	Dostoevsky, Fyodor. *The Brothers Karamazov*. Translated by Constance Garnett. New York: New American Library, 1980.
Horace	Sand, George. *Horace*. In *Oeuvres complètes*. Paris: Calmann-Lévy, 1825–1926.

Who is to Blame?

Herzen, Aleksandr. *Who is to Blame? A Novel in Two Parts.* Translated by Michael R. Katz. Ithaca, N.Y.: Cornell University Press, 1984.

A Common Story

Goncharov, Ivan. *A Common Story.* Moscow: Foreign Language Publishing House, 1959.

Rudin

Turgenev, Ivan. *Rudin.* Vol. 3 in *The Novels and Stories of Ivan Turgenieff.* New York: Charles Scribner's Sons, 1904.

A Note about Translations
and Transliterations

George Sand's *Jacques* and *Horace* are not readily accessible in French and have not yet been translated into English. Translating Sand's work poses a challenge, in that her prose style features difficult grammatical structures and long, involved sentences. Because I would be greatly remiss in presenting her work only in my own English renderings, and because most nineteenth-century Russians who read Sand's novels read them in the original, I have cited them in French and have provided an accompanying English translation.

With the Russian texts, I have cited professional translations when available. When other translations have not been available, I have translated the passages myself.

All transliterations from Russian in this study conform to the Library of Congress style. Transliterations of texts cited in the bibliography, however, retain their original form.

George Sand

and the Nineteenth-Century
Russian Love-Triangle Novels

1
Introduction:
Toward an Erotics of Reading

À force de parler d'amour, on devient amoureux (In speaking of love, one falls in love).

—Blaise Pascal

Parler de l'amour c'est faire l'amour (To speak of love is to make love).

—Honoré de Balzac

That which makes lovemaking and reading resemble each other most is that within both of them times and spaces open, different from measurable time and space.

—Italo Calvino

An American champion of George Sand, Henry James, noted that the French novelist "wrote as a bird sings; but unlike most birds, she found it unnecessary to indulge, by way of prelude, in twitterings and vocal exercises; she broke out at once with her full volume of expression."[1] In conveying the impact of an artist who wrote so naturally and so prolifically—over one hundred novels, numerous volumes of correspondence and several plays—I shall limit my study to a discussion of Russian borrowings of the love-triangle theme from three of George Sand's most influential works in that country: *Jacques* (1834), *Mauprat* (1837), and *Horace* (1842).

These works comprise a part of Sand's "romantic rebellion," featuring themes of ill-matched marriages, torrid romances, and soul-searching confessions. They include didactic pronouncements on how lovers and spouses should fulfill their respective roles, an aspect of Sand's work that takes a revolutionary turn in the Russian novels that acknowledge her impact.

My review and comparison of love-triangle novels is placed against the historical background of the social position of women. In studying these

13

novels of human connection through love relationships, I shall consider the political dimension of Sandism with which these narratives are imbued. To discuss "relationship" at the heart of texts representing two different cultures entails a distinctly humanistic study. I will examine these literary works by combining, juxtaposing and recombining them in accordance with a remarkably simple proposition: that literature tells us how we live (and should live) and records that which we fail to see in our own lives.

I shall also consider the sociopolitical aspects of George Sandism in nineteenth-century Russia to ascertain why many readers devoured her works and Russian works that had borrowed from her, and why readers committed themselves to follow these novels as guidebooks to life. What is comparative literature if not linkage, juxtaposition, and assembly? In composing this study I have been struck by the exciting congruence between relationships in my subject matter and the possible ways of illuminating those connections.

Discerning linkages and patterns calls attention to and defamiliarizes relationships, causing us to recognize their oddness and arbitrariness. At the same time we perceive the common ground between the linking of people and the linking of texts.

Rather than subscribe to a single methodology, I have allowed the study to determine its own comparative angle. Various critical texts inform this study of desire and culpability in George Sand's work and in the Russian borrowings. Tony Tanner's *Adultery in the Novel: Contract and Transgression* (1979) explores the psychosocial dynamics of adultery, sketching out a dialectic play of desire and a weakening of traditional codes. Arnold Weinstein's *Fiction of Relationship* (1988) examines the narrative literature of relationship, as well as the prospect that relationship may be a fiction, something made rather than given, built out of belief instead of fact.

Chapter 2 of this study explores the ironic relationship of women and fiction in nineteenth-century Russia. Chapters 2 through 5 examine specific examples of Russian borrowings from and adaptations of Sand's works. Chapter 6 continues the discussion of women writers and political activists to ascertain "who was to blame" for the failure of women writers to address the Woman Question and examines the various resolutions to the dilemma of "what was to be done" in the aftermath of George Sandism.

In considering the love triangle and its ramifications in nineteenth-century literature and culture, I shall explore three aspects of desire and culpability. Chapter 3 examines Jacques, the character type of the forgiving, enlightened spouse whose wife takes a lover. In this portion of the study I examine narrative desire and reader conspiracy. Wolfgang Iser discusses in *The Act of Reading: A Theory of Aesthetic Response* (1978) the manner in which the aesthetic quality of a text lies within its "performing structure," which clearly cannot be identical to the final product, because without the participation of the individual reader there can be no performance. "It is, then, an integral quality of literary texts that they produce something which they themselves are not."[2]

In *Reading for the Plot: Design and Intention in Narrative* (1985), Peter Brooks defines narrative desire as desire for closure and completion. The play of desire in time compels the reader to turn pages and strive toward narrative ends. This desire for completion or consummation extends itself to love relationships, as well.

In chapter 4, on Sand's *Mauprat,* I examine the archetypal qualities of the self-actualizing "woman as hero" type exemplified by Sand's Edmée, and I consider Carolyn Heilbrun's *Toward a Recognition of Androgyny* (1973) in this discussion of desire for human completeness. Here, too, the fiction of relationship comes into play as male Russian authors create idealized woman characters who could never really live up to the "terrible perfection" with which they are endowed.[3]

Narrative desire compels the reader to implicate herself into the text. Steven G. Kellman explains in *Loving Reading: Erotics of the Text* (1985), that reading, like love, aims at dissolving personal boundaries. Both reading and loving are processes that are betrayed when reified.[4] As the reader implicates herself through her close connection with the text, desire assumes a dimension of shared culpability. As the reader conspires with the narrative voice, the act of reading becomes a far from innocent process. The narrator's motivation to recount the tale stems from her need and desire to implicate her listeners in a tainting secret with which she cannot live alone. If the listener or reader has truly engaged himself, he has assumed the role offered by the text, mentally pronouncing "I" in reference to another. In connecting with "the other" the reader has perpetuated the intersubjective and reversible pattern of dialogue. Kellman writes in *Loving Reading:*

> . . . for the past two centuries adultery has not only been the preoccupation of Western fiction; it has been a description of the literary experience itself. In place of a love that is public and sacramental, authors have increasingly embraced one that is private and illicit.[5]

This private or illicit connection refers to the conspiratorial aspect of narrative desire.

In chapter 5 on *Horace,* I examine René Girard's notion of the triangulation of desire, as he elaborates it in *Mensonge romantique et vérité romanesque (Deceit, Desire, and the Novel)* (1961). *L'homme inutile* (the useless man) or *llishchnii chelovek* (the superfluous man) constitutes the third character type in the love triangle featured in so many Sandian novels and incorporated into numerous Russian novels. This superfluous man exemplifies the traditional characteristics of "le jaloux" (the envier) as defined by Girard: a character whose desire emulates that of another. The challenge of supplanting his rivals, coupled with a secret longing to be like the "other," compels him to pursue the spouse or love interest of someone else.

Although Sand often employed love triangles in her romance novels, she did not initiate this basic plot form in fiction. The 1830s and 1840s in Russia ushered in an era of intense absorption of Western ideas. Sand, a contemporary of Balzac, Hugo and Dickens, did not dominate Western influence on the Russian novel. Moreover, several parallels between Sand's works and those of the masters of Russian fiction (Dostoevskii, Turgenev, Herzen, Chernyshevskii and Goncharov) stem from common sources, in particular Rousseau, Ann Radcliffe, and Walter Scott. The Russian artists had read Sand in their youth as literary apprentices and later employed ideas they had assimilated from these common philosophies. I intend through this study to indicate Sand's pervasive appeal to Russian readers and writers, a force which compelled many to alter their personal lives, citing the actions of one of Sand's literary prototypes as a precedent. Her novels pervaded Russia during a time of intellectual and social ferment and coincided with the beginnings of the Russian novel in the 1840s. This coincidence earned her the epithet, "the mother of Russian realism."[6]

In speculating about the wonder of human connection and the mysterious, arbitrary and fictitious nature of relationship, I will venture to consider some of the less tangible aspects of George Sand's exceptionally warm reception in Russia. In exploring the fascinating aspects which comprise the "Russian soul," I refer to Vladimir Weidlé's interpretive study of cultural history entitled *Russia: Absent and Present* (1952). Weidlé identifies four principle components of this spiritual entity. He contends that Russians share an extraordinarily strong feeling for family and community life; a fear of law and of the mechanical; a hatred of all forms; and a deep spirit of humility and charity. Weidlé emphasizes particularly that which he perceives to be a Russian aversion to "forms," to all excessive regulation of human relationships.[7] In a much more contemporary observation, Milan Kundera reflects in his novel *Immortality* (1990), "Russia and France are two poles of Europe that exercise eternal mutual attraction. . . . Oh France, you are the land of Form, just as Russia is the land of Feeling."[8]

Sand's prolific, improvisational writing lacks fundamental plan and "form." Perhaps a comment made by the nineteenth-century metropolitan of Moscow, Philarète, best explains the communion between George Sand and the Russians. He characterized the Russian soul as having "little light, but plenty of warmth."[9] Henry James offered the assessment, "Mme. Sand's novels have plenty of style but they have no form. Balzac's have not a shred of style, but they have a great deal of form."[10] Were we to equate style with warmth and form with light, we might ascertain why Russian readers heeded George Sand's didactic romance novels with such enthusiastic abandon.

2
Women and Fiction:
Who is to Blame?

> The title women and fiction might mean, and you may have meant
> it to mean, women and what they are like; or it might mean, women
> and the fiction that they write; or it might mean women and that
> which is written about them; or it might mean that somehow all three
> are inextricably mixed together and you want me to consider them
> in that light.
>
> —Virginia Woolf, *A Room of One's Own*

Following a humiliating defeat in the Crimean War (1854–56), the Russian intelligentsia engaged in an exercise of self-assessment and in an evaluation of the urgent need for reform. Out of their discussions and debates arose a series of burning questions, not the least of which was the "Zhenskii vopros," or "Woman Question." Critics of the old society vied for women who would play a vital role in the building of the new one. Literature played a prominent role in the emancipation of the Russian woman and served to reflect the sociological and ideological problems of her time. The literary proponents of the Woman Question were to create a fictional prototype that has recurred throughout the recent history of Russian fiction: the strong and decisive heroine who serves as a counterpart to vacillating, superfluous men.

The evolution of the relationship between women and fiction in nineteenth-century Russia is extremely ironic and controversial in nature. In the era of the Woman Question the issue was propagated significantly through fiction by male writers (as I shall examine in the borrowings from George Sand). The Russian women's own literary voice resounded in fields that remained outside the realm of male dominance, perhaps through a lack of interest in them on the part of the male literary giants. Women writers of the nineteenth-century turned to the genres of autobiography and poetry to reflect on their lives. These works by women writers, which have largely remained obscure, must be rediscovered by contemporary readers if we are to appreciate fully the various aspects of the Woman Question and attempt to judge the efficacy of the resolutions to this question of individual and social concern.

The role of women as fiction of the male imagination in nineteenth-century Russia derives from a tradition rich in misogyny. "The woman must obey her husband, reside with him in love, respect and unlimited obedience, and offer him every pleasantness and affection as the ruler of the household."[1] This article, culled from the 1836 Code of Russian Laws, served as the legal basis of a married woman's subservience to her husband.

Custom further reinforced this law of unqualified obedience by allowing the husband to use force in chastising insubordinate wives and children. Without her husband's express permission, a noblewoman could not travel, work or study. Prior to her marriage, her parents hindered her actions equally zealously in a relationship not unlike that of serf and master. Sons grew up subservient to their parents, consoled by the knowledge that as adults, they would exercise the same authority over their wives and children.

Russians of the intelligentsia of the nineteenth century learned to submit to patriarchal authority in their immediate families. The family hierarchy both reflected and perpetuated the state's patriarchal leadership. Consequently, to be a woman in nineteenth-century Russia entailed being first a daughter, then a wife and mother, all the while remaining subservient to men. Society valued women according to their capacity to bear children and to maintain their households. Peasant women labored often in the fields in order to contribute to the family's economic resources. Their work, considered "unproductive," did not entitle them to share in the allocation of household assets. Perhaps this refusal on the part of male peasants to acknowledge the contributions of their female counterparts accounts for the blatant misogyny of the following folk proverbs: "I thought I saw two people, but it was only a man and his wife."[2] "A chicken is not a bird, and a woman is not a human being."[3]

Surprisingly, noblewomen bore children more frequently in tsarist Russia than did peasant females. Not surprisingly, more of the noblewomen's children survived. The women and children of the landed aristocracy enjoyed better health and diets than their counterparts in the lower classes. Because noblewomen hired wet nurses, they lacked even the most ineffective means of birth control. Biographical studies conducted on women in nineteenth century Russia reveal that upper-class women gave birth every sixteen to twenty-four months during their years of marriage.[4]

Among the Russian gentry prior to the advent of the heightened awareness of the plight of women known as the Woman Question, marriage proved to be more a socioeconomic union than a conjugal one. Matrimony tended too often to be a parsimonious arrangement at the expense of the bride's contentment. Only a small minority of Russian women inherited land, and that to a lesser degree than their brothers; all too frequently, marriage offered a woman her only hope to ameliorate her social status and to escape the tyranny of her parents' home.[5]

A woman's religious education perpetuated her subjugation perhaps even more than her family or husband. Russian Orthodoxy considered matrimony a holy union. For a woman to rebel against her husband entailed revolting against God. Since the time of Peter the Great, authorities would grant a divorce only in cases of impotence over a period of three years, adultery (as attested to by several witnesses), or five years unexplained absence.

Education in nineteenth-century Russia reinforced the differences between the sexes and the social classes. While boys attended school to acquire Western European values and a notion of service to the state, girls passively received a traditional religious orientation. To fulfill the objectives of serving as wife and mother, noblewomen received schooling as girls which would enhance their marriageability. According to Gogol's satirical assessment in *Dead Souls*, this entailed mastering the three subjects comprising all of human virtue: "French, indispensable to family happiness, the pianoforte, to afford pleasant moments to one's spouse; and finally, the knitting of purses and other presents with which to surprise one's husband."[6] Consequently, prior to the advent of the Woman Question, schooling for girls, which was limited to the privileged classes, provided vocational training for wifehood, motherhood and domestic trivialities.

A girl in a wealthy gentry family grew up in a dream world. She practiced her future vocation with dolls and learned from her governess to speak French, to sew and to play the piano. She anxiously awaited her first ball and her initial taste of life as a woman. As Dolly Oblonskaia relates in Tolstoi's *Anna Karenina*, "With maman's upbringing I was not more innocent, I was stupid, I knew nothing."[7] The aristocratic way of life so artfully depicted in Tolstoi's novels accounted for less than 1 percent of the contemporary Russian nobility. Ten percent lived in relative comfort. Their sons were raised on Western ideals while their daughters were groomed for marriage. The remaining 90 percent, however, struggled with financial hardships and often lived as peasants. Their birthright determined class distinction.[8]

A vast chasm separated the women of the aristocracy from their middle-class and peasant sisters. Aristocratic women enjoyed relative leisure. Although she bore children frequently, the wealthy gentry woman employed serfs to rear them. Often the children of Russian nobles would develop close friendships with the family domestics. Combined with their naïve and idealistic formation, this warm rapport with servants compelled many gentry girls to ally themselves with the populist movement as women. The peasants played virtually no role in the initial stirrings of the Woman Question, except as the recipients of the populists' support and as the future beneficiaries of revolutionary change. Until the 1860s, the gentry women, as the sole recipients of organized education (limited though it was), were pioneers among Russian women in posing the terrible question, "Is there nothing more to life?"[9] In doing so, the nineteenth-century noblewomen presented to tsarist Russia the larger, more encompassing enigma of the Woman Question.

The relationship between women and fiction extends also to the role of women as consumers of fiction. During the 1830s and 1840s, Russians who had any pretense of revering European culture formed a veritable cult in appreciation of the fiction of George Sand, originally Aurore Dupin Dudevant.[10] So pervasively did Sand's work (and personal life) influence tsarist Russia that a special term was coined to describe the literary phenomenon. The term *Zhorzhzandism* was applied to the many Russian novels written in the 1830s and 1840s that dealt with themes similar to those of Sand's early novels. The international opera star Pauline Viardot attested to Sand's enormous popularity in Russia. She wrote to Sand that her works were immediately translated there from the time they first appeared, that everyone read them from the top rungs of the social ladder to the bottom, that the men adored her, the women idolized her—that, in short, she reigned over the Russian people more sovereignly than the tsar.[11] Talk about Sand took the Russian literary salons by storm. Pushkin wrote in a letter to his wife, "If her [Evgenia Tur's] translation is as faithful as she herself is a faithful copy of Madame Sand, then her success is undoubtable."[12] His letter reflected the fashionable attitude toward Sand in Russian high society. Diaries, memoirs and letters testify to her immense popularity among the Russian people and to the fact that young Russians seized each Sand novel as quickly as it arrived in their motherland, and devoured her prose.[13]

Almost all educated Russians in the nineteenth century read French flu-
ently, but nonetheless many of her works were translated into Russian
almost as quickly as they appeared in the original. Often the literary borrowings from Sand were so blatant, as with Druzhinin, that the essence of
her philosophy was rendered into Russian through a literary medium other
than translation. The Sand novels that Russians did translate were chosen
without regard to the order in which they were written, their popularity, or
their literary merit. Moreover, translators often took great liberties in alter-
ing Sand's prose, privileging instead their own feminist or socialist biases.
Sand was translated by men and women of renown in Russia, including
Mme. Kern (Pushkin's mistress), Ivan Panaev and Alexandr Herzen. Even
Dostoevskii undertook the translation of one of Sand's novels, *La dernière
Aldini* (1838), only to discover to his dismay that it had already been ren-
dered into Russian.

Annenkov, Herzen, and Botkin saluted Sand as an apostle and mis-
sionary of the future. Turgenev avowed his indebtedness to her writings.
Dostoevskii spoke of the new hope the world gained through her visionary
works.[14] Reflecting on her enormous impact, he noted that

> Sand was not a thinker but one of the clairvoyant seers of a happy
> future awaiting mankind; . . . she based her socialism, her convictions,
> her hopes and her ideals upon the moral feeling of man, upon the
> spiritual thirst of mankind and its longing for perfection and purity.[15]

The renowned Russian literary critic, Vissarion Belinskii, publicly converted in 1840 to the humanitarian socialism preached by Pierre Leroux in
L'encyclopédie nouvelle and by Sand's novels, particularly *Spiridion*. One
chronicler of the period, Ivan Panaev, who claimed to have translated the
final chapters of Sand's novel for Belinskii, attested to the stunning transformation of the Russian critic's attitude toward the French novelist:

> All of his former literary authorities and idols: Goethe, Walter Scott,
> Schiller, Hoffmann—all paled before her. . . . Now he spoke only
> about George Sand and Leroux. His enthusiasm was so strong that he
> decided to study French in order to read them in the original.[16]

Vissarion Belinskii was never successful in this endeavor, but his friends,
Herzen and Panaev, prepared translations for him of some of Sand's most
important works. Under the influence of his mentors, Sand and Leroux,
the father of the Russian intelligentsia publicly revised his former opinions

on women and marriage. Belinskii had once avowed, "George Sand is writing a whole series of novels, each more scandalous and absurd than the last." He later revered her as "the Joan of Arc of our time, the rising star and the prophetess of a grand future." He exclaimed further, "This is not the first time that humanity will have been saved by a woman."[17]

Sand's novels greatly inspired the young anarchist-to-be, Bakunin, who felt that the time for theorizing was over and who found in Sand's work a turn toward practical considerations. He wrote in French to his family: "Every time that I read her, I become better, my faith strengthens and grows . . . no poet, no philosopher is as likeable as she, no one has explained to me so well my own thoughts, feelings and needs."[18]

D. S. Mirskii's highly regarded *History of Russian Literature* (1958) presents perhaps the most authoritative testimony we have to Sand's impact on nineteenth-century Russian literature. In his text, Mirskii credits Sand for her significant role in the development of the Russian realist novel:

> Russian realism was born in the second half of the forties. . . . In substance it is a cross between the satirical naturalism of Gogol and an older sentimentalism revived and represented in the thirties and forties by the then enormously influential George Sand. Gogol and George Sand were the father and mother of Russian realism and its accepted masters during the initial stages.[19]

The remarkable power of Sand's voice in Russia stems partially from the fact that her novels imported revolutionary Western ideas that the tsarist censors had banned. Readers were forced to smuggle in and read in secret Fourier and Saint-Simon, for instance. In an article dedicated to Sand, Dostoevskii recalls,

> In those days fiction was the only thing permitted, whereas the rest, virtually every thought, especially coming from France, was strictly forbidden. . . . Nevertheless, novels were permitted and right here, specifically in the case of George Sand, the guardians committed a grave error . . . that which in those days burst into Russia in the form of novels . . . proved the most "dangerous" form; . . . there came forth thousands of lovers of George Sand.[20]

Sand's novels frequently funneled into Russia the very ideas the government sought to suppress. Whereas the developing literary circles of Moscow held George Sand as an object of veneration, the dominant St.

Petersburg press, representing the viewpoint of "official" Russia, severely reproved her work. They frequently censored her translated novels as a matter of course, since her immense popularity made her politically suspect even when her ideas were innocuous. Although censors excised portions of Sand's works capriciously, without regard to content, Russians could easily secure her unexpurgated works in French.[21]

By 1834, Sand had published four major novels, *Indiana* (1832), *Valentine* (1832), *Lélia* (1833) and *Jacques* (1834). At this time, the Russian press launched a full-scale attack on this "shameless," "immoral," "immodest," "indecent," "insidious," "Machiavellian" author (epithets they applied to Balzac, Hugo, and Sue as well).[22] From the time of the publication of *Indiana*, her reception throughout Europe followed a course of malicious gossip about her love affairs, her androgynous garb, and her carousals in bars. As late as 1845, Sand again shocked her Russian reading public with *Lucrézia Floriani*, a coda to her nine-year relationship with Frederic Chopin. This novel features an opera star who has four children by three lovers. She rejects marriage and revels in her independence. This work revived the scandal, controversy, and charges of immorality hurled against Sand. Her reception by the Russian intelligentsia was mixed but passionate on both fronts. Sand's critics claimed that her promiscuous notions and manlike audacity compelled high-born women to repudiate traditional family bonds by cavorting around Europe with Italian lovers and assuming a guise of decency upon their return, all in the name of *zhorzhzandism*. Defenders of morality such as Bulgarin and Grech warned the Russian reading public against Sand, dwelling on sordid details about her bobbed hair, trousers and cigar smoking.[23] Nikolai Strakhov, the close friend of Tolstoi and a Slavophile journalist who commented indignantly upon *Lucrézia Floriani*, complained that Sand was inflicting upon Russia a Catholic extremism. He contended that Catholic contempt for the flesh had necessitated the dissolute reaction of Sand's emancipated heroine, Lucrézia.[24] However, Khomiakov, the most influential of the conservative Slavophiles, refused nonetheless to attribute society's ills to George Sandism. He noted: "The depravity of men presupposes the depravity of women. . . . And thus, the teachings of George Sand are justified. I don't see why Lucrézia Floriani would not have been a very nice man, and even a very respectable gentleman."[25]

Sand's most important literary influence in nineteenth-century Russia lies in her early novels about love and marriage, rather than in the pastoral or utopian socialist works. Russians absorbed her passionate personal quest into three subjects crucial to them as well: religion, politics and love. Sand conducted her philosophical search from the adopted point of view of the underprivileged rural classes. This beckoned directly to the habitual reader of Turgenev, Chekhov, and Tolstoi, among others. Sand loved her home, Nohant, as fervently as Chekhov did Melikhova or Tolstoi Iasnaia Poliana.[26]

Her influence extends beyond the structural elements of the text. Although some Russian novelists emulated her style transparently, as did Druzhinin with his novel *Polinka Saks*, Sand tended to raise controversial questions with her works. Herzen and Chernyshevskii, for example, looked for solutions to her "problem novels." Sand asks in the preface to *Jacques*, "A qui la faute?" (Who is to blame?). These novelists responded to her topical dilemmas rather than to her writing techniques. Sand's work pervaded the early formations of these great Russian novelists, and her influence lasted years beyond her immediate notoriety. In the introduction to her extensive biography on George Sand, Vladimir Karenin, a Russian woman who, like Sand, published under a male pseudonym, wrote:

> It is precisely by considering George Sand as a Russian force, as one of the primary roots of the Russian social conscience of our time, that we have determined that our duty as a Russian writer was to dedicate a serious study to her.[27]

George Sand's ideas and philosophy became Russian ideas and philosophies in a natural, organic manner. Dostoevskii explains: "Much of what we have taken from Europe and transplanted to Russia we did not copy like slaves from their masters, as the Potugins invariably insist [a character in Turgenev's novel *Smoke* (1867)], but we have inoculated it into our organism, into our flesh and blood."[28] George Sand contributed to nineteenth-century notions of matrimonial conflict, the problem of the love triangle, sex as the normal and necessary culmination of passion of the heart (both inside and outside of marriage), and the question of culpability in these conflicts. Sand promoted sentimental emancipation as an individual solution rather than as a social one. She subscribed to an abiding faith in the capacity of the individual to move rapidly while society merely stumbled toward a higher goal. These Russian novels convert Sand's notions of emancipation to a social plane, extending culpability in the love triangle, for example, to the shortcomings of the collective.

Although the freedom of the heart espoused by George Sandism appeased the discontented noblewomen in the 1830s and 1840s, their daughters clamored for more than a mere sentimental emancipation. Russian intellectuals revolutionized Sand's philosophies. Perhaps Nikolai Cherny-shevskii's *What is to be Done?* (1863) illustrates this best. Borrowed quite liberally from *Jacques,* his work was revered by radicals in the latter part of the nineteenth century as a virtual bible.

As a new generation of women began to work resolutely for political and economic liberation, they perpetuated the admiration for Sand's work. They no longer sympathized with her ideas to the extent of their mothers and grandmothers, but they acknowledged a debt of gratitude to the French novelist for having been the educator of the preceding two generations of Russian radicals. A Russian encyclopedia printed in 1894 credited Sand with a direct influence in having raised the Woman Question.[29]

Mikhail L. Mikhailov (1829–65), considered the spiritual leader of the Russian woman's movement, undertook the first serious considerations of the Woman Question. He proved to be the first Russian thinker to synthe-size the separate considerations of love, work, and education into an an-thropological argument. The antifeminist writings of Jules Michelet and the socialist P. J. Proudhon aroused Mikhailov's interest in the Woman Question. Employing George Sandism as evidence, both antifeminist French thinkers used female peccadillos to discredit reform.[30] Michelet, a strong proponent of female subordination in marriage, contended that menstrual problems and pregnancies were debilitating distractions to work and serious study. He argued that a woman's husband should be respon-sible enough "to instruct her and elevate her in things pious and holy."[31] Proudhon pointed to a woman's physical smallness and passivity in sex as proof of her weaker nature; to the largeness of her pelvis, hips and breasts as proof of her sole function as childbearer; and to the relative smallness of the female brain as proof of her mental inferiority.[32] Proudhon attributed coquetry and prostitution to an allegedly innate female vice, contending that they manifested a woman's obscene nature.

Mikhailov refuted these allegations, arguing that man rather than woman had the perpetual lust and constantly sought gratification of depraved de-sires. He attempted to de-emphasize sexual differences and to affirm woman's capacities. "There should be nothing feminine in women except their sex," he wrote. "All other traits should be neither masculine nor feminine, but purely human."[33] This desire for androgyny plays a promi-nent role in the emergence of the self-actualizing "woman as hero" pro-tagonist in Sand's novel, *Mauprat.*

Mikhailov contended that child bearing should require no more than eight to ten years of a woman's life. A woman could subsequently devote the rest of her life to work. He argued, moreover, that marriage should be an institution based on love and that women should be allowed to seek divorce. Mikhailov assured his readers that the emancipation of women would not endanger the family, but rather render it more durable.

Strongly influenced by the French feminist, Eugénie d'Hercourt and her scientific approach to the Woman Question, Mikhailov drew his arguments largely from European works on anthropology, medicine and feminism.[34] Like N. I. Pirogov and D. I. Pisarev, he regarded education as the key problem in Russia. In his 1860 article entitled "Women: Their Education and Significance in Family and in Society," Mikhailov attempted to prove that flaws in the female character were conditioned rather than innate. Her unworldly upbringing compelled a woman of the gentry to seek refuge in marriage (often with the first eligible man she encountered) from the oppression of her family and the intolerability of lessons intended to make her marriageable.

So how, then, did a French woman novelist prompt consideration of the Woman Question in nineteenth-century Russia, and why was it that Russian male authors perpetuated the cause? Although most women novelists of nineteenth-century Russia attempted to emulate George Sand in their fictional accounts of conjugal conflict and in their discussions of woman's inferior condition, none created a comparable impact.

Baroness Elena Gan (Zinaida R-va, pseud.), a wealthy noblewoman salon figure and writer of the 1840s, wrote novels to escape boredom. Because she wrote from a woman's point of view, critics have often compared her to George Sand. Her typical heroine, a talented and sensitive woman, "vegetates in a wasteland in ignorance, far from the world, from all the great models, from all means of education for which her soul thirsts . . . just because she is a woman."[35] In 1837, this young novelist made her literary debut with "The Ideal," a story published in *The Library for Reading* that transparently emulated Sand's *Indiana*. Gan's heroine, Olga Goltzberg, languishes for love, as does Indiana, and lacks compassion and understanding from everyone around her. Sand describes her heroine as "toute fluette, toute pâle, toute triste. . . . Semblable à une fleur née d'hier qu'on fait éclore dans un vase gothique" (so thin, so pale, so sad. . . . She resembled a fresh, budding flower made to bloom in a Gothic vase).[36] Similarly, Gan depicts Olga as "an adorable and intelligent woman, born to adorn the flower of mankind . . . a poetic soul surrounded by a swarm of insects who delight in stinging her from all sides."[37] Unlike the French novelist, however, Gan was a proponent of the "odno-liubka," the woman of one love.

For this Russian novelist who died young, adultery or sexual freedom did not resolve the Woman Question. She did acknowledge that problems for women existed; she herself was acutely aware of the scorn heaped upon women of talent who refused to conform to society's expectations. For Gan and others, the security of marriage in itself failed to endow life with meaning.[38]

Another novelist who, like Elena Gan, earned the epithet of the "Russian George Sand" was Countess Evdokia Rostopchina (1811–58), a society woman who dabbled in poetry and novels. She published two novels, *The Duel* (*Poedinok*) (1838) and *The Happy Woman* (*Schastlivaia zhenshchina*) (1851), in *The Muscovite* (*Moskvitianin*). Her stories about the beau monde lack Sand's humanism and wide appeal, however.[39]

Evgenia Tur, author of "The Mistake" ("Oshibka") (1849) translated excerpts of Sand's autobiography *L'histoire de ma vie* for the *Russian Herald* (*Russkii Vestnik*), praising its author: "George Sand is not only a great writer, but an even greater thinker; and not just a thinker, but a doer, a public-spirited, socially conscious person."[40]

The 1830s ushered in the epoch of "zhorzhzandschina" (female enthusiasts of George Sand). Women readers, particularly those who were not very emancipated, read George Sand's novels and realized that they could correct the wrong in their lives. Many, like Indiana, dreamed of leaving their unsatisfactory husbands, or of leading the free life, like Lélia. Russian women novelists who attempted to write in the Sandian mode also included Avdotia Panaeva and Vladimir Krestovskii (pseud.). All are nearly forgotten today, relegated to the obscure margins of historical record.

The George Sands and George Eliots of Russia were men. In the following three sections, I will discuss specific examples of borrowings from three of Sand's most influential novels in Russia: *Jacques* (1834), *Mauprat* (1837), and *Horace* (1842). In examining structural and thematic parallels, I shall further explore the relationship of women and fiction by considering the implications of desire and culpability in these works.

3

Jacques, the Enlightened Husband:
Narrative Desire

I saw a woman sleeping. In her sleep she dreamt Life stood before her, and held in each hand a gift, in the one Love, in the other Freedom. And she said to the woman, "Choose!"

And the woman waited long: and she said, "Freedom!" And Life said, "Thou hast well chosen. If thou hadst said, 'Love,' I would have given thee that thou didst ask for; and I would have gone from thee, and returned to thee no more. Now the day will come when I shall return. On that day I shall bear both gifts in one hand."

I heard the woman laugh in her sleep.

—Olive Schreiner, "Life's Gifts" (1892)

In addressing the issue of desire and culpability in the love triangle, I will focus on the narrative level and examine the reader's role with regard to desire (for the end) and culpability (conspiracy). Narratives both tell of desire—in our case the desire of the protagonists involved in the friendship *à trois*—and arouse and make use of desire as a dynamic of signification.[1] Peter Brooks links narrative desire to Freud's notion of Eros in *Reading for the Plot: Design and Intention in Narrative* (1985). Desire, like Eros, constitutes a force including sexual desire, but is larger and more polymorphous. It is a force which seeks "to combine organic substances into ever greater unities."[2] Brooks evokes the notion of Eros, desire in its plastic and totalizing function, as an integral part of our experience of reading narrative and because he finds in Freud's work the best model for a "textual erotics."[3] The epistolary form of Sand's *Jacques* reflects particularly well on the narrative level those issues of desire and culpability that in other texts in this study I discuss on the level of sociology, politics, and intertextuality.

According to the theory of reader response criticism outlined by Wolfgang Iser in *The Act of Reading: A Theory of Aesthetic Response*, "the liter-

29

ary work is in no way a mere copy of the given world—it constructs a world of its own out of the material available to it."[4] In creating this world, the author employs elements familiar to the reader in order to construct a background against which the new elements in the foreground can be construed by the reader. Were it not for the familiarity of the background, these new elements, which might not be consistent with the reader's disposition, would remain incomprehensible because of the reader's incapacity to link them to elements already known. George Sand creates the world of *Jacques*, through the dynamic of the relationship between the background and the foreground.

The era following romanticism obliged works of fiction to refrain from presenting themselves as such. They were to appear rather as documents or as direct witnesses of reality. Similarly, the epistolary novel presents itself as a series of documents emanating not from a novelist, but from true characters who corresponded. The editor serves as the passive collaborator, whose existence contributes to the background, as defined by Iser.

In *Forme et signification: Essais sur les structures littéraires de Corneille à Claudel* (1962), Jean Rousset describes the need of characters in epistolary novels to reveal everything to a confidant. This ardent desire to divulge secrets and profound thoughts becomes particularly strong during a person's periods of crisis or transition. Sand bases the plot of *Jacques* primarily on psychological observations. The epistolary form suits this work particularly well since no correspondent has the privileged point of view. The secondary letter writers serve primarily for expository purposes. Fernande's confidante, Clémence, serves as the younger woman's stuffy superego or conscience figure.[5] Fernande shares with her widowed friend her need to express her insecurities regarding Jacques's past, as well as her concerns and elation at the prospect of becoming his wife.

Rousset also discusses the correspondent's capacity to express spontaneous, immediate emotions. The letter records directly the contradictory and incoherent fluctuations of a heart which opens voluntarily to confide to another. As the period of crisis or transition comes to a close, the frequency of the letters slows and the urgency of their contents diminishes. During the first months of contentment following her marriage to Jacques, Fernande no longer feels the compulsive need to confide in Clémence. Later she excuses herself for not having written, explaining that her friend is right to reproach her for her silence after all of the letters Fernande had submitted to her when she was tormented and in need of counsel. Love is egotistical, she explains. It calls out to friendship only when it suffers.

The letter itself enjoys a privileged triumph of form. Letters, as Jean Luc Seylaz has shown in his well-known study of Choderlos de Laclos's *Les liaisons dangereuses*, carry out the will's colonization of experience. Written after the fact, letters serve as tools of organization and analysis, and they may offset the pressures of feeling.[6]

Besides conflict, a necessary element which provokes one character to write another is absence. Because Jacques and Fernande live together during the greater course of time addressed by the novel, they correspond only once. The "real" reader is informed of the progress of their marriage through the contents of the letters that each addresses to a confidant physically removed from the scene. Moreover, the "real" reader has the occasion to read all of the letters gathered by the fictitious editor; these supply him with various versions of the same event from different points of view.

In Sand's epistolary novel, Clémence serves purely as a functional character. Her distance from Fernande enables the young bride to recount her experience and impressions to an interlocutor. Often, a principal character refers to a letter deleted by the fictitious editor, mentioning briefly its contents. Fernande writes Clémence: "Tu veux les détails sur mon habitation, sur le pays, sur l'emploi de mes journées . . ." (You want details on my home, on the region, on the way I spend my days) (*Jacques*, 101). This reference to questions posed by Clémence provides the motivation to Fernande to recount her own story.

The "real" reader of the epistolary novel is led (or seduced) to implicate himself in the text upon assuming the role that the text offers him to play. The "intended" reader of the epistolary novel is the fictitious confidant or the "addressee" of the letter. The "real" reader implicates himself progressively more in continuing his reading. In *Fictions of Feminine Desire: Disclosures of Héloïse* (1982), Peggy Kamuf says the reader's desire to pursue the narrative can be attributed to his indiscreet curiosity at the prospect of reading mail intended for someone else. This links desire to culpability. By assuming the role of the "intended" reader (addressee), the "real" reader undergoes a loss of innocence simply by intercepting the secrets intended for another interlocutor. Competent readers conspire. The reading of the letter implicates the secret-sharing reader. Desire and culpability merge in a type of voyeurism as the "real" reader reconstructs the plot of *Jacques* by selecting elements from the point of view of the various correspondents. The presence of a fictitious editor intensifies the reader's implication in Sand's text. In *Jacques*, the editor remains anonymous. The reader does not know how the editor has secured the letters because the novel lacks an explanatory preface. Instead the fictitious editor provides the reader with a literary disclaimer:

> Le lecteur ne doit pas oublier que beaucoup de lettres ont été supprimées de cette collection. Les seules que l'éditeur ait cru devoir publier sont celles qui établissent certains faits et certains sentiments nécessaires à la suite et à la clarté des biographies; celles qui ne servaient qu'à confirmer ces faits . . . ont été retranchées avec discèrnement. (Note de l'éditeur) (*Jacques*, 227)

> The reader mustn't forget that many letters have been omitted from this collection. The editor felt obligated to publish only those which establish certain facts and feelings necessary to the story line advancement and to the clarity of the biographies; those which served only to confirm these facts . . . have been deleted with discretion. (Editorial note)

In Sand's work, this editorial note, along with a final explanation regarding Jacques's death, serves an important function in developing the relationship between the background and foreground, as defined by Iser. These editorial asides address the reader as an observer from outside the text and interrupt the flow of the narrative voice, reminding the reader of his role as voyeur, as outsider looking on. As the accidental recipient of letters intended for someone else, the "real" reader mentally pronounces the pronoun "I," upon adopting the role of the character who has penned the letter, the fictitious "addresser." At the same time, he plays the role of the "déstinataire," the intended reader of the letter. In adopting the role of the fictitious "addressee," the "real" reader foresees the reaction of this character to the contents of the epistle. With every letter, the "real" reader experiences a transition in point of view, as he takes on the role of the assigned "addresser." The editorial asides direct the "real" reader's attention outside the text, reminding him of his status as voyeur.

This rupture in the text fulfills two goals. It lends an illusion of verisimilitude to the work, which presents itself as a collection of real letters. Moreover, it intensifies the tension that the reader experiences between his own disposition and the role offered by the text.

Iser explains further in *The Act of Reading* that a literary work must provoke a point of view that will permit the reader to perceive elements that would never have become apparent as long as his own disposition had determined his selective vision. The epistolary novel explicitly treats the interpretation of a text (the letter) by a reader (the fictitious "addressee"). This interpretation enables the "real" reader to observe the manner in which a reader might experience a transformation in his habitual way of perceiving things because of the act of reading.

In Sand's novel, Jacques recognizes that Fernande acts oddly, voicing concerns that must emanate from another. Unaware that she is corresponding with Clémence, he intuits nevertheless that something in Fernande's correspondence is causing her grief. He recounts in a letter to Sylvia that he suspects that Fernande's mother is sending her letters that depress her. When Sylvia comes to live with the couple, Clémence cautions Fernande that Jacques and Sylvia must pretend to be brother and sister, otherwise their ménage à trois will provoke the derision of neighbors and the gossip of servants. She warns: "Je te conseille d'en parler à ton mari, de lui présenter mes craintes comme venant de toi, et d'obtenir qu'il mette en ceci la prudence qui convient" (I advise you to discuss this with your husband, presenting my fears as your own, and to make certain that he will treat this matter with the necessary prudence) (*Jacques*, 122).

Jacques recognizes that the letters his wife receives have altered her disposition. When Fernande follows Clémence's advice, a dispute erupts between husband and wife about public opinion regarding Sylvia's presence in their home. Jacques pardons her promptly, however, telling Fernande that it is obvious that it is not she but another who is speaking through her. "Tu es bonne, ma pauvre Fernande; aie donc la force de n'écouter d'autres conseils que ceux de ton coeur" (You are good, my poor Fernande. So have the strength to listen to no other advice than that offered by your heart) (*Jacques*, 173).

One of the most striking examples in *Jacques* of the impact of a text on its reader takes place in the scene where a letter falls into the hands of someone besides the addressee. The incident of the accidental reading takes place in the scene where Jacques enters Fernande's room searching for ink and paper in order to write Octave. He catches a glimpse of a letter and perceives in Octave's handwriting the sentence, "Les enfants que nous aurons ensemble ne mourront pas" (The children that we will have together will not die) (*Jacques*, 385). Jacques's unintentional interception of a letter written to his wife determines his destiny. He writes Sylvia that the letter has informed him of his duty to Fernande, to console and to heal her. He sees now that all she desires is to be liberated from her husband's love. Jacques relates to his sister that once he informed Fernande that his love for her had died, he saw Fernande reborn and her eyes seemed to tell him,

"Je puis donc aimer Octave à mon aise" (I can now love Octave freely) (*Jacques*, 385).

The epistolary novel, then, provides the reader with the possibility of discovering a fictitious reader's interpretation of a letter she has received. At the same time, the "real" reader's interpretation of the same letter is affirmed, contradicted or modified when he reads the addressee's response to the addresser's letter. The "real" reader's assembly of the disparities between the different interpretations of the same text will contribute to his construction of the "meaning" of the work as a whole.

George Sand frequently employs the technique of shifting viewpoints in *Jacques* by providing several different versions of the same event. In this manner, *Jacques*, like other epistolary novels, reveals itself as a series of reconstructions. The "real" reader ultimately reconstructs and assimilates these as he interprets the entire work through a series of partial interpretations. The use of gaps to separate the epistles facilitates this process. Sand severs the narration at the end of each letter to change to another narrative voice that recounts other events and features other characters. This intensifies the activity in the imagination of the reader. The gaps between the letters provoke the reader to identify with the characters as he attempts to discern the outcome. This natural curiosity and desire for the end compels the reader to implicate himself progressively into the text.

The negations in the text function in a similar manner. These evoke elements in the reader's mind only to annul them. That which has been negated remains in the background of the reader's view, while the modifications remain in the foreground. From the beginning, each text provokes certain expectations and then proceeds to change them or to fulfill them when the reader had ceased to anticipate them. *Jacques* illustrates this technique in the series of accusations and denigrations featured in Clémence's letters to Fernande. Clémence argues from the beginning that Fernande has chosen a poor match in Jacques, warning that her husband is much too old for her, and that a woman with experience and a calm temperament would be better prepared to adapt to the shortcomings of such a union. She cautions Fernande, " mais pour une petite tête exaltée comme la tienne, un homme aussi expérimenté que M. Jacques est le pire mari que tu pouvais rencontrer" (but for a little idealist like you, a man as experienced as Monsieur Jacques is the worst sort of husband that you could encounter) (*Jacques*, 129) .

Although Fernande denies these allegations, they remain in the background for the reader, and these expectations that are evoked in the beginning are realized in the end. Blanks and negations lead the reader, then, to reconstruct the interpretation of partial elements in the text and to link them to the work in its entirety.

The concept of reconstruction is fundamentally tied to the nature of the epistolary novel. As writers, the individual characters recount the immediacy of their fears, joys, sorrows and doubts to the intimate interlocuter. Moreover, the tone of each letter varies according to the character recounting his relationship with the addressee, and his mood at the time he composes the epistle. These variations reflect ambiguities generally present in any dialogue. Hilary Corke explains in "New Novels" (1957) that a dialogue is "not a transcript of what a character would have said in 'real life' but rather of what would have been said plus what would have been implied but not spoken plus what would have been understood though not implied."[7]

Sand illustrates this phenomenon particularly well with an exchange between Jacques and Sylvia in which he intuits that which she does not state expressly. She writes:

> Jacques! reviens, Fernande a besoin de toi; elle est malade de nouveau parce qu'elle vient d'éprouver une grande douleur. Rien ne peut la calmer. Elle t'appelle avec angoisse, elle dit que tous les maux qui lui arrivent viennent de ton abandon; que tu étais sa providence et que tu l'as quittée. (*Jacques*, 368)

> Jacques! Come back, Fernande needs you. She is sick again because she has just suffered a terrible blow. Nothing can calm her. She calls to you in anguish, saying that all the misfortunes that have befallen her have come from your abandonment, that you were her Providence and that you've left her.

Jacques responds that he will arrive two days after the arrival of the letter. Due to the urgency of Sylvia's tone and because of their manner of understanding each other intuitively, Jacques correctly assesses that his son has died.

Similarly, Jacques composes his last letter to Fernande scrupulously, relying on the reader's capacity to guess that which is implied but not stated. He does not want her to know the true cause of his death and he writes in such a manner that Fernande will never attribute his accident to suicide. Jacques relates to Sylvia that in his letter to Fernande he has written about his next return home and domestic projects for improving the house. He states that he has taken care to adopt a calm and hopeful tone in writing Fernande in order to safeguard against her assuming the blame upon hearing of his death. His caution indicates an important function of narrative voice in the text. Jacques practices a sort of literary criticism in discussing the manner in which he has manipulated his own language to avoid the possibility that Fernande might discern the truth.

The protagonist's suicide fulfills another important function of the literary text: that of social commentary. During the nineteenth century, literature served to balance the shortcomings of the prevailing scientific, religious and philosophical systems, each of which claimed to possess universal truth. George Sand's *Jacques* became a particularly significant social commentary because of its treatment of the love triangle. The novel outraged public opinion and left an indelible impression on Sand's contemporaries. Husbands charged that it undermined the institution of marriage. Reflecting on the unjust sufferings of married women during his era, the novel's hero laments:

> Les améliorations que rêvent quelques esprits généreux sont impossibles à réaliser dans ce siècle-ci; ces esprits là oublient qu'ils sont de cent ans en avant de leurs contemporains, et qu'avant de changer la loi il faut changer l'homme. (*Jacques,* 39)

> The improvements dreamed of by a few liberal souls cannot come to pass in this century; those great minds forget that they are a hundred years ahead of their contemporaries, that before we can change the law we must change man.

A reader's assembly of initial interpretations of the first reading belongs to the reader's background during a second reading of the novel. Consequently, this assembly can never be repeated in a manner identical to the initial reading. Because the reader now has knowledge of the outcome that he had lacked before, the imaginary objects that accumulate along the temporal axis cannot be duplicated in exactly the same way. A second reading of *Jacques* renders an impression completely different from the first. The beginning of the first reading provokes the reader to question the nature of Jacques's relationship with Sylvia. The tremendous affection exhibited in their letters lends the impression that they are former lovers. Jacques tells her never to forget that there exists between them a sentiment stronger than love, that she has but one word to say to send him from one end of the world to the other.

After roughly the first quarter of the novel, the reader learns that Jacques and Sylvia may be children of the same father. In a second reading, the reader knows that Robertine de Theursan, Fernande's cold, fortune-hunting mother, had abandoned at birth her daughter Sylvia, and that the identity of her father was never determined. On his deathbed, Jacques's father had asked his son to take charge of the child who might be his daughter. The marriage between Jacques and Fernande appears in a second reading as the hero's attempt to somehow consummate his forbidden love for Sylvia. Clearly regretting the impossibility of coupling with her, Jacques writes Sylvia before his suicide:

> Si nous avions su plus tôt et d'une manière plus sûre que nous pouvions être un homme et une femme l'un pour l'autre, notre vie à tous deux eût été bien différente; mais l'incertitude eût rendu la seule idée de ce bonheur odieuse à tous deux. (*Jacques*, 394).

> If we had known earlier and with greater certitude that we could be a man and a woman for each other, both our lives would have been greatly different; but uncertainty would have made the very idea of this happiness loathsome to us both.

By marrying the woman he knows to be Sylvia's sister, Jacques attempts to unite himself as closely as possible with his true beloved.

The "real" reader of the epistolary novel serves as a voyeur looking on from the outside. The fact that he reads the epistles without the accompaniment of an omniscient voice is important. This permits the reader to assemble the contradictions between the various versions and to evaluate those that are more precise than others. In this manner, the reader has the occasion to experience the symphonic nature of the narrative voices and to select those elements that lend "meaning" to his interpretation.

Iser indicates in *The Act of Reading* that each reader interprets that which he is reading at different stages of the reading process. There exist moments when the reader observes as an outsider (during editorial asides addressed to the "real" reader) and others when he feels as though he is taking part in the action recounted by the text. Rather than extract a concrete "meaning" from the text (which does not exist because each reading of the same text varies even if the reader remains the same), the reader experiences what the novel does. The act of reading entails remaining simultaneously within the text as a participant (and in the epistolary novel as addressee of the letter) and outside the text as an interpreter. This double location gives the reader the capacity to envision the point of convergence where the principal perspectives reunite. This is the point where the disparate elements of the text coalesce into a comprehensible whole. The reader's implication in the text, as well as the tension which arises between his two roles, allows him to envision this point of convergence and to experience a meaning of the text. The epistolary novel demonstrates particularly well the act of reading and of interpreting within a text. Moreover, the variance between the reaction of the fictitious addressee of a letter and that of an accidental reader (real or fictitious) places in high relief the innumerable possibilities of aesthetic response. Sand's *Jacques* demonstrates further the reader's role as voyeur, which incorporates narrative desire with the reader's conspiracy with the characters, owing to his engagement in the act of reading.

Polinka Saks—Aleksandr Druzhinin

If the reader and the literary text interact in a process of communication, our prime concern should no longer remain the *meaning* of that text but rather the text's *effect*.[8] Herein lies the function of literature. Herein lie the fascinating implications of George Sand's literary impact on nineteenth-century Russia. Sand had not intended *Jacques* as a marital blueprint for her readers to follow literally. Russian readers and novelists took her at her word, however. *Jacques* led Sand's other novels in creating the most controversy with regard to the bourgeois marriage contract. Both Belinskii and Herzen referred frequently in their letters and diaries to Sand's enormously successful 1834 novel, often quoting the hero's lament about the barbarous institution of marriage. In spite of the abundant idealizations that contemporary readers perceive in Sand's work, Bakunin and other "men of the forties" revered the French novelist's practicality.[9] In contrast to the purely theoretical works of the German idealists whose writings had dominated the intellectual arena in Russia prior to George Sandism, the French writer's novels gave the intelligentsia concrete solutions to prevalent problems. Bakunin praised Sand's warmth and human goodness as being "a true charity, because it [was] practical." He wrote to his family, "The time for theorizing, thank God, is past. Everyone feels it more or less; the dawn of a new world is already illuminating."[10]

One of the precepts featured in *Jacques* that garnered tremendous support in Russia dealt with the treatment of jealousy. Those who endeavored to achieve intellectual and moral superiority to others and complete equality with their mates had to renounce jealousy as a petty emotion unworthy of great beings. In an episode in Druzhinin's *Polinka Saks* (1847), modeled transparently after *Jacques*, the former *institutka* interrogates her much older husband as to how he would contend with a rival. Polinka asks,

> "Tell me, what would you do if I were unfaithful to you?"
> "Nobody is unfaithful nowadays" [Saks replied].
> "Well, what would you do?"
> "How would you be unfaithful?"
> "Well, is it impossible to imagine that I could fall in love with one of your friends?"
> "Would you really fall in love?"
> "Yes, for my whole life—eternally, mindlessly."
> His eyes gleamed with such anger that I became frightened.
> "Why would I need such a wife? I would kiss you and retreat from you as far as possible." (*Polinka Saks*, 12)

Hoping to hear that Saks would challenge his rival to a duel, Polinka asks, "What would you do to him?" Echoing Jacques's "A qui la faute?" (Who is to blame?) Saks asks simply "Why is he guilty?" (*Polinka Saks*, 12).

Sand sought to refute charges that her novels presented men in a brutal light. Jacques, a sympathetic husband, espouses an implicit code of behavior for husbands designed to ensure the wife's happiness by allowing her to love as God wills her to do so. Sand's plan clearly fails to consider the husband's happiness, as he commits suicide in such a manner that it will appear to have been an accident, in order to assure his wife's guiltless quest of a happier marriage. The husbands of the Russian versions of *Jacques* either feign suicide or retreat peacefully from the scene. The romantic *mal du siècle* attitude espoused by Jacques regarding the legitimacy of suicide in the face of complete hopelessness failed to win favor with Russian writers. As with Sand's gothic elements of near-rapes, seductions in private chapels, or moments of delirious passion, suicide had fallen out of fashion. However, *Jacques*, which proved to be the single most influential of all of Sand's novels in Russia (although it remains surprisingly neglected by critics), was not translated for ten years. Even then, the final printing lacked the last seven chapters containing the hero's suicide.[11]

Druzhinin's epistolary novel *Polinka Saks* (1847) became one of the most famous literary successes of the 1840s. This blatant imitation of Sand's novel converted its twenty-three-year-old author into an instant celebrity. Starchevskii, a writer of memoirs of the period, noted that "there was not a family where the mother and daughter did not carry this story in their hands [and] to speak with Druzhinin, that dear advocate of the female heart, was the height of bliss for every young woman."[12]

Ironically, Druzhinin, who had won his fame from imitating Sand, was one of the first defectors from the ranks of her ardent admirers as debates about her morality and controversy over her literary influence raged in the 1850s. Feeling that he had "outgrown" Sand, Druzhinin became an ardent Anglophile. Turgenev related to his younger colleague in a letter, "For you she represents a delusion to be uprooted. For me she represents an incomplete truth when complete truth is unattainable."[13]

Ironically, Druzhinin had his own imitator. Mikhail Avdeev published *The Reef (Podvodnyi kamen)* thirteen years after *Polinka Saks.* Like Druzhinin's work, this novel features a revised ending to a story based on *Jacques;* the erring but repentant wife returns to her tolerant husband and receives his forgiveness. The novel appeared within a year of Goncharov's *Oblomov* and Turgenev's *On the Eve* and failed to win a wide readership. In a review for *Biblioteka dlya chteniya* (The library for reading), Pisemskii summed up the novel in two words: "Polinka Saks."[14] Dostoevsky's journal, *Time,* dismissed *The Reef* as "an imitation of an imitation."[15] Moreover, to demonstrate the degree to which readers and reviewers knew of the literary antecedents of Avdeev's work (and to satirize its improbable plot), the contemporary humor magazine *Iskra* (The spark) featured a cartoon in which a wife abandons her husband for his friend, tires of the latter, telegraphs the former begging to return, and is welcomed back politely.[16] The same issue of *Iskra* features a letter supposedly written by the five-year-old "son" of Avdeev's heroine. Defending his parents from accusations that they behaved unnaturally, the child writes: "People forget that Papa descends from grandfather Jacques, a native Frenchman . . . and Mama is kin to Polinka Iakovlina through her husband, Saks . . . so we have family scandals in our blood, so to speak."[17]

Druzhinin provides another striking instance of intertextuality in the episode in which Polinka strives to please her husband by memorizing his favorite author's work. Initially, Saks's attempts to implement Jacques's educational scheme by encouraging Polinka to read some of the early George Sand romances. Quite certain that one woman will be able to understand the genius of another, Saks watches in disillusionment as his child-bride "yawns and yawns and throws the books aside with disgust" (*Polinka Saks,* 7). Later, she tries to please her husband by trying to read Sand in earnest. Taking *Mauprat* from the bookshelf, she asks Saks:

"Is this any good?"

"It's very good, Polinka, but you hate George Sand. . . . Do you

remember that you complained that you did not understand anything
in it?"

"I read it without any real desire," she replied. "Now I'm going to
try hard" . . . she added, smiling, "I'm going to learn it by heart the way
they forced us to learn in school."

"How can you pound something like this into your memory? Who
memorizes to learn at your age?" he asked in desperation. (*Polinka
Saks*, 29)

The patient Saks seizes the novel from Polinka's hands excitedly. She fails
to comprehend her husband's exasperation, having been praised in board-
ing school for her ability to recite from memory.

In *Na zare zhizni* (At the dawn of life) (1964), E. Vodovozova recounts
that the closed institute protected its students from evil influences, a security measure that also fostered excessive innocence. The language in the
early letters of Polinka and Fernande reveals the immaturity of both heroines. Her correspondence with Clémence reveals Fernande as a chatty,
puerile, exuberant schoolgirl, naïvely fascinated by love. She confides:

Vraiment, il n'y a pas longtemps que je lisais encore des contes de
fées; c'était toujours la même chose, mais c'était bien beau! C'était
toujours une pauvre fille maltraitée, abandonnée, ou captive, qui, par
les fentes de sa prison, ou du haut d'un des arbres du désert, voyait
passer, comme dans un rêve le plus beau prince du monde escorté de
toutes les richesses et de toutes les joies de la terre. Alors la fée entassait
prodiges sur prodiges pour délivrer sa protégée; et un beau jour
Cendrillon voyait l'amour et le monde à ses pieds. (*Jacques*, 76)

Really, not such a long time ago, I was still reading fairy tales. It was
always the same thing, but it was always so beautiful! There was
always a poor, mistreated, abandoned or captive girl who, through the
bars of her prison or from the top of one of the trees in the desert, saw
the most handsome prince in the world pass by, as in a dream, with all
of earth's riches and joys. So then, the fairy lavished one marvel upon
the next to save her goddaughter; and one fine day, Cinderella saw
love and the whole world waiting at her feet.

Similarly, Polinka's hyperbole, exaggerated French endearments and
memories of frolicking in the dormitory reveal her equally ingenuous schoolgirl mentality. She writes her former schoolmate, "The day I received your
letter, ma toute belle, mon incomparable Annette, was the happiest day of

my life!" (*Polinka Saks*, 5–6). Upon leaving the sheltering walls of the institute, these girls assimilated only with great difficulty to the society from which they had been assiduously kept apart.[18] Not surprisingly, the figure of the *institutka* attracted numerous writers of fiction. When innocence suddenly encounters corruption, the outcome tends to be dramatic. Prince Galitskii, a superficial, shallow, superfluous rake (a common component of the love triangle in Russian fiction) seduces the enchanting, childlike Polinka while Saks is away on business. In contrast to Saks, who encourages her to challenge herself and to grow intellectually, Galitskii loves Polinka precisely because she is an angel rather than a woman. Unlike Fernande, Polinka soon grows disillusioned in her second marriage. As she outgrows the ignorance that had been a product of her upbringing and institute education, (and that had so completely exasperated her first husband), Polinka appreciates Saks's real worth and rebels against the empty existence. Her language undergoes a sudden transformation during her second marriage. The naïve *institutka* adopts the serious, introspective qualities evident in Saks's own language.

Suddenly, everything Saks had tried to impress upon her hits Polinka like a bolt of lightning, clarifying that which had formerly been dark in her soul. She recognizes, too late (for she will die before they can ever be reconciled), that she had always loved Konstantin. She simply had not encountered a sufficient amount of life's trials to appreciate his sober enlightenment.

Although he adopts the principles of *Jacques* in dealing with his wife's infidelity, Konstantin, a reasonable, educated man, contrasts sharply with Sand's lofty, fatalistic hero. He suffers tremendously from having lost Polinka and questions his decision of having passively stepped aside for his rival. "Maybe someday flaming youth will call me a new Jacques, but I am a man in love; . . . why are the rights of women important to me? Why do I need to know the theory of love and its laws? It's only words, words" (*Polinka Saks*, 54). Druzhinin shifts the emphasis in *Polinka Saks* from the emancipation of the heart to the right of a woman to be treated as an equal adult rather than as a child. He makes *Jacques* the basis of a treatise on women's education, condemning Polinka's social formation for her marital tragedy.

"Iakov Pasynkov"—Ivan Turgenev

Turgenev's story "Iakov Pasynkov" (1855) contrasts sharply with Druzhinin's tale in the manner in which its author borrowed from George Sand's work. Whereas Druzhinin established his literary career with a blatant imitation of a Sand novel, Turgenev employs only generic likenesses. George Sand was only one major influence, and Turgenev transforms any borrowings through own invention.

Of all her Russian devotees, only Turgenev developed a close personal relationship with George Sand. They did not initiate this friendship until 1872, when Turgenev was already in his fifties and George Sand nearly seventy. Sand's influence on Turgenev preceded their acquaintance by many years, beginning when Turgenev was a sixteen-year-old student at Petersburg University and Sand's first novels were being published.[19] Throughout their lives, they shared a mutual love for the opera singer Pauline Viardot. The French novelist dedicated her lengthiest novel, *Consuelo* (1842), to the opera star and claimed to have modeled the novel's ideal heroine after Viardot. Turgenev pined for her for years in yet another ménage à trois, a prominent feature of nineteenth-century intellectual life. This study examines the pervasive impact of the love triangle in fiction, but this proved also to be a common element in a society where reality often imitated fiction. Among Turgenev's associates who formed these ménages à trois were the Panaevs and Nekrasov, the Shelgunovs and Mikhailov, the Bokovs and Sechenov (after whom Chernyshevskii modeled Vera Pavlovna and Kirsanov in *What is to be Done?*) and the Ogarevs and Herzen.[20] Herzen again suffered from a tragic love triangle later when his beloved wife Natalia took a lover, a dilettante German poet named George Herwegh, whom Herzen had befriended. Although his wife had employed the theory of love outlined in *Jacques* in taking a lover, it never occurred to Herzen to acquiesce and step aside self-effacingly for his wife's happiness, as had the literary prototype. Instead he grew irate and lambasted Herwegh as a "Horace," after the insincere and bombastic character in Sand's novel, whom he had earlier labeled as "petty" and "egotistical."[21] Turgenev's position in his own ménage à trois, however, appears to have been less a case of freedom for a woman than of thralldom for a man. Public opinion had it that Viardot had enslaved Turgenev, reducing him to the state of her "cavalier servant" and luring him away from Russia, thereby hindering his understanding of his own country. Critics condemned his love for the married opera star as "a sign of his chronic weakness of will, at the root of his pessimism and his melancholy."[22]

Sand's influence on Turgenev strongly resembles the impact she had on another mutual friend, Flaubert. They both adored her as a great and humane woman, but acknowledged her limitations as an artist of form. Both disagreed with her aesthetics. Flaubert once wrote to Sand that he felt an unconquerable repugnance to writing "from his heart."[23]

Russian critics have long been in search of Sandian influences in Turgenev's work. *Jacques* and *Horace* are two works often neglected by critics with regard to Turgenev's borrowings and adaptations. In 1834, the Russian novelist completed a poetic drama, *Steno*, likely named after the idealistic young poet in *Lélia* (1833).[24] Many critics have postulated a relationship between Sand's so-called "rustic novels" or *romans champêtres* and Turgenev's *Notes of a Hunter*. In these works, which coincide significantly in their dates of publication, both authors employ elaborate, poetic descriptions of nature, replete with folklore and folk superstitions.[25] When Sand's popularity reached its peak during the reign of the "generation of the forties," of which Turgenev was an important member, the French author was still one of Turgenev's most revered writers. Upon reading Sand's pastoral novel *François le Champi* in *Journal des Débats*, Turgenev wrote to Pauline Viardot in January 1848:

> It is done in the best possible way: simple, true, poignant. She blends in a few too many peasant expressions perhaps; it lends an affected air to her narrative from time to time. . . . This woman has the talent to render the most subtle, fleeting impressions in a firm, clear and comprehensible manner. She knows how to conjure the (subtlest) scents and the slightest sounds.[26]

In spite of Turgenev's criticisms of Sand, this letter demonstrates the scrupulous detail with which he studied the stylistic effects Sand had achieved. He openly acknowledged to the French novelist her impact on his work. In response to Sand's praise of his *Notes of a Hunter*, Turgenev wrote her, "On the way to Nohant I promised myself to tell you of the immense influence which you [have] had upon me as a writer."[27]

Although I discuss Sand's *Mauprat* in relation to Turgenev's *On the Eve* in this book, I would be remiss in failing to mention the parallels between Sand's Patience, a character in that work, and Turgenev's Kasian in *Notes of a Hunter*. A noted critic, M. Sumtsov, says in "Vliianie Zhorzh Zand na Turgeneva" (The influence of George Sand on Turgenev) that Kasian bears an uncanny likeness to his literary predecessor through his intelligence, his gentleness, and his loving attitude toward nature. Moreover, they resemble one another physically; both have thick, black hair. Both are reputed to be sorcerers by the neighboring peasants and share an inclination to philosophize. Like the educated Patience, Kasian can read and teaches his daughter Aniushka to read as well, a detail which accords poorly with the life of the Russian peasantry of the forties. Both live isolated, solitary lives and share an aversion to physical labor. An interesting parallel exists in Patience's horror at the killing of the owl by the young Mauprat and in Kasian's reaction to the killing of the corncrake by the hunter.[28]

Halpérine-Kaminski notes, however, that one must refrain from seeking Sand's effect upon Turgenev's talent in the details of characters and inventions. The effect is larger, the critic contends. "One finds in Turgenev's writing Sand's compassionate pity for the weak and for victims of social class and her taste for rustic milieux. The similarities extend to the sobriety of the descriptions in Turgenev's work and in the picturesque reality of his characters."[29] Halpérine-Kaminski regrettably provides little concrete evidence to substantiate these remarks. Even more unfortunate is the fact that Turgenev's hesitant nature prevented him from making a public statement about George Sand in the name of Russian people. He would have been the ideal candidate to testify to the enormous effect which her works had had upon his generation. He admitted to Flaubert that upon hearing of Sand's death, he had wanted to send a message of condolence to Nohant in the name of the Russian people. He regretted that he had been restrained by "a kind of ridiculous modesty, by a fear of the *Figaro*, or publicity—stupid things in fact!" "The Russian public," he wrote,

> was one of those upon whom Madame Sand had the most influence—and it should have been said, by God!—and I had the right to do it after all! But there you have it![30]

Turgenev did submit one of his finest letters to A. Suvarin, the editor of the newspaper *Novoe vremia* (*New Times*) after Sand's death in June 1876. Reacting strongly to an indifferent obituary, Turgenev summed up extremely well both the essence of his friendship with the French novelist and her significance for him. An ardent admirer and faithful supporter of Sand, Turgenev reveals in his eulogy that if he had reservations about her abilities as a novelist, he had none whatsoever about her qualities as a human being:

> When, about eight years ago, I first became close friends with George Sand, the ecstatic admiration which she had once aroused in me had already disappeared. I no longer adored her; but it was impossible to enter into the circle of her private life—and not become her adorer in another, perhaps better sense. . . . Believe me, George Sand is one of our saints; you will understand certainly what I mean by this word.[31]

Sand described the type and invented the term *homme inutile* (the useless/ superfluous man) in *Jacques*. The eponymous hero, a former officer of Napoléon, maintains lofty, romantic notions about the impossibility of perfect love. Incest taboos prevent him from pursuing a romantic encounter with the woman he loves because she may be his half-sister. Instead he marries her half-sister, a woman whose temperament contrasts sharply to his own. Disillusioned and out of his element in the dreary reactionary period after Waterloo, this ineffectual romanticist kills himself to enable his wife to marry the man she loves.[32]

Similarly, Turgenev's hero sacrifices his prospects for happiness so that the girl he loves can marry his rival, and the choice of name (Iakov = Jacques) indicates that the Russian novelist certainly intended to remind readers of the French prototype.

Like Jacques's love for Sylvia, Pasynkov's great loves for both Fräulein Frederika and Sofia remain purely platonic. The narrator, a close friend of Pasynkov's from school days, reveals:

> He only saw his beloved on Sundays, when she used to come and play at forfeits with the Winterkeller children, and he had very little conversation with her. But once, when she said to him, "Mein lieber, lieber Herr Jacob!" he did not sleep all night from excess of bliss. It never even struck him at the time that she called all his schoolfellows "mein lieber." ("Iakov Pasynkov," 157)

When Fräulein Frederika becomes engaged to Herr Kniftus, Iakov reveals his sorrow to his confidant, the narrator. Like Jacques, Pasynkov never seeks the society of anyone, but remains courteous and gentle to all. If rudely treated, he is neither humiliated nor sullen. He simply withdraws and holds himself aloof, with a sort of regretful look, as if he is biding his time. Upon learning of the fräulein's impending nuptials, Pasynkov presses Herr Kniftus's hand and sincerely wishes him complete and enduring happiness. Later, while discussing the matter with his confidant, he concludes in abdication, "Seek consolation in poetry and in friendship" ("Iakov Pasynkov," 158–59). Like Sand's hero, Pasynkov encounters conflict with self-effacing resignation.

Later, the narrator confides to Pasynkov his love for Sofia Zlotnitsky. Iakov, too begins to spend a great deal of time with Sofia and her sister Varvara. When the narrator learns in a drinking bout with his associate Asanov that Sofia is deeply in love with the latter, the narrator confronts her the next day with excerpts he has memorized from her letters to Asanov.

Reviled and deeply ashamed, the narrator retreats to his home where his friend Pasynkov overhears Asanov's confrontation with him later that day. Confiding his agonizing jealousy to Pasynkov, the narrator falls sobbing on his friend's neck. Iakov assures his friend that he will talk to Sofia and to Asanov (whom he dislikes) on his behalf to resolve the conflict. Unbeknownst to the narrator (and therefore to the reader), Iakov himself has fallen deeply in love with Sofia, a fact which he will only reveal on his deathbed. Pasynkov unselfishly resolves the argument and restores peace between Sofia and the narrator, encouraging his friend to continue his visits to her, lest his intentions be misconstrued. Knowing he has acted abominably, the narrator fears he has lost Iakov's respect. Pasynkov counters, "'Me! Despise you? . . .'" (His affectionate eyes glowed with love). 'Despise you . . . silly fellow! Don't I see how hard it's been for you, how you're suffering'?" ("Iakov Pasynkov," 172). Even in moments of personal despair, he sympathizes unselfishly and genuinely with others.

Similarly, Fernande writes Octave of Jacques's generous forgiveness:

Tu as raison, Octave, c'est un homme excellent; il est impossible d'avoir plus de générosité, de douceur, de délicatesse et de raison. Je vois bien qu'il sait tout. (*Jacques*, 376)

You are right, Octave, he's an excellent man; it is impossible to have more generosity, sweetness, tenderness and fairness. I see now that he knows everything.

As he lies dying from an arrow wound to the lung, Pasynkov recounts the incident to the narrator and finally avows his secret love.

"Yes," Pasynkov began again; "that explanation with her . . . I shall never forget it. It was then I found out, then I realized the meaning of the word I had chosen for my self long before: resignation. But still she has remained my constant dream, my ideal. . . . And he's to be pitied who lives without an ideal!" ("Iakov Pasynkov," 189)

This self-proclaimed dreamer resigns himself to fate. Like Jacques, his goodness and romantic notions translate tragically into dark self-fulfilling prophecies. The most ironic connection between these two ineffectual dreamers stems from their tragic mistakes in having loved the wrong sister! Jacques marries Fernande to save her from Sylvia's tyrannical mother, and because her blood relationship to Sylvia (of which both sisters are unaware) enables Jacques to sublimate his forbidden love as completely as possible. But Sylvia remains his soul mate and Fernande is a poor match for the lofty romanticist. Similarly, the narrator mourns Pasynkov's death with his former love interest, Sofia, and laments:

> And a man like that . . . has left us unnoticed, almost unappreciated! But that's no great loss. What is the use of man's appreciation? What pains me, what wounds me, is that such a man, with such a loving and devoted heart, is dead without having once known the bliss of love returned. ("Iakov Pasynkov," 199)

Sofia astounds the narrator by revealing that her sister Varvara had deeply loved Pasynkov over the years. Her dedication to him had deterred her from ever marrying another. Ironically, Sofia might have requited Pasynkov's love had her sister not desired him. His most endearing qualities—his genuine commitment to ideals and his romantic notions of a perfect love—condemn Iakov to an open-ended existence, during which he never enjoys the fulfillment of closure, completion or consummation.

What is to be Done?—Nikolai Chernyshevskii

Nikolai Chernyshevskii virtually worshipped George Sand for her socialist idealism and her proclamation of Saint Simon's "rehabilitation of the flesh." He derived the plot of his novel, *Chto delat? (What is to be Done?)* (1863), from Sand's *Jacques*, a fact known to Soviet scholars but which, if not suppressed, rarely received mention.[33] Chernyshevskii's interest in Sand dates from the early 1840s, when he read his father's copies of *Fatherland Notes* at his home in Saratov. The fascination continued throughout his lifetime. Before departing for his exile in Siberia, Chernyshevskii had with him four Sand novels in the Peter-Paul Fortress. It was during his incarceration there that he wrote his only published novel, the revolutionary *What is to be Done?*

The title itself dramatizes the move from the question of culpability (as with Herzen's *Who is to Blame?)* to the question of practical activity. The subtitle, "Tales about New People," indicates that Chernyshevskii's characters subscribe to a new, more radical breed of heroism. His heroes, Kirsanov and Lopukhov, his "woman-as-hero" Vera Pavlovna, and his "superhero" Rakhmetov (modeled after Laravinière in Sand's *Horace*) all focus the attention of readers and critics on the new generation of the sixties with their unprecedented aspirations and achievements.[34]

The Russian scholar A. Skaftymov traces thematic and structural parallels between *Jacques* and *What is to be Done?* and concludes that Sand's novel exercised the single most important influence on Chernyshevskii's ideas regarding women. Believing that women should enjoy complete freedom in love, Chernyshevskii extended these options to his own wife, who took full advantage of them. Prior to their marriage, she had inquired what actions he would take if she were ever to deceive him. He told her to read *Jacques*. Later, while in prison, Chernyshevskii wrote and counseled his son to read Sand as a means of self-improvement.[35]

Both Sand and Chernyshevskii employ the plot of a developing love triangle to raise such issues as woman's rights as man's equal partner, an indictment of marriage as a constricting institution, overcoming guilt, succumbing to desire, and, in Chernyshevskii's case, the need for women to establish themselves as financially independent partners. The novelists recount the nature of a woman's submission first as a daughter and later as a woman. Both heroines dedicate themselves zealously to their extraordinarily sensitive husbands. Jacques and Dmitrii have delivered Fernande and Vera, respectively, from oppressive mothers. In spite of their gratitude, however, both women experience a sexual awakening that only a beloved family friend can satisfy.

By comparing Sand's *Jacques* and Chernyshevskii's *What is to be Done?* I shall demonstrate the degree to which Sand's work influenced the Russian writer by examining the roles of both heroines first as daughters and mothers, then as wives and lovers, and finally as members of society. The last stage of my discussion will reflect Chernyshevskii's variation on Sand's theme of emotional emancipation.

Jacques serves as a point of departure for the Russian novelist's more revolutionary social solutions to the subjugation of women. *What is to be Done?* served as a virtual bible to members of the Russian intelligentsia raised in the last decades of the nineteenth century. Students debated feverishly the issues raised by the novel. Many of them established co-operatives and communal living arrangements comparable to those in Chernyshevskii's work.

Like Sand, Nikolai Chernyshevskii insisted on freedom in love, at the same time celebrating the joys of a lasting union. Chernyshevskii revered Sand, whose novels convey persuasive objections to family relations that are based on social convention and domestic tyranny rather than on mutual love and respect.[36] Greatly interested in the theoretical question of how men and women relate to one another, Chernyshevskii echoed the contention of George Sand and other feminist romantics that marriage constitutes a thoroughly dehumanizing experience for women unless they are completely free to choose their spouses and to terminate their marriages at will. They considered that to be nothing but a wife and mother was to renounce much of one's productive and creative capacity in return for "servant status."[37]

In *What is to be Done?* Vera Pavlovna feels repugnance and pity for her mother, Maria Alekseevna, a woman who steals goods and pawns them for cash. Vera laments to her tutor, Dmitrii Lopukhov, while still living in her parents' wretched home:

> Akh! but if you only knew, my friend, how hard, how hard it is for me to remain here. When there was no near possibility for me to escape from this degradation, from this misery, I kept myself by main force in a deathly apathy. But now, my friend, it is too suffocating in this foul, wretched atmosphere! (*What is to be Done?* 99)

Maria will do anything to her daughter—beat her or cosset her—to force her into marrying Mikhail Ivanych Storeshnikov, a moderately well-off nobleman and wastrel. When she finally comprehends, at the gates of the "School of Pages," that Vera has disappeared and has married the tutor, Maria exclaims all the way home, "She has robbed me! She has robbed me!" (*What is to be Done?* 143). Lopukhov, a young nihilist medical student who marries Vera Pavlovna solely to save her from her tyrannical mother, ushers in an era (during the 1860s and 1870s) of "the fictional marriage," whereby a man married in order to rescue a girl from her family or to enable her to attend a university. Tatiana Bogdanovich recounts in her work, *Love Among the People of the '60s,* the convoluted stories of these unconsummated unions, many of which led to conflicts as great as those in Sand's novels.[38] Instead of making love to Vera, Dmitrii encourages his bride to read from his collection of utilitarian tracts.

Chernyshevskii indicates clearly, however, that Maria Alekseevna has herself fallen victim to difficult circumstances common to many women of her time. Moreover, many of the mother's evil machinations have yielded positive results for her daughter. The money procured through Maria's stolen goods has financed Vera's education. Further, the young woman's sense of decency has developed in reaction to Maria Alekseevna's example of maternal corruption. Had her mother been good, she rationalizes in her dream, Vera would have been made a doll. "Such a mother must have a doll in her daughter, because she herself is a doll, and she is always playing dolls with dolls" (*What is to be Done?* 170). In Vera's dream, her mother reproaches her for her ingratitude:

> Be grateful, you selfish girl! Do not love, do not respect me! I am a vixen; why should you love me? But you understand, Vera, that if I were not what I am, you would not be what you are. You are good because I am bad. (*What is to be Done?* 169)

Similarly, in Sand's novel, the young Fernande suffers the wrath of a calculating, gold-digging mother. Jacques takes tremendous pride in delivering Fernande from her depraved mother, Mme. de Theursan, the former mistress of his father and the mother of his soul mate, Sylvia. He writes to Sylvia: "[Je] l'épouse . . . pour deux raisons: la première, parce que c'est l'unique moyen de la posséder; la seconde, parce que c'est l'unique moyen de l'arracher des mains d'une méchante mère, et de lui procurer une vie honorable et indepéndante" (I am marrying her for two reasons: the first, because it is the only way she can become mine; the second, because it is the only way to tear her from the hands of a cruel mother and to offer her an honorable and independent life" (*Jacques*, 38). Moreover, in spite of her misgivings about Fernande's marriage to an older man, Clémence admits that as much as she dislikes Fernande's mother, she is charmed that Fernande is nothing like her, and that if anything can console her for the haste with which Fernande is determined to marry Jacques, it is the knowledge that she can fall into no worse hands than those she is leaving.

Unlike Vera Pavlovna, however, Fernande eventually assumes many of her mother's faults, albeit unwittingly. Sand's portrayal of Fernande as a mother indicates that although the young woman considers her children an enhancement to her happiness, she accords true priority to her love relationships, first with Jacques, then with Octave. In *Jacques*, Fernande bears twins, who later die as if in punishment for her guilty love for Octave. Later she carries Octave's child. Children remain peripheral to the novel, though. The central concern of *Jacques* deals with desire and culpability.

Chernyshevskii takes yet a step further with this love of pleasure at the expense of the traditional female role as wife and mother. Vera appears to lack maternal instincts entirely. The narrator of *What is to be Done?* leads the reader to believe that after five months of marriage to Dmitrii Lopukhov, Vera is pregnant:

> Dmitrii Sergeytch, returning from one of his lessons, found his wife in a peculiar state of mind. Her eyes were shining with pride and happi-

ness. This caused Dmitrii Sergeytch to remember that for several days past he had seen in her some signs of mental exaltation, joyful thoughts, and tender pride. (*What is to be Done?* 153)

As it turns out, Vera gives birth to an idea. She resolves happily to establish a sewing union. This will offer poor girls the opportunity to build their own community and to become self-sufficient.

Sand's *Jacques* proved to be revolutionary in its denouncement of the stifling confines imposed on women. But whereas Sand's prescription for improvement lay in the liberation of the heart, Chernyshevskii's proposed reforms extended from the nuclear family to all of society.

The parallel developments of the love triangle in the two novels further demonstrate the degree to which Chernyshevskii implemented (and revolutionized) Sand's ideas in *What is to be Done?* The husbands featured in both novels denounce the traditional roles prescribed by matrimony. Jacques criticizes the "barbarous institution of marriage," believing the wifely vows of fidelity and obedience to be base and degrading. He writes Fernande that the improvements to which a few generous spirits aspire will never be realized in this century. When he marries the young, inexperienced Fernande, he pledges to her his lifelong respect. He promises that, should she one day cease to be attracted to him as a lover and find him too old, he will leave her in peace to pursue her destiny as she sees fit. He later forgives Fernande her love for Octave. Seeing her pale, incapable of lying, suffering the ordeals of a conscience laden with guilt, ready at any moment to confess her sins to him, Jacques writes Sylvia:

> Nulle créature humaine ne peut commander à l'amour, et nul n'est coupable pour le ressentir et pour le perdre. Ce qui avilit la femme, c'est le mensonge. Ce qui constitue l'adultère, ce n'est pas l'heure qu'elle accorde à son amant, c'est la nuit qu'elle va passer ensuite dans les bras de son mari. (*Jacques*, 339)

> No human being is capable of manipulating love, and no one is guilty for experiencing it or for losing it. What degrades a woman is lying. What constitutes adultery is not the hour she spends with her lover, but the night she is going to spend afterwards in her husband's arms.

Dmitrii demonstrates the same respect for Vera in *What is to be Done?* Lopukhov leaves medical school to marry Vera Pavlovna. They take every precaution to ensure their peaceful cohabitation, dwelling in separate bedrooms with a common room between them. Lopukhov encourages his wife to learn practical skills that she may employ in the service of humanity. Establishing a Fourierist sewing cartel composed of poverty-stricken women who become productive members of society, Vera Pavlovna later pursues medical studies in order to serve humankind (and particularly womankind) in an even greater capacity. When married to Kirsanov, she reflects:

> One of them [the professions] is far more convenient to me than the others. My husband is a doctor. He devotes all his leisure time to me. With such a husband, it is an easy matter for me to try to be a doctor. It would be a very striking thing if there should spring up at last a class of women doctors. They would be very useful for all women. It is much easier for a woman to talk with a woman than with a man. How much suffering, death, and misfortune would be removed. I must try it. (*What is to be Done?* 356)

When Lopukhov's wife and his best friend fall in love, in spite of themselves, he does not condemn Vera for her change of heart. "It makes no difference," he tells her, "how or why it came to you; you cannot help it. Now there is only one choice: either you should suffer and I suffer also through it, or you should cease to suffer, and I too" (*What is to be Done?* 263). He assures Vera that regardless of her decision, they shall always remain friends. For Chernyshevskii, marriage must provide a rational, free, and equal partnership, dissoluble if true love for another intervenes but always courteous and respectful. They should shun each other's company unless they can appear before one another with the same politeness and good humor that they would accord to strangers.

The novels differ in one important aspect: the manner in which the wife struggles for equality in the partnership of marriage. This variation further indicates the degree to which Chernyshevskii employed Sand's ideas as a basis for a much more revolutionary work, one that prescribed specific measures for sweeping social reforms and that redefined societal roles.

In *What is to be Done?* Vera explains to her tutor before they marry that although she does not yet know how she will feel when she loves a man, she does know that she will allow no one to enslave her. She wants to be free, under obligation to no one: "I want to do only what I have it in my heart to do, and let others do the same; I do not ask anything of anybody; I do not want to curtail anybody's freedom. I want to be free myself" (*What is to be Done?* 45).

Shortly after their marriage, in fact, Vera begins to assert her insistence on being treated as her husband's equal. She chastises Dmitrii for kissing her hand, considering it inappropriate for a woman's hand to be kissed when a man's is not. Vera forbids him from placing her on a pedestal and from engaging in excessive flattery:

> What is that? Do you mean to give me a compliment? You want to be very polite; but I know too well how people flatter so as to reign under a mask of humility. I beg of you to speak more simply hereafter. My dear, you are praising me to death. I am ashamed, my dear; don't praise me, lest I become too proud. (*What is to be Done?* 120)

Vera's independence awes even the progressive Lopukhov. He tells her, "There is so little femininity in your nature, Vera Pavlovna, that most likely you have nothing but men's thoughts" (*What is to be Done?* 121). She replies:

> Akh! my dearest, what does that word "femininity" mean? I understand that a woman speaks in a contralto voice, a man in a baritone; but what of that? Is it worthwhile to ask us about such things? Why do people keep telling us that it is our duty to remain feminine? Isn't it a piece of nonsense, dear? (*What is to be Done?* 121)

Vera Pavlovna insists on working, refusing to live at her husband's expense. The narrator of Chernyshevskii's novel reflects, "There can be no full happiness without full independence. Poor women, how few among you have this happiness" (357). When Dmitrii questions Vera as to how she has come to adopt these ideas, she replies incredulously, "Akh! and now he is asking me who gave me that idea. Why, weren't you yourself saying this very thing? And in your books—fully half of them say so" (119).

Vera's later commitment to medicine demonstrates once again the revolutionary nature of Chernyshevskii's novel. *What is to be Done?* does not really constitute a novel at all, but rather a manual (often quite didactic) disguised as a novel ("Tales of the New People") which translates *Jacques*'s ideas on marriage into terms designed to appeal to the progressive young utilitarians of the late 1800s. They had supposedly outgrown notions of romantic love and its accompanying jealousy and yearned for action in lieu of further speculation. Vera Pavlovna reads George Sand's books and cites their limitations:

Now here is George Sand —such a good and noble woman! —and yet, she thinks that these ideas are only visionary. And our own writers—but no; our writers have nothing of the kind at all. Or take Dickens; he has something of the sort, but it seems as though he did not hope for it at all, as though he only wished that it might be, for he is kind-hearted, but he is sure that it cannot be. But how is it that they don't know that this cannot help being, that this state of things must actually come about, that it will be accomplished without fail, that no one will be poor or unfortunate? (*What is to be Done?* 73)

Whereas Sand's books present goodness and morality only in dreams, Lopukhov has taught Vera that these dreams and utopias will come to fruition without fail. Chernyshevskii consequently establishes his work as a revolutionary improvement on Sand's original.

As Vera develops a strong sense of self, she channels her energies directly into an effort for the benefit of a collective. *What is to be Done?* provides a (debatably) tangible solution to the question it raises. Historically considered Belinskii's successor as the leader of the Russian intelligentsia, Chernyshevskii wrote his novel while serving a prison term for having denounced tzarist injustice. The novel demonstrates Chernyshevskii's socialist efforts to make young people think about the future, reducing complex public and private phenomena to basic values. Whereas Sand's novel also challenges fundamental injustices with regard to prescribed marital roles, *Jacques* lacks the didactic platform of *What is to be Done?* Moreover, the solution to the love triangle presented by Sand proves to be a tragic and unsatisfactory resolution to a condition in which everyone is a victim. For a being whose existence proves futile to all, Jacques rationalizes, suicide constitutes a legitimate act (*Jacques*, 391). Although Chernyshevskii adopted Sand's plot, he added a bracing, rational revision; Dmitrii fakes his death with joyous and socially positive results. A nihilist, Chernyshevskii espoused a doctrine of "enlightened self-interest." According to its policies, a man would step aside if his wife were to fall in love with another; he would wish her well and secure a new partner. Moreover, this doctrine proclaimed that as a rational creature, man does nothing that is not in his own best interest. Lopukhov, though passionately in love with Vera Pavlovna, cannot, according to this code, constrain his wife or friend. He resolves the situation brilliantly:

Now the sapient reader will not fail to have guessed who shot himself. "I saw long ago that it was Lopukhov," says the sapient reader in triumph at his perspicacity. Where could he have hid himself, and how did his cap have a bullet hole through the top? "There is no need of asking; it is only a trick of his, but he caught himself in a net, the rascal," says the sapient reader. Nu! God be with thee; decide it just as thou pleasest; there's no reasoning with thee. (*What is to be Done?* 269)

News that he lives comes through Rakhmetov, the emerging hero of history. When Vera and Kirsanov learn that Lopukhov is alive, they dine voraciously, kissing and caressing all the while. A double row of dots suggests that they fulfill their passions.[39] Their joy upon learning of his survival dispels all of the guilt Vera had suffered initially. Having been tormented by an inexplicable passion for Kirsanov, Vera had tried everything in her power to fully reciprocate Lopukhov's love for her. For a brief period she had even shared her first husband's bed. In her third dream, however, Vera must read the painful pages of her innermost diary. Here, Chernyshevskii succeeds in achieving recognizable human feeling. Vera laments the fact that she feels gratitude rather than passion for Lopukhov, and that except for establishing her sewing cartel, she has behaved like a self-indulgent tease. Rakhmetov later reveals to Vera the inevitability of her separation from Dmitrii. Because of their intelligence, Vera and Dmitrii had not quarreled and fought when they first sensed an uneasiness with each other. Rakhmetov explains:

> Your dissatisfaction could not have taken such a form because both of you were enlightened people, and therefore it was developed in only its easiest, gentlest, and least offensive form,—love towards another. Consequently there is no use in talking about love to another, that is not the main trouble at all. The essence of the matter lies in your dissatisfaction with your former position, and the cause of this dissatisfaction was the discordance of your characters. Both of you were good people, but after your character became mature, Vera Pavlovna, and lost its childish indefiniteness, and acquired definite features, it proved that you and Dmitrii Sergeyitch were not very well suited to each other. (*What is to be Done?* 303)

Lopukhov explains in retrospect that the mistake was exacerbated by the fact that Vera had revered him too highly after marriage. Dmitrii relates, "There was never any equality between us. She took for a universal human feature any peculiarity of mine, and for a time she was drawn away by it" (319).

In Sand's novel, the same issues provoke the adulterous affair between Fernande and Octave. Daily proximity between two people poorly matched in age, temperament, experience, upbringing and expectations of each other leads to tension and poor communication. After a few short months of delirious happiness, Fernande begins to suffer from jealousy, anxiety and insecurity, as she realizes that "tout n'est pas joie dans l'amour; il y a aussi bien des larmes, et je ne les répands pas toutes dans le sein de Jacques, car je vois que j'augmente sa tristesse en lui montrant la mienne" (all is not joy in love; there are also plenty of tears, and I do not shed them all in Jacques's embrace, because I see that I only increase his sadness by showing him my own) (*Jacques*, 119–20). She reasons that Jacques treats her childish behavior unjustly, claiming that in her place, he would suffer perhaps more than she, since he had no rivals in the past. Before Sylvia's visit, Fernande forces her husband to swear solemnly that he has never been nor ever will be in love with this beautiful woman. She explains her need to have him assure her: "Ah! tu sais que je suis faible et qu'il faut me traiter avec condescendance; . . ." (Oh, you know that I am weak and that you must treat me with understanding) (*Jacques*,154). She implores her husband to refrain from rebelling against her in his pride and to try to soften a bit and understand her.

Jacques relates to Sylvia that it now appears as though Fernande is embracing her childish fears, which she had initially attempted to hide and to overcome. He regrets having to treat her like a ten-year-old child, but he fears at the same time that he is too much of a pedant and is too old to show her that "qu'au lieu d'avancer dans la vie morale elle recule, et perd, à écarter les moindres épines de son chemin, le temps qu'elle pourrait employer à s'ouvrir une nouvelle route, plus belle et plus spacieuse" (that instead of making progress in her moral life, she is falling backward and that, by removing the tiniest thorns from her path, she is wasting the time she could spend opening up a new, fairer and wider way) (*Jacques*, 156).

Jacques grows disillusioned by the insecure, melodramatic behavior of his child-bride. Imagining that he has lost interest in her, Fernande throws herself at his feet to beg his forgiveness. This repulses rather than moves him, however. Jacques is reminded of turbulent scenes with former lovers who, after having lost his esteem, tried in vain to reclaim his love. To see Fernande employing the same desperate tactics distresses him greatly. Fernande and Jacques begin to reflect in their letters to Clémence and Sylvia, respectively, that their short-lived bliss has degenerated into disappointment, disillusionment, and an inability to communicate.

After the birth of their twins, Jacques and Fernande refrain from making love for over a year. (Their abstinence stems from the common belief that sexual arousal affects the nursing mother's milk.)[41] The arrival of Octave, a handsome twenty-four-year-old man initially interested in Sylvia, compounds the difficulties of the marriage. Jacques and Sylvia, possibly children of the same father, are kindred spirits. Both share the same progressive notions about love and independence. Jacques and Sylvia serve as subject doubles (egos) who demonstrate ambivalent reactions to the two object doubles(alter egos), Fernande and Octave.[42] The subject or ego of each pairing exercises authority over the dependent object or alter ego. Fernande illustrates this dependence particularly well. She exists only through her investment in another. She fails to sustain her relationship with Jacques because he imposes on her a contradictory injunction. He has taken great pride in having rescued a weak girl from an oppressive home life, but he wants her to behave strongly and decisively without making clear to Fernande what he expects of her. Recognizing that "on n'aime que son pareil en ce monde" (one only loves one's equal in this life) (*Jacques*, 206), Fernande laments her incapacity to fulfill her husband's elusive expectations of her. She writes Clémence in resignation, asking , "Que faire maintenant?" (What is to be done now?) (*Jacques*, 142). Fernande relates that Jacques appears to grow progressively more disgusted with her through no fault of her own. She says, "Nous nous faisons du mal mutuellement par une sorte de fatalité" (We keep hurting each other as though by fate) (*Jacques*, 142).

Octave, too, has fallen from Sylvia's ethereal pedestal and treads the ground of the physical world. Fernande and Octave console each other by forming a new couple. He demands nothing else of the young woman than that she remain weak so that he may protect (and make decisions for) her. Fernande recognizes that she needs this status of submission and childlike security, confiding: "Je n'ai jamais souhaité d'autre bonheur que d'être protégée, aidée et consolée par l'affection d'un autre" (I have longed for no other happiness than to be protected, helped, and consoled by the affection of another) (*Jacques*, 227). The object doubles, Octave and Fernande, find in each other the ideal soul mate, as Jacques and Sylvia have. Fernande writes Octave that when the four of them are together, they form two pairs who are like two friends that sustain each other in both their pleasures and pains (250).

The fact that Jacques and Octave love the same two women indicates the complementary aspects of the two sisters, Sylvia as subject, Fernande as object: "l'une [Sylvia] brune, grande, fière et audacieuse, l'autre blanche, timide et sentimentale" (one [Sylvia] brunette, tall, proud and daring, the other, fair, shy and sentimental) (*Jacques*, 169). Like Rousseau's Julie and Claire, Fernande and Sylvia have a single sister spirit. Only through his attraction to Sylvia does Octave make Fernande's acquaintance. Similarly, Jacques's marriage to Fernande increases his proximity to Sylvia both mentally and physically.

Sand extends her doubling even to Jacques and Fernande's children, the twins. Janis Glasgow has made an interesting argument regarding the novel's relationship to Sand's personal life. Written in Venice after Sand's painful break with Alfred de Musset, *Jacques* features Octave, Fernande's male object double. Octave was the name of one of Musset's subject doubles in *Les caprices de Marianne* (1834). Glasgow asserts, moreover, that Alfred de Musset himself served as Sand's model for the object double.[43]

In the tradition of *Jacques,* Chernyshevskii introduces a fourth love object into the original love triangle, resulting in a balanced, harmonious quartet. Because the incest barrier does not exist between Lopukhov (Beaumont) and Katia, as it does between Jacques and Sylvia, everyone in Chernyshevskii's novel emerges personally fulfilled and socially productive. Several parallels link the four protagonists of the quartet. Vera has three rescuers throughout the course of the novel (Lopukhov, Rakhmetov and Kirsanov), two of whom also save Katia. Vera falls in love with Lopukhov's best friend, Kirsanov, who (unlike Jacques and Octave) serves as a virtual replica of Lopukhov:

> He, as well as Lopukhov, had regular and handsome features. Some regarded the former, others the latter, as the better looking. Lopukhov was rather thinner, had dark chestnut hair, gleaming dark eyes, which seemed almost black, an aquiline nose, thick lips and a rather oval face. Kirsanov had blond hair inclining to a brownish shade, dark blue eyes, a straight Grecian nose, a small mouth, an oblong face, and a remarkably light complexion. Both were men of very tall stature and straight; Lopukhov somewhat broader across his shoulders, Kirsanov somewhat taller. (*What is to be Done?* 201)

Lopukhov and Kirsanov share an interest in medicine, and have the same progressive ideology and taste in women. Their differences are physical and these are negligible. Lopukhov later remarks of his marriage that once he had realized that Vera's passion "was directed towards one who was absolutely worthy, and generally speaking, was absolutely able to fill [his] place, [he] became extremely glad" (*What is to be Done?* 325).

Much like Jacques's letter to Octave interrogating him about his intentions toward Fernande, Lopukhov attempts to discuss the matter rationally with Kirsanov in hypothetical terms:

> Let us suppose that there are three people in existence—a supposition which contains nothing impossible; let us suppose that one of them has a secret which he would like to keep from the second, and particularly from the third; let us suppose that the second finds out the secret of the third, and says to him: Do as I tell you, else I shall expose your secret to the third. What do you think about this matter? (*What is to be Done?* 252)

In a mixture of enlightened self-interest and faithfulness to Jacques, Lopukhov feigns suicide (though not troubling himself with the emotional scars he would leave behind, as had Jacques) and escapes to America. Free to marry, Vera and Kirsanlov wed a week later. A new wife, Katia, soon consoles Lopukhov for his loss. When he returns to Russia as Charles Beaumont, he and Katia rejoin the Kirsanovs. The two couples live and work together, free of jealousy and pettiness.

Like Dmitrii, Jacques can dismiss his rival, kill him, or merely pardon him. Instead he asks Octave whether he really cares for Fernande, whether he would take care of her if her husband were to abandon her, and whether the attachment would be durable. Like Lopukhov, Jacques puts his interrogation into hypothetical terms, referring to Fernande as "une personne qu'il n'est pas besoin de nommer" (someone we needn't bother naming) (*Jacques*, 328). The younger man answers that he knows that Jacques has been informed of his relationship with Fernande. He explains further that he has come to offer his life to Jacques in reparation for the damage he has caused. Octave writes further, however, that if Jacques should seek vengeance on Fernande, he (Octave) will risk his own life to save her, killing Jacques if necessary. Finally, Octave answers Jacques's inquiry by assuring him that he has such a profound and true attachment for Fernande that if Jacques should die or ever leave her out of bitterness, he (Octave) will devote his entire life to her. Quite satisfied with the result of this examination, Jacques leaves Fernande and Octave free to pursue their passion.

Unlike Dmitrii Lopukhov, who discusses Vera's passion for Kirsanov directly with her, absolving her of any blame, Jacques protects Fernande like a child until the very end. Early in the novel, she complains to Octave, "Voyez-vous, on me traite ici en enfant de quatre ans; mon mari et Sylvia s'imaginent que je ne suis pas en état de comprendre leurs sentiments et leurs pensées" (You see, I'm treated here like a four-year-old child; my husband and Sylvia fancy that I'm in no condition to understand their feelings and thoughts) (*Jacques*, 210). Jacques maintains his sovereignty over his wife by exercising his role as father figure. He takes every precaution to protect Fernande from the knowledge that he has been informed of the affair. He has Madame Borel send Fernande a letter stating that Monsieur Borel's letter to Jacques disclosing her indiscretion had never been sent.[44] Jacques insists that Fernande is not at fault for the passion she feels. He writes Sylvia that it would be a travesty to condemn one so sensitive and repentant as Fernande simply "parce que Dieu [l']a faite si faible et si douce" (because God has made her so frail and so sweet) (*Jacques*, 340).

Jacques's enlightened attitude toward his wife's desire for another is tainted by his condescension toward Fernande. Because she is innately weak and childlike, he reasons, it would be impossible to discuss a rational solution with her. Instead he magnanimously demonstrates to the woman he truly desires that he is kind, self-effacing, and doomed in love because the barrier of incest prevents him from pursuing Sylvia. He explains to his sister that Fernande and Octave are not to blame because they love each other. Desire is natural and culpability is superseded by sincerity. Jacques argues, "Il n'y a pas de crime là où il y a de l'amour sincère" (There is no crime where there is sincere love) (*Jacques*, 340). Marriage is a human institution, Sand's protagonist reasons, but passion is part of the divine essence.

Living in an age which does not permit divorce, Jacques fulfills his prenuptial promise to Fernande and discreetly disappears to take his own life in the Tyrol. To avert the suspicion of suicide, so as not to punish Fernande, Jacques falls over a precipice in such a manner that his death appears to be an accident. In Sand's *Jacques*, the hero's sacrifice yields irrevocable consequences. This is not the case, however, in Chernyshevskii's *What is to be Done?* Here Dmitrii, realizing that Vera and his own best friend Aleksandr will continue to torment themselves on his behalf, stages his own suicide in order to liberate them from the restraints imposed by his marriage to Vera. Later, Dmitrii reemerges as the American Charles Beaumont, in love with Katerina Vasilevna, another self-actualizing "new woman" of Russia. Through Kirsanov's help, Katia has rejected Solovkov, for whom she had previously been willing to sacrifice her life. A person of imagination, Katia falls in love with and marries Beaumont. George Sand is her favorite author and Geneviève her favorite heroine. When Beaumont insists that women need a man's experience in order to marry wisely, Katia counters, "Then only widows should marry?" (*What is to be Done?* 18).

Together, the Beaumonts and the Kirsanovs live an idyllic existence in which the doors between the rooms now remain open. All of the protagonists appear to enjoy comfortable circumstances and a larger block of time than the regular twenty-four-hour period allotted to those who are not "new people." Vera savors pastries and cups of tea-tinged cream, and enjoys long hot baths and lolling late in bed. All this Chernyshevskii's "new woman" can enjoy as a wife, mother, proprietor of a sewing cooperative, and as Russia's first woman medical student.[45] Vera and her husband leave for work midmorning and devote virtually every evening to parties, theater or the opera. Somewhere, out of sight (and certainly out of Chernyshevskii's consideration) someone has taken charge of cooking, cleaning, laundering, ironing and child care (or supervision of the children while they perform all of these tasks).[46] As the novel ends, the couples are living in delightful, innocent harmony. What the old morality would condemn as bigamy, the new morality reveals as an authentic and truly uncompromised communal life. Chernyshevskii answered the dilemma of desire and culpability posed in Sand's novel a generation earlier, and thereby greatly intensified and extended the original impact that Sand had made on the reading public.

Serving as a holy text to the "new people" of the 1860s, Nikolai Chernyshevskii's revolutionary novel *What is to be Done?* catapulted into action scores of progressive men and women with big aspirations. Whether the women had feminist, nihilist, or radical leanings, Chernyshevskii's novel provided them with specific devices for liberating themselves. Bourgeois feminists saw the novel as teaching the necessity of economic independence and education for women, as well as presenting a moral imperative for them to support each other in these endeavors. The *nigilistka* saw *What is to be Done?* as summoning women to free themselves from social incarceration and as espousing a doctrine of personal emancipation and sexual freedom. The effect of the novel on radicals was more subtle due to their dedication to the cause of "joining the people." Chernyshevskii did, however, encourage women through his fiction to join the ranks of the "new people" who would one day effect a social revolution.[47]

Vera Pavlovna, the heroine of *What is to be Done?*, appeared as the first female *raznochinets* (member of mixed classes) to play a prominent role in the emancipation of women. She was the first woman character in Russian fiction to try to initiate social change for women through economic independence. By establishing a sewing cooperative, the heroine goes beyond the bounds of the limited feminism of the time by becoming one of the "new people" in Russia. She expresses the necessity of economic emancipation as follows: "Money lies at the root of all things; . . . whoever has the money has the might and the right; . . . consequently so long as a woman lives at her husband's expense, she will be dependent upon him" (*What is to be Done?* 119–20).

The impact of Chernyshevskii's novel on Russia in the 1860s reveals particularly well the function of literature as a reflection and refraction of sociopolitical reality. Vera Pavlovna reflects the extent of self-evaluation and reassessment conducted by the Russian women of her era. This reflection bore such a striking similarity to the external world that many Russian girls and married women attempted to emulate Vera Pavlovna's rules of life. According to an official report of the censorship, many women ran away from their parental or conjugal home under the influence of the novel. They moved to the big cities and often to countries in Western Europe in search of employment, personal freedom, and education.[48] Chernyshevskii's novel significantly sensitized men to the Woman Question by linking the solution of women's oppression to socialism.[49] Through his fiction, Chernyshevskii reflected the social ills of his day, and by embodying his own notions of economic, romantic and educational emancipation for women, his work refracted a vision for reform and served as a tribute to the impact of a remarkable pioneer, George Sand.

4

Edmée, the New Woman: Desire for Androgyny

L'enracinement est peut-être le besoin le plus important et le plus méconnu de l'âme humaine. (The need for roots is perhaps the most important and the least recognized need of the human soul.)
—Simone Weil, *L'enracinement: Prélude à une déclaration des devoirs envers l'être humain*

Ultimately, the goals of spirituality and of revolutionary politics are the same: to create a world in which love, equality, freedom, and fulfillment of individual and collective potential are possible.
—Hallie Iglehart, "The Unnatural Divorce of Spirituality and Politics"

While separating from her husband, Casimir Dudevant, George Sand abandoned the bitter cynicism of her early novels in which unhappy women were paralyzed by tyrannical husbands. In its place she embraced a loving, active socialism. The leitmotif of love which Sand employed throughout her life in her works, as well as in her personal life, prevails particularly in her fifth novel, *Mauprat* (1837), one of her most revered works in Russia. In one of her rare communicative moods, Sand related to her friends:

Yes, love is the key to the enigma of the universe! Always to come forth again, to grow and cling to life, to seek one's opposite for the purpose of assimilation, continuously to accomplish the marvel of commingling and combining, whence springs the miracle of new productions—these are the laws of nature.[1]

Sand's fifth major novel and her first to preach utopian socialism and eternal love won a wide readership in Russia. Vissarion Belinskii, powerful arbiter of Russian literary taste in the 1840s, praised *Mauprat* in 1841, shortly after his conversion to French utopian socialism. His fervent enthusiasm set the tone for Sand's reception in Russia in the 1840s and 1850s. There she was proclaimed "the advocate of women as Schiller had been the advocate of humanity."[2]

Sand never abandoned the belief that a marriage between equal partners was inherently good. She contended that subservience or tyranny could claim no role in a valid marriage. Sand addressed members of the Central Committee of the Provisional Revolutionary Government in 1848, demanding that the state protect the rights of married women. She wrote:

> give back to the woman the civil rights that only marriage takes away from her, which the unmarried only can keep for herself; detestable error of our legislation which in effect puts woman into the greedy grasp of the man, and which makes marriage a state of eternal minority; whereas the majority of the young girls would decide never to marry if they had the slightest notion of the civil legislation at the age at which they renounce their rights.[3]

Sand's novel *Mauprat* features a "woman hero" who finds happiness in marriage after having served as the savior and educator of her spouse. By the 1860s, most educated Russians had also passed through Sand's early "romantic rebellion" and a breed of "new women" characters began to appear. In *Toward a Recognition of Androgyny* (1973), Carolyn Heilbrun differentiates the "woman as hero" from the traditional heroine, who is the woman the hero pursues, loves or marries, and whose consciousness is in no way central to the novel.[4] Unlike her predecessor, who at most served in a pivotal episode in the hero's life, the "woman as hero" begins with a purpose of which she believes herself capable. But to be human is to act on partial knowledge. Like any hero/protagonist, the "new woman" must contend with events she has not foreseen. The past which she has forgotten rises up to thwart her. She undergoes a passion and suffers to attain the ends she has set for herself.[5]

Heilbrun contends that our future salvation lies in a movement away from sexual polarization and the prison of gender, and toward a world in which individuals may choose freely their modes of personal behavior.[6] The condition of androgyny seeks to liberate the individual from the confines of rigidly assigned sex roles. Heilbrun explains that during the period in which women heroes predominated in fiction, the demands of their artistic vision forced male authors, possibly against their habitual inclinations, to use a woman as hero. These men were not engaged in a feminist

battle, she argues. Rather, the place of women provided the proper meta-
phor for the place of the heroic in a work of literary art. Henrik Ibsen, for
instance, continually denied that he was writing about women's rights. "I
am writing about humanity," he insisted.[7]

Great periods of civilization, however much they may have owed their
beginnings to the aggressive dominance of the male principle, have featured some sort of rise in the status of women. This historical phenomenon
manifests something more profound: "the recognition of the importance of
the 'feminine' principle, not as other, but as necessary to wholeness."[8]

In this section I will demonstrate how this desire for human wholeness
relates to narrative desire. These works also exemplify this historical tendency to revere women as strong characters in their own right. In *Mauprat*,
Sand links contemporary socialism with feminism by featuring a woman
hero who imparts a social and humanitarian message to her lover. Significantly, the main events of the novel take place immediately prior to the
French Revolution. The nascent spirit of *liberté, égalité* and *fraternité* gov-
erns the work, and Edmée champions the revolution.[9]

Chernyshevskii's Vera Pavlovna served as a heroic model for all "new
people"—men and women alike—to emulate during the period preceding
the Russian Revolution. Not surprisingly, Lenin hailed this as a great work.
Sand's almost messianic call to action in *Mauprat* inspired the attempts of
various Russian women characters to undertake Edmée 's actions. Fictional women now became rescuers.

Mikhail Mikhailov, a journalist and strong advocate of the new woman,
argued for this androgynous ideal. "There should be nothing feminine
about a woman except her sex," he wrote. "All other traits should be neither masculine nor feminine but purely human."[10] In Sand's *Mauprat*, as in
the Russian novels that emulate this character of "woman as redemptress,"
the woman hero rescues through love. Love leads to social justice. Love
shifts its emphasis from the personal and petty to the universal and utopian. Love contributes actively here to man's betterment. Through the
agency of love, the heroic beauty renders the beast a gentler, more enlightened creature.

Desire for androgyny derives from a desire for completion. This relationship extends, as well, to the act of reading and to the motivation behind
narrating. Desire is always there at the start of a narrative, often in a state of
initial arousal (as with Bernard's attempt to rape his cousin Edmée when
both are seventeen), after having reached a state of intensity such that
movement must be created, action undertaken, and change begun.[11] Edmée

recognizes her own sexual arousal and undertakes Bernard's sentimental education in order to civilize the barbarous cutthroat and to create her ideal mate. The narrative voice belongs to a much older, wiser Bernard. His wife Edmée has recently died. *Mauprat* documents the hunger of the self for union (Mauprat is the surname shared by both cousins and refers to Edmée's quest, as well as to Bernard's). At the same time, the narrative illuminates the spectacular subversion which is at work, since the greatest single impediment to mutuality is precisely the hungry self. Bernard repeatedly retreats to his brutish ways when confronted with the prospect of losing Edmée to her fiancé, M. de la Marche. In trying to force her to return his love (which originates as a carnal, immature desire), Bernard repels Edmée and compels her to place more obstacles in his path. He must completely prove his love before he wins her acceptance. Bernard strives toward completeness (and consummation of his passion) just as the reader yearns for closure. If the motor of narrative is desire—totalizing, building ever larger units of meaning—the ultimate determinants of meaning lie at the end of the text. Narrative desire is inexorably a desire for the end. Relationship (between characters, between the reader and the text, between cultures) yields a centrality and an immediacy that few other themes can claim. Relationship constitutes not only an essential "subject" of literature; very often, it provides the very "goal" of the text, a goal pursued by readers and protagonists alike.[12] Indeed, the blood relationship between the young cousins compels both to nurture their connection until, at the narrative's end, they manage to assimilate their differences and to become one eternally, blissfully married couple.

In the end, Bernard virtually becomes Edmée. Except for the reference to Edmée's delicate beauty, Bernard's early description of his beloved applies perfectly to the man he becomes:

> Elevée aux champs, elle était forte, active, courageuse, enjouée; elle joignait à toutes les graces de la beauté délicate toute l'énergie de la santé physique et morale. C'était une fière et intrépide jeune fille autant qu'une, douce et affable chatelaine. Je l'ai trouvée souvent bien haute et bien dédaigneuse; Patience et les pauvres de la contrée l'ont toujours trouvée humble et débonnaire. (*Mauprat*, 117)

> Raised out in the country, she was strong, active, brave, playful; she joined all of the graces of delicate beauty with all of the energy of physical and moral health. She was a proud and dauntless young girl, as well as a sweet and gracious hostess. I often found her quite haughty

and rather disdainful; Patience and the other poor people of the area always found her humble and good-natured.

The interchangeability of the two protagonists attests to their androgynous wholeness. Each maintains qualities common to both traditional sex roles. This "Bernard larmoyant" (tearful Bernard) (*Mauprat*, 293) does not correspond to the traditional male. His beloved cousin, who has a "virile" writing style, is a first-class rider and hunter. She has enough reason and strength for two ("de la raison et de la force pour deux") (*Mauprat*, 309) and hardly conforms to the feminine ideal of the traditional heroine. This inversion of traditional sex roles extends to the behavior of both protagonists. Edmée chastises, commands, makes fun of, humiliates, forbids, punishes, and wields power over Bernard. In contrast, Bernard cries, suffers, obeys, begs forgiveness, is hurt, is disheartened, and loses consciousness.

But each maintains traditional qualities at the same time. Edmée longs for action and an opportunity to implement her republican principles, fulfilling her destiny ultimately through her love for her father, Bernard, and their children. Bernard ventures off to America to fight, while Edmée remains behind to nurse her ailing father. Sand espouses a different approach to sexual freedom in *Mauprat*. During Bernard's absence, both remain faithful. His love for Edmée, who is not yet even his fiancée, keeps Bernard from yielding to temptation for six years while he is in America with Lafayette. Although rare in Sand's work, sexual renunciation functions here as a plea for a single standard of sexual behavior, the *équation prénuptiale*.[13]

The androgynous feature in *Mauprat* reveals itself distinctly toward the middle of the novel. Bernard recalls:

> Edmée m'apparaissait sous un nouvel aspect. Ce n'était plus cette belle fille dont la présence jetait le désordre dans mes sens; c'était un jeune homme de mon âge, beau comme un seraphin, fier, courageux, infléxible sur le point d'honneur, généreux, capable de cette amitié sublime qui faisait les frères d'armes, mais n'ayant d'amour passionné que pour la Divinité. (*Mauprat*, 147)

> Edmée appeared to me in a new light. She was no longer the beautiful girl whose presence had so disoriented my senses; this was a young man of my own age, as handsome as a seraph, proud, brave, unyielding on the point of honor, generous, capable of the sublime friendship which made brothers in arms, but feeling passionate love only for the Deity.

Simone Lecointre outlines in her study "George Sand: Le Discours amoureux: Deux aspects d'une écriture poétique" a series of actions without distinguishing whether they pertain to Edmée or to Bernard. No masculine/femi-
nine opposition exists to establish the gender of the actions' agent.

Desire, moreover, entails a certain aggressive tendency toward possession, a sexual tension exemplified by both protagonists. Bernard particularly, employs the terms, "s'emparer," (to seize), "saisir," (to grasp)
"poursuivre" (to pursue), "dévorer (des yeux)," (to devour with his eyes)
"emporter (dans ses bras)" (to carry in his arms), "serrer" (to press), "tenir"
(to hold), as well as "appartenir" (to belong to), "posséder" (to possess),
"céder" (to surrender), and "être a moi" (to be mine)—all of which feature
clear sexual connotations.[14] These aggressive/possessive qualities of desire
reflect Bernard's upbringing among a band of brigands and also indicate
the lengths to which he must go in order to have Edmée reciprocate his
passion. Bernard joins completely with his cousin only after having sym-
bolically killed her and having confronted death himself. This pleasure/
pain-charged desire reveals itself particularly well in the scene during which
Bernard inadvertently wounds Edmée . The wall (hymen) of her chapel
separates them (reminiscent of the long conversation between Pyramus
and Thisbe) and shelters the woman hero from the intrusion of male desire.
He inscribes his desire on her physically, however, and the wound carries
an erotic charge for its aggressor. They argue:

> Edmée, je vous commande de m'embrasser.
> —Laissez, Bernard, s'écria-t-elle, vous me cassez le bras. Voyez,
> vous m'avez écorchée contre le grillage.
> —Pourquoi vous êtes-vous retranchée contre moi? lui dis-je en
> couvrant de mes lèvres la légère blessure que je lui avais faite au bras.
> (*Mauprat*, 127)

> "Edmée, I order you to kiss me."
> —"Leave me alone, Bernard," she cried, "you're breaking my arm.
> Look, you've scraped me against the railing."
> —"Why did you pull away from me?" I asked her, covering with my
> lips the light wound that I had inflicted on her arm.

Bernard does not kiss the wound merely to heal it. In a subsequent
scene, the bandage which covers the scratch excites him; and he again
kisses the site of the wound as if to stake out his own territory. The gesture
is intended to enrage his rival, M. de la Marche:

Elle avait les coudes appuyés sur les bras de son fauteuil et les mains gracieusement entrelacées sous son menton. Les femmes avaient à cette époque et presque en toute saison les bras demi nus. J'aperçus à celui d'Edmée une petite bande de taffétas d'Angleterre qui me fit battre le coeur. ... Je soulevai doucement la dentelle qui retombait sur son coude, et, enhardi par son demi-sommeil, j'appuyai mes lèvres sur cette chère blessure. (*Mauprat*, 136)

She had propped her elbows on the arms of her chair and had her hands gracefully interlaced under her chin. At that period during practically every season, women had their arms half-naked. I saw on Edmée's a little band of English taffeta which caused my heart to beat faster. . . . I gently lifted the lace that fell over her elbow, and, emboldened by her half-sleep, I pressed my lips against the dear wound.

After his sojourn in America, Bernard still succumbs to the violent desire to possess Edmée. He reveals in a letter (which later nearly costs him his life at a trial) that passions still rage in that part of his nature that the rebel angels rule. He confides shamefaced that in the delirium of his dreams, he seems at times to be plunging a dagger (more sexual imagery) into her heart, forcing her to love him as if by some somber magic (*Mauprat*, 293). Naomi Schor examines in her article "Female Fetishism: The Case of George Sand" the unlikelihood of a man fetishizing a wound. Because fetishism has always been defined in terms of male sexuality, Schor proposes an alternative. She contends ultimately that to read Sand's recurrent scenes of fetishistic eroticism in the perspective of female fetishism entails giving full play to what she terms "Sand's insistent and troubling bitextuality."[15] This bitextuality abounds in Sand's *Mauprat*. By employing a male narrator, Sand indicates her solidarity with men and uses it politically to create an impact. Having her male readership identify with her safeguards against patronizing dismissals as a silly woman writer. The use of a male narrator distinguishes the French novelist from other women writers and enables her unthreateningly to adopt the role of chivalrous defender of women. Having lulled men into a false security with a conspiratorial wink, Sand freely assaults their laws and contemporary mores. *Mauprat*, like other Sand novels, conceals some very clever sex-change operations. Edmée educates Bernard, who in turn educates the male narrator, a "*little young man*" (emphasis Sand's) belonging to an effeminate generation. Ultimately, it is a woman who writes the novel, and she is known as such by her readership despite her male pseudonym.[16]

Family relationships abound in *Mauprat*. Patience describes himself as Edmée's foster father and admits to Bernard that he has come to love him as his own child. Sand employs various family terms to describe the relationship between Bernard and Edmée. These range from cousin (their real blood tie) to brother and sister (one of Sand's favorite references to true soul mates, i.e., Jacques and Sylvia), to mother and son. This last term is used from the beginning of their acquaintance. Although they are both seventeen, Edmée calls Bernard "mon enfant" twice right after their first meeting. Her kiss reminds Bernard of his mother's last kiss.[17] Edmée rejoices with a "mother's pride" at Bernard's intellectual progress (*Mauprat*, 242). Even upon his return from America, the mature Bernard expresses his gratitude that Edmée has been a true mother to him. Edmée transforms her wild, rascally cousin into a new man worthy of her, and she does so not through self-sacrifice but rather by withholding love. She insists on herself as an autonomous subject and behaves as "une véritable mère" (a true mother) (*Mauprat*, 242). George Sand was extremely close to her own son, Maurice, and may have perceived that a woman's role as mother to a son may impart to her more power and autonomy than any other role she plays.[18]

Although Edmée is engaged to a perfectly proper gentleman when she first meets Bernard, she falls in love with her less refined, uneducated cousin. She reveals to the abbé years before her marriage that she refuses ever to suffer the tyranny of a man, whether it is the violence of a lover or a husband's slap across the face. She indicates early her awareness of the masculine power to which marriage would subject her.[19]

Bernard bitterly dislikes his rival and tries to provoke him into a confrontation whenever possible. He finds this a far from easy task, as M. de la Marche seems bent on being all politeness and goodness (*Mauprat*, 146). Patience encourages Bernard to seek his cousin's hand, believing that any gentleman who smells as sweet as a whole flower garden will be a poor match for Edmée (*Mauprat*, 137). Edmée resolves the dilemma of the love triangle by choosing the suitor who offers her the challenge of transforming him into a noble and courageous mate. Never having experienced a twinge of passion for M. de la Marche, Edmée freely admits to the abbé that he will quickly recover from the announcement that she can never be his wife. She assures him that her former fiancé is a man of no depth and is somewhat cold (*Mauprat*, 157). In making this choice, Edmée demonstrates that she, too, has changed along with Bernard. Her sentimental education began at La Roche-Mauprat at the initiation of Bernard's general education. Her realization of her progress comes well before his, however.[20]

Edmée, the first of Sand's women characters to use her feminine virtues to teach, enlighten and console, designs Bernard's education to teach him moral principles and the ability to reason. Given the belated nature of her cousin's schooling, Edmée excludes Latin from his curriculum. She places emphasis instead on shaping the heart of the vicious rascal, teaching him to control his natural impulses and to live with her (and others) without oppressing or dominating. This essentially constitutes Sand's agenda for her readers, as well. Recognizing, of course, that sweeping educational reforms would take years to enact, Sand has her male protagonist indicate how individuals can serve each other as educators through love:

> Je crois bien que si l'on m'eût mis au collège à dix ans, j'eusse été sociable de meilleure heure; mais eût-on su corriger mes violents appétits et m'enseigner à les vaincre comme Edmée l'a fait? J'en doute, tout le monde a besoin d'être aimé pour valoir quelque chose, mais il faut qu'on le soit de différentes manières. Celui-ci avec une indulgence infatigable, celui-là avec une sévérité soutenue. En attendant qu'on ait résolu le problème d'une éducation commune à tous, et cependant appropriée à chacun, attachez-vous à vous corriger les uns les autres. (*Mauprat*, 314)

> I do believe that, had I been put in school at the age of ten, I would have become sociable much earlier; but would anyone have known how to correct my violent appetites and how to teach me to overcome them as Edmée has? I doubt it, for everyone needs to be loved to be worthwhile, but each in a different way. One might have to be indulged tirelessly, another might require consistent strictness. While waiting to resolve the problem of establishing a common education for all that is appropriate for each individual, set yourselves about the task of reforming one another.

The androgynous ideal derived from this perfectly suited education and from the "kind fairy" who masterminded it, triumphs in the end (*Mauprat*, 33). Completion and perfection accompany closure. The *maison paternelle* of Bernard's uncles falls. In place of the wild, vicious, thieving branch of his father's family, the new Mauprats—Bernard, Edmée and their four surviving children—embrace the values of the branch of the family headed by Edmée's father. The revitalized, reborn house of Mauprat features the best qualities of both parents. The formerly dreaded bastion of Roche-Mauprat stands in the end as a stable, thriving, happy home, a monument to the potential goodness and wisdom of humanity.[21]

Oblomov—Ivan Goncharov

Among contemporary Russian women heroes in literature, Olga Ilinskaya of Goncharov's *Oblomov* (1859) comes closest to emulating Edmée's success in saving a man's soul from perdition. Unlike the lawless savage Bernard, however, Olga's subject displays no aggressive, brutal tendencies. He succumbs to idleness with a dreamy acquiescence. He embraces the boredom that plagues other superfluous men who find no worthy outlets for their energies. Olga undertakes the arduous task of regenerating both spiritually and physically this incorrigible, lazy, gluttonous Russian nobleman. She literally tries to "create" her ideal mate in him. Like Edmée, Olga sees her subject as a kind of Galatea to whom she has to act as Pygmalion. Goncharov endows the classical myth with an androgynous twist, however. Olga becomes a Pygmalion *manqué* in the end. She fails to breathe life into a male but rather womanish Galatea.[22] The woman hero has more masculine traits than her male counterpart. Her determination initiates their love affair, and she establishes all of the policies in the relationship. Oblomov's "pure and virginal soul" compels him to rejoice passively at the prospect of being loved by a strong maternal force. His very appearance suggests passivity and feminine gentility:

> The smooth and excessively white skin of his neck, his small soft hands and plump shoulders, suggested a certain physical effeminacy. His movements were restrained and gentle; there was a certain lazy gracefulness about them even if he were alarmed. If his mind was troubled, his eyes were clouded, his forehead wrinkled, and an interplay of hesitation, sadness and fear was reflected in his face; but the disturbance seldom took the form of a definite idea and still more seldom reached the point of a decision. It merely found expression in a sigh and died down in apathy or drowsiness. (*Oblomov*, 1)

Olga begins resolutely to galvanize Oblomov's physical and mental energy from a state of virtual inertia. She compels Oblomov to set his life in order by getting out of bed before noon, eating less sweets, taking fewer naps, changing from his dressing gown and slippers, and taking charge of his estate.

Olga's determination, courage, and pride establish her role as a conventionally masculine one. Her methods remain, however, both maternal and seductive. Like Sand's woman hero, Olga alternately threatens and teases Oblomov. She is tender and maternal in her role as teacher, an approach which wins the complete confidence of Ilia, who had been doted on dreadfully as a child at Oblomovka. In describing little Ilia's upbringing, Goncharov indicates the harmful effects of being catered to by a host of servants.[23] Stolz explains to his friend, "It began with your not knowing how to put on your socks and ended with your not knowing how to live" (*Oblomov*, 403). Goncharov hints that Olga and Stolz may have been too late in attempting to educate Ilia, whose heart and mind had been imbued with the slow, lazy rhythms of Oblomovka from the cradle.[24]

The narrator recalls an incident during which the entire matriarchal household of Oblomovka had mobilized in a panic to retrieve Ilia when he was missing. The boy, who had rushed out one winter day to join the neighbor children in a snowball fight, was detained "three days in bed, though only one thing could have done him any good—playing snowballs again" (*Oblomov*, 147). These overreactions to real and imaginary childhood ailments have led to a strong case of hypochondria in Ilia as an adult. Unable to face the prospect of waking up early and dressing for work, Oblomov has his physician certify that his job jeopardizes his health. The certificate reads:

> I, the undersigned, certify and append my seal thereto that the collegiate secretary, Ilia Oblomov, suffers from an enlarged heart and a dilation of its left ventricle (*Hypertrophia cordis cum dilatione ejus ventriculi sinistri*) and also from a chronic pain in the liver (hepatitis), which may endanger the patient's health and life, the attacks being due, it is to be surmised, to his going daily to the office. Therefore, to prevent the repetition and increase of these painful attacks, I find it necessary to forbid Mr. Oblomov to go to the office and insist that he should altogether abstain from intellectual pursuits and any sort of activity. (*Oblomov*, 56–57)

With this oversolicitous, doting conditioning, Oblomov, not surprisingly, demands from Zakhar and from Olga a loyalty and love as absolute as the love of a mother for her child. The strong ideological component in her love compels Olga to abandon her efforts to reform Oblomov when she recognizes that her strict view of life and moral passion can never be reconciled with Oblomov's poetic dream of married life. When he does eventually marry, Oblomov merges the image of his mistress, Agafia, with that of his mother, endowing the relationship with an incestuous quality. Accustomed to having been fed, dressed, and educated by mother figures, Oblomov reveres his passive role as an unconditionally beloved beneficiary. In a particularly revealing episode with Stolz (a name which means "pride" in German) Oblomov, drunk on homemade currant vodka, greedily attacks the mutton. He praises Agafia's culinary talents repeatedly. Olga may sing "Casta diva," he remarks, "but she can't make vodka like this" (*Oblomov*, 449).

Olga's shortcomings extend beyond her inability to compete with Agafia in the kitchen, however. The spirited young woman fails, in spite of her forceful character, to combat Oblomovism, the irremediable apathy of a character devoid of will power and self-confidence. Her personal defeat in regenerating Oblomov's life force condemns Olga to a new mediocrity. The lively, intelligent, mildly ironic young lady becomes a somber, dull, conforming adult. She recognizes her own tendencies to succumb to an Oblomov-like apathy and treats herself as a fallen woman. Convinced that she has failed at her one chance for true love, Olga grows despondent, associating the image of the withering lilac with her own past. Her defeatist attitude places Stolz in the position of noble rescuer. Regrettably, Olga loses her status as redemptress and is herself redeemed by Stolz, a representative of the new generation. Half-German and half-Russian, he accomplishes efficiently the tasks that he sets out for himself. He rescues both the wan, lovesick Olga from her dejection, and the other member of the love triangle, Oblomov, from the claws of greedy crooks. Olga's natural vivacity is overshadowed by her husband's meticulous control over life. Stolz attempts to weave a rational existence for her. He lives "according to a set plan and tries to spend each day as he spends each ruble, keeping a firm and unremitting watch over the expenditure of his time, his labor, and his mental and emotional powers." Moreover, Stolz "seems to govern his joys, and sorrows like the movements of his hands and feet" (*Oblomov*, 167–168). Unfortunately, this efficiency tends to put Olga in a position of subservience. Although she likes him because he always amuses her and does not allow her to be bored, Olga is "still a little afraid of Stolz too, for she feels too much of a child in his presence" (*Oblomov*, 192–93). Later, as her love for Stolz dawns, Olga resents her lack of control. She laments that up till then she had managed her own life and another's so confidently and intelligently. Shame for her past and wounded vanity now cause her to tremble like a little girl.

> Before this dangerous adversary [Stolz] she had none of the penetration, self-control, strength of will and character which she had always displayed with Oblomov. She understood that if she had so far succeeded in hiding from Stolz's keen gaze and fighting him successfully,

she owed it not to her own power as in her struggle with Oblomov, but solely to Stolz's reticence and obstinate silence. (*Oblomov*, 431)

In contrast to the mother-son relationship associated with the Olga-Oblomov romance, Goncharov employs brother-sister references to indicate the close familiarity between Stolz and Olga. At first, Olga fails to recognize her old friend. But then her brows straighten and her eyes shine with a quiet and profound light of joy. The narrator comments, "A brother would be happy if a sister he loved had been as glad to see him" (*Oblomov*, 417). As each day passes and he rekindles her despondent spirit, Olga reflects what happiness it would be to have Stolz as a brother . . . to have permanent rights over a man like that, not only over his mind but his heart as well, to enjoy his presence openly and legitimately, without having to pay for it by heavy sacrifices, misery and confessions" (427).

Their romance proves to be less than ideal, however. Stolz never succeeds in fulfilling the "whole depth of her soul" (464). After several years with Stolz, Olga feels empty and sad, although she has no ostensible cause for complaint.[25] Afraid of sinking into an apathy like Oblomov's, Olga seems to prefer the prospect of any privation and disaster to her unadventurous married life. With an effort, she tries to shake herself free from brooding by quickening the pace of her life and enjoying the society of others, absorbing herself completely in small domestic cares and talking with Andrei "of dull and serious things" (474). Guiltily, she tries to discern what her soul is missing:

> "What is it?" she thought in terror. "Is it necessary, is it possible to wish for something else? Where am I to go? Nowhere! the road does not lead any farther. . . . Doesn't it? Have I, then, completed the circle of my life? Is this all . . . all?" her heart asked, and left the question unfinished . . . and Olga looked round anxiously lest someone should overhear this whisper of her heart . . . (*Oblomov*, 477)

Her despondency is hardly surprising, considering the chasm between her natural vivacity and her husband's well-regulated character. Her moral and psychological malaise stem in part from Stolz's egotistical streak, as when he complains of the trouble that Oblomov has given him.

Olga ultimately fails to emulate Edmée's status of woman as hero. Unlike Edmée, she never confronts the danger of rape or death. An inherent part of the love triangle, Olga never really exists independently of the two men she loves. Goncharov portrays her in relation to the one or the other. The novelist describes Olga as the "soul" of the novel, referring to her position as the touchstone of both male characters (reminiscent of the pattern between Peter, Lizaveta and Alexander in *A Common Story*) but does not endow her with an autonomous personality.[26]

Radical critics of the day lamented that Olga's strong, practical nature is wasted, having failed to identify a worthy outlet for her energies. N. A. Dobroliubov contended that she was capable of dedicating herself to the right causes. D. I. Pisarev, on the other hand, could discern in her nature no proclivity for revolutionary work. He criticized her lack of "practical activity" despite her energy and vitality.[27] Unlike Edmée, who stands to reestablish the honorable foundations of the family name and please her beloved father, Olga is a strong woman who simply lacks a task worthy of testing her powers.

Turgenev's woman hero Elena of *On the Eve* also exemplifies the spirit of the wise and courageous Edmée. In a letter written in 1859, Turgenev described to Goncharov an "exalted" woman character he was creating. The latter replied that "a heroine of that type could only be found in George Sand's novels, . . . a woman pure and chaste who loves only an ideal and not a man."[28] At the end of *On the Eve,* Turgenev chooses Venice as the site for the couple to spend their last days together. Like their attendance at a performance of *La Traviata* on the night Insarov dies of tuberculosis, Venice evokes romantic associations with Sand in the mind of the contemporary reader. Goncharov asked Turgenev why he would send the protagonists to Venice en route to Bulgaria. Venice, with its Sandian associations, allowed Turgenev to imply much more than he chose to state expressly.[29]

The publication of *On the Eve* brought with it another painful quarrel between Goncharov and Turgenev, which had its roots in something more than ordinary literary jealousy. For many years, they had met on occasion to read to each other their works in progress. Turgenev enjoyed these sessions, often taking Goncharov's advice about deleting passages and editing.[30] Goncharov both admired and resented Turgenev's ease in writing. A slow, awkward writer himself, Goncharov often took years to produce a completed work. Unlike his aristocratic colleague, Goncharov was forced to earn his living as a civil servant. Envious of Turgenev's education, talent, income of ten thousand rubles, and freedom to travel, he charged, "You slide through life superficially; . . . I plough a deep furrow."[31]

When Goncharov accused Turgenev of having stolen *On the Eve* from him, a committee of colleagues sat in arbitration to resolve the scandal. They agreed that any resemblances stemmed from "the events [that] were common to the times and to the Russian soil."[32] Angry that the committee had not been more explicit, Turgenev dissolved his ties to Goncharov, although he later forgot the incident in a dignified manner. V. S. Pritchett explains in *The Gentle Barbarian* (1977) that Goncharov's fantasy turned to frenzy. He charged that besides plagiarizing his works, Turgenev was passing them on to his European friends so that Alphonse Daudet, Flaubert, the Goncourts, and George Sand were using them at his expense.[33] Besides the chronological improbability of these allegations, *On the Eve* reflects a clearly different approach to the woman as hero, vindicating Pritchett's dismissal of what he considered to be paranoid ravings on Goncharov's part.

On the Eve—Ivan Turgenev

Less than a year later the publication of *Oblomov*, Turgenev's *On the Eve* (*Nakanune*) (1860) appeared. This novel features a woman hero, Elena Stakhova, who fulfills Edmée's mission to serve the people and embodies the revolutionary aspirations of the radicals of the 1860s. A solitary, dreamy Russian girl "on the eve" of adulthood, Elena leaves her family and homeland to serve with her beloved husband, Insarov, a Bulgarian patriot fighting for the liberation of his homeland. At last the radicals enjoyed two literary characters who exemplified their passion to serve a cause. They received little consolation, however, in the fact that one of these was a woman and the other a Bulgarian.[34] Dobroliubov published a famous article entitled "Kogda zhe pridët nastoiashchii den?" (When will the real day come?), referring to the day on which Russian men like Insarov would appear and women like Elena could find purposeful activity in their own homeland.[34] Turgenev's own character laments at the end of *On the Eve:*

> We still have no real men, however, much as we look for them. What we have is either small fry, rodents, little Hamlets, brutes, ignoramuses groping in subterranean darkness, or pushers, millers of the wind, and drumsticks. Or it's that other sort of people, those that have analyzed themselves with disgusting precision, that keep feeling the pulse of every single sensation and reporting to themselves: this is what I feel and this is what I think. A useful and sensible occupation! Surely if there were any real men among us, that girl, that sensitive soul, wouldn't leave us, wouldn't slip away like a fish escaping into the water. What does it all mean, Uvar Ivanovich? When will our time come? When will real men be born in this country? (*On the Eve*, 153)

Dobroliubov found much to praise in the novel. He fully approved of Elena, saying she was an "ideal figure, composed of the best elements developing in our society."[35] Another contemporary critic, Kropotkin, later recalled that in *On the Eve*, Turgenev had not only revealed the redeeming qualities of Russian womanhood; he had also prescribed how these women should be treated. He wrote, "This aspect of Turgenev's writing produced on me and on thousands of my contemporaries an indelible impression, much stronger than the best articles in defense of women's rights."[36] Elena Stakhova appeared when the campaign for women's rights had not yet gathered momentum. Although Turgenev would not likely have considered himself a feminist (particularly in light of some caricatures, such as that of Kukshina in *Fathers and Children (Ottsy i detii)*, which gave emancipated women a bad name, he was friendly with Mikhail Mikhailov and L. P. Shelgunova, with whom Mikhailov was living. No record exists to indicate the topics of conversation between Turgenev and Mikhailov, the first truly coherent spokesman on the Woman Question. It is quite likely that they discussed women's issues, however, and their friendship began during the gestation period of *On the Eve*.[37]

Turgenev's woman hero prefigured the "new woman" and her frustration and dissatisfaction with the limited alternatives available for an individual who yearned to play a positive role in society. Leo Tolstoi, far from supporting women's rights, scorned Turgenev's novel and female protagonist. Forty years later, however, he revealed to Chekhov that he found Turgenev's portraits of women truly remarkable. "Perhaps there weren't any women such as he described, but after he had written about them, they appeared. That's true; I myself later observed Turgenev's women in real life."[38]

After the publication of *On the Eve*, new Elenas did appear everywhere, many of these Russian women far surpassing their literary prototype in their commitment to a cause. Turgenev's friend, Baroness Iuliia Petrovna Vrevskaia, for example, lost her life in a bout with typhus at the front while working as a nurse in the Russo-Turkish war.[39] Chernyshevskii's Vera Pavlovna eventually swept aside the conservative model established by Elena, as did real life women such as Vera Zazulich and Sophie Perovskaia, who were prepared to commit acts of terrorism and to die for their beliefs if necessary.[40]

Edmée's humanitarian sympathies and exalted character are reflected in Elena. Like Edmée, she selects her own destiny. Although Elena feels an attraction to both the dilettante sculptor Shubin, who is handsomer and wittier than Insarov, and to the scholarly Bersenev, who is more intelligent, she chooses the Bulgarian patriot because he affords her the opportunity to serve mankind. "From childhood she had longed for action, for good deeds. Beggars and the sick and hungry preoccupied and worried her, tormenting her mind. She saw them in her dreams, and used to ask her acquaintances whether they saw any" (*On the Eve*, 35). Insarov possesses some of the best qualities of the other two suitors. He shares Shubin's taste for the concrete without the accompanying frivolity, and he emulates Bersenev's commitment to humanistic values without the accompanying vagueness.[41]

Bersenev plays the awkward role of the third wheel in the love triangle with Elena and Dmitri. He laments:

> So that's how much she loves him, . . . I hadn't expected it; I didn't imagine it could be so strong already. . . . She says I'm kind. . . . Who knows what feelings or motives made me tell Elena all that? It certainly wasn't out of kindness. It was just my accursed desire to find out if the dagger was really stuck deep in the wound. I ought to be glad— they love each other, and I am the man who helped them. "A future mediator between science and the Russian public"—that's what Shubin calls me. Apparently I'm destined to be a go-between. (*On the Eve*, 93)

Andrei Petrovich does serve as a go-between for Elena and her husband. When Dmitrii falls ill, Andrei nurses him back to health and alerts and consoles Elena. While Insarov is recovering, he asks Elena if Bersenev is in love with her.

> Elena cast down her eyes. "He loved me," she said in an undertone. Insarov squeezed her hand. "You Russians have hearts of gold! To think that he, of all people, should have tended me and spent sleepless nights over me!" (*On the Eve*, 139)

Elena chooses the Bulgarian patriot because he inspires her with passion, an aspect lacking in her relationships with her deeply admired suitors (as with Edmée and her first fiancé). Like her French counterpart, moreover, Elena refuses to limit herself to the expectations which society and her family have for her future. Confident in the knowledge that she has made her own free choice in loving Insarov and that nothing will deter her from it, Elena laughs at the pompous Kurnatovskii, the suitor her father has brought home for me.

Although Elena does not literally create her husband in Edmée's manner, she actively participates in her lover's cause, embracing it as her own. In many ways, she exceeds Edmée's humanitarian principles. Whereas Edmée waits to proclaim her love for Bernard until his life is at stake, long after he has proved his unequivocal devotion to her, Elena makes the courageous decision to marry Insarov, while he, the dedicated activist, hesitates. He plans to leave Russia without bidding her good-bye, knowing that it would be too much to expect a well-to-do member of the gentry to leave her home for a dangerous, uncertain future with an impoverished foreign revolutionary. Elena, however, has recognized her passion for Insarov and his cause. She professes her love to him and delays his departure. Edmée's years of explaining and analyzing her love for Bernard pale in comparison to Elena's irrepressible determination to shape her own life and to link herself with Insarov. Her resolution is complete. Elena is never contradictory, capricious, or self-analytical. She simply acts on her decision once she has resolved to fight by Dmitrii's side in liberating his homeland.[42]

Turgenev more than once noted that Sand's most fascinating women were "un peu trop pédante" (a bit too pedantic). He avoids the kind of obstacles Edmée uses to educate and tame Bernard. Turgenev reveals economically Elena's complete devotion to Insarov in their last idyll in Venice through her three visits to his room as he lies dying. Turgenev employs the relationship of brother and sister to analogize their closeness, a favorite tactic of Sand's in describing lovers:

> The calm of bliss, of a peaceful harbour, of a goal attained, that heavenly calm which imparts both meaning and beauty to death itself, swept over her in a divine wave. She desired nothing because she possessed everything. "Oh my brother, my friend, my darling!" whispered her lips, and she wondered whether it was his heart or hers beating and melting so sweetly in her breast. (*On the Eve*, 101)

Insarov provides a purpose for which each is willing to die. Elena, in teaching him to love, provides them with something for which to live. Had they survived the rigors of revolution and produced a family, their romance might have taken on the historical dimension of *Mauprat*.

Elena's strength and devotion exceed even those of her revolutionary husband. She assures him that she will follow him because her duty is to love him. The Bulgarian quails before her determination. "Oh, Elena," he says, "what unbreakable chains every word you utter puts on me!" Like Edmée, Elena knows that love is a liberating force rather than an enslavement. "Why talk of chains? . . . we are both free human beings," she responds (*On the Eve,* 138).

Elena further proves to be a true woman hero in her dedication to her husband's cause. She undertakes the archetypal action of the hero—purpose through passion to perception—in pursuing her quest even after Dmitrii's death.[43] Unlike Edmée, who ends her days with Bernard, Elena has to carry on alone, exemplifying Goncharov's description of the Sand heroine, who "loves not [just] a man, but an ideal."[44]

Like other self-actualizing female prototypes in Russian fiction, including Chernyshevskii's Vera Pavlovna, Goncharov's Olga, Herzen's Liuba *(Who is to Blame?)* and Turgenev's Natalia *(Rudin),* Elena spends a great deal of time in solitude and becomes an introspective, sensitive woman at an early age. Similarly, Edmée's first understanding of life is shaped by Patience and her father. They instill in her principles of freedom, equality and brotherhood. Later, isolated from society, Edmée, like her Russian literary counterparts, develops the habit of reflecting alone on all she has learned.

Elena's elders allow her to run free from an early age. Soon she rejects altogether any attempt at supervision, despising her father, feeling a "cold sympathy" for her mother, and ignoring her governess. The narrator recounts that from the age of sixteen, Elena has enjoyed complete independence.[45] Like these other woman heroes, Elena utilizes the freedom of her circumstances to cultivate her moral sensibility. These women exist apart from society but must identify a means through which to act upon society. When they do at last act, these women heroes demonstrate the force of a carefully nurtured personality.[46]

These Russian novelists often employ the device of a personal journal to indicate the introspective natures of their female protagonists. Vera Pavlovna confronts the bitter truth contained within the pages of her mental journal. In a dream, Liuba seeks refuge from an unhappy home life and later, through her journal, reflects upon her dilemma in loving two men. Finally, Elena comes to recognize her dawning love for Insarov by transcribing her thoughts and feelings. Prior to that recognition, she records her frustrations and fears in her diary, revealing the extent of her sensitivity and perception:

I wonder what has come over me today: I feel dizzy and am ready to drop on my knees and ask for quarter. I do not know who is doing it or how, but I feel as if I were being killed, and I cry out inwardly in my indignation, and weep, unable to control myself. Tame these passions in me, O Lord! Thou alone canst do it, for all else is powerless: neither my paltry alms, nor my occupations—nothing, nothing whatsoever—can help me. I would gladly hire myself out as a maid, for then I should feel much better. (*On the Eve*, 87)

It remains a sad irony, however, that Elena's gesture of greatest purpose consists in devoting herself to a man whom she believes will best be able to realize her ideals for her! She cannot impart power to Insarov because she ultimately has no more power than he. Her heroic status is diminished by the fact that, although she holds center stage, her main role consists of endorsing someone else (albeit someone of her choosing).

Bersenev and Shubin look to her to have her validate one of their respective visions of love. Her choice will sustain that vision. Turgenev's work is revolutionary in that woman's approval becomes energetically solicited.[47]

This proves to be the novel's burden as well, however. Elena is only a woman, no less but also no more. Turgenev triumphs in not endowing her with an unattainable terrible perfection. Instead, she must contend at the novel's end with the mundane ugliness of salvaging her broken life. References to burial preparations and travel arrangements predominate in her last letter to her parents. Love is dead; the world must be attended to. Turgenev exposes her role for the extremely fragile mechanism it is. Russians would have to continue their search for a more prosaic means of dealing with the pernicious circumstances of reality.[48]

Crime and Punishment and *The Brothers Karamazov*—Fëdor Dostoevskii

The reader can discern Sand's presence in the female protagonists of Goncharov's *Oblomov* and Turgenev's *On the Eve*. Neither of these novels, however, combines "woman hero," social mission, historical setting, and melodramatic technique in the same manner as do Dostoevskii's novels.

Mauprat, consistent with other early Sand novels, features effusive love letters, a threatened suicide, passionate encounters in isolated spots, and other Gothic elements. The calamities that befall Sand's persecuted women perpetuate the Gothic plot. In this manner, Sand manages to convert a potentially dull and pedantic social message into an exciting tale, replete with terror, torture, and ecstasy. The Gothic plot lends to Sand the device she needs to convey her revolutionary ideas. Had Bernard not tried to rape her, Edmée would never have undertaken his redemption and education.

Dostoevskii, too, employed elements of the *roman-feuilleton* and the Gothic novel in order to stimulate the reader's interest and to express his philosophy. In creating in his novels "the world of daemonic heroes in ample capes, of maidens poised between torment and dishonor, of beggared virtue and malignant wealth," Dostoevskii paid tribute to a kindred spirit, to the French novelist who drew on the same literary traditions and novelistic conventions as he.[49] Like Turgenev, Dostoevskii wrote a moving eulogy to Sand, having been a fervent admirer of hers in his young, formative years as a writer. He wrote in his *Diary of a Writer* in 1876 that George Sand had "promptly assumed in Russia virtually the first place among a whole Pleiad of new writers who, at that period, rose to fame and won renown all over Europe."[50] Most significantly, Dostoevskii refers to a specific female character-type established by Sand and exemplified in his own novels by Dunia in *Crime and Punishment* (1866) and by Katerina Ivanovna in *The Brothers Karamazov* (1879–80). He defines this prototype in his *Diary of a Writer:*

> A straightforward, honest, but inexperienced, character of a young feminine creature is pictured, one possessing that proud chastity which is neither afraid of, nor can even be contaminated by, contact with vice—*even if that creature should accidentally find herself in the very den of vice.* The want of magnanimous sacrifice (supposedly specifically expected from her) startles the youthful girl's heart, and unhesitatingly, without sparing herself, disinterestedly, self-sacrificingly and fearlessly, she suddenly takes the most perilous and fatal step. That which she sees and encounters does not in the least confuse or intimidate her; on the contrary, it forthwith increases courage in the youthful heart which, at this juncture, for the first time, realizes the full measure of its strength—the strength of innocence, honesty and purity.[51]

Characters such as Dunia and Katerina "thirst for sacrifices and heroic deeds." Indeed, Sand's own description of her first heroine, Indiana, applies perfectly to many of Dostoevskii's female characters:

> C'est la femme typique, faible et forte, fatiguée du poids de l'air et capable de porter le ciel, timide dans le courant de la vie, audacieuse les jours de bataille, fine, adroite et pénétrante pour saisir les fils déliés de la vie commune, niaise et stupide pour distinguer les vrais intérêts de son bonheur, se moquant du monde entier, se laissant duper par un

seul homme, n'ayant pas d'amour-propre pour elle-même, en étant
remplie pour l'objet de son choix, dédaignant les vanités du siècle
pour son compte et se laissant séduire par l'homme qui les réunit
toutes. Voilà, je crois, la femme en général, un incroyable mélange de
faiblesse et d'énergie, de grandeur et de petitesse, un être toujours
composé de deux natures opposées, tantôt sublime, tantôt misérable,
habile à tromper, facile à l'être.[53]

She is woman herself, frail and strong, exhausted from the weight of
the air and yet capable of carrying the sky, timid in the course of life,
yet audacious on the days of battle, refined, clever, and adept at grasp-
ing the subtlest threads of life, silly and stupid at distinguishing the
true interests of her happiness, making fun of the entire world, allowing herself to be duped by one man alone, having no self-esteem but
being full of esteem for the object of her desire, disdaining the vani-
ties of her era for his sake, and allowing herself to be seduced by the
man who embodies them all. Here, I believe, is the essence of woman,
an incredible mixture of weakness and energy, of greatness and pettiness, a being always composed of two opposing natures, sometimes
sublime, sometimes miserable, clever at deceiving, easily deceived.

Unlike other nineteenth-century novelists, Dostoevskii responded to
Sand's language and style rather than to the programmatic aspects of her
work. Several critics speculate that if Dostoevskii had finished *Netochka
Nezvanova*, a work that, like "The Landlady," directly emulates Sand's
diction and style, he might have left a tale of a successful woman who
redeems an unfortunate hero. Dostoevskii's completed stories of the 1840s
all reflect prevailing attitudes toward women.[54]

His second wife, Anna, stated that among his favorite authors,
Dostoevskii always included George Sand.[55] He noted the purely evangeli-
cal spirit of Sand's works—certainly an aspect of *Spiridion* (1839)—and
several critics have directly attributed to this the deep spiritual affinity that
he felt toward her works. Dostoevskii accorded Sand an ultimate Slavophile
compliment. He suggested that she unconsciously adhered to the Russian
Orthodox faith:

Of course, being a Frenchwoman, in accord with the conceptions of
her compatriots, George Sand could not consciously adhere to the idea
"that in the whole universe there is no name other than his [Christ's]
through which one may be saved"—the fundamental idea of Orthodoxy—yet despite this seeming and formal contradiction, George Sand,

I repeat, was perhaps, without knowing it herself, one of the staunch-
est confessors of Christ. She based her socialism, her convictions, her
hopes and her ideals upon the moral feeling of man, upon the spiritual
thirst of mankind.[56]

Dostoevskii consciously borrowed and transformed Sand's literary techniques to suit his own artistic goals. Isabelle Naginski describes the literary
relationship between George Sand and Dostoevskii as "the serenity of
influence," as opposed to Harold Bloom's notion of "the anxiety of influence," through which one artist denies the impact of another upon his work
and deliberately misreads and misinterprets the other.[57] The literary work
itself did not awaken his artistic receptivity so much, however, as did the
circle of ideas behind it.[58] He essentially converted the "new word" that
Sand brought to Russia in the 1840s into a "Russian force." Critical of
Westernizers who assiduously copied anything fashionable from Europe,
Dostoevskii managed to venerate Sand without relinquishing the notion of
Russia's individual character. A Soviet approach to Sand perpetuated this
strategy. F. I. Kuleshov, for example, considered that Sand served not to
innovate in Russia but rather to reinforce indigenous Russian traditions.[59] In
one of his notebooks for 1876 and 1877, Dostoevskii made this assessment:

> In Russia, criticism is amateurish (*ot ruki*), impressionistic (*po vdoxno-
> veniiu*). Someone reads a few novels and immediately starts writing
> the criticism section [of a journal]. That is why there is so much lack
> of content. If one has a great deal of talent (like Belinskii), one can
> express many feelings, but a (scholarly) study of how writers (Schiller,
> George Sand) influenced Russia and to what an extent would be an
> extraordinary and serious undertaking. But we will have to wait a long
> time for that. The history of the metamorphosis (*perevoploshchenie*) of
> an idea into another idea.[60]

The metamorphosis of an idea into another idea reflects very appropriately
the manner in which Dostoevskii adopted elements of Sand's works only
to make them organically his own. A. L. Bem refers to the Russian novelist
as a "reader of genius" with a great capacity for recalling disparate literary
works and synthesizing them into his own writing.[61]

Although Dostoevskii's women characters do not tend to occupy center stage, they do reflect the lives of complete human beings and are often
just as tormented and disturbed as their male counterparts. Dostoevskii
occasionally employs as comic relief the passive, stereotypical *institutka*

type whose life revolves around trapping a husband and immersing herself in domestic inertia.

Avdotia Romanovna (Dunia) in *Crime and Punishment* is beautiful, self-reliant and strong. Her position in regard to her two suitors, Luzhin and Svidrigailov, reveals that her kindness offsets her pride. Luzhin's attraction to her stems from his desire to marry an honorable girl who has no dowry and knows what it is like to be poor, a wife who will consider her husband her benefactor (*Crime and Punishment*, 44–45). Knowing that a wealthy husband would lighten the family burden in educating her brother, Raskolnikov, Dunia refuses nevertheless to compromise her principles in a loveless match. When Luzhin charges that she has shown him disrespect, Dunia explodes, knowing she has always acted honorably toward him: "What! I place your interest beside everything I have treasured in my life until now, everything that until now has been my *whole* life—and suddenly you're offended because I assign you too little worth!" (296–97).

In a key scene which presents some fascinating parallels with Sand's *Mauprat*, Dunia proves herself to be the kind of feminine creature about which Dostoevskii wrote in his *Diary of a Writer*. Both Edmée and Dunia possess "that proud chastity which is neither afraid of, nor can even be contaminated by, contact with vice—even if that creature should accidentally find herself in the very den of vice." Both Dunia and Edmée confront the frightening prospect of rape in their respective dens of vice, yet each emerges undefiled, having appealed to the would-be perpetrator's generosity. Dunia fears Svidrigailov, but is like Edmée, who is "fort troublée" but "forte et ferme dans sa pureté" (very upset but firm in her purity) (*Mauprat*, 50). Unlike Edmée, who at seventeen meets Bernard for the first time after she is duped into entering the castle of La Roche Mauprat and accidentally finds herself in the very den of vice, Dunia intentionally places herself at Svidrigailov's mercy, knowing him to be a jaded roué in the grip of an uncontrollable sensual passion. While Edmée, standing trembling and terror-stricken like a victim before the executioner, threatens to stab herself if Bernard will not release her, Dunia anticipates her precarious position, and takes measures (as does Svidrigailov). He tells her that Raskolnikov murdered the pawnbroker, but offers to save her family if she will yield. Nearly fainting, she looks around wildly, imploring him to release her. Like Bernard, Svidrigailov has locked the door and points out her vulnerable position. He coaxes her menacingly:

You mentioned "force," Avdotia Romanovna. If it's force, then you may judge that I have taken measures. Sofia Semionovna's not at home. It's a long way to the Kapernaumovs'—five locked rooms. Finally, I'm at least twice as strong as you are. I don't, what's more, have much to be afraid of, because you cannot appeal—after all, you don't want to betray your brother in the process, do you? Nobody would believe you anyway: why would a single girl go alone to a man's apartment? So that even if you sacrifice your brother, you would have little to show for it. Rape is quite difficult to prove, Avdotia Romanovna. (*Crime and Punishment*, 476)

Suddenly she draws a revolver from her skirt (his own revolver, he notes ironically) and cocks it, ready to kill him (rather than herself).[62]

Svidrigailov clearly yearns for moral redemption and he has convinced himself that Dunia alone can redeem him. Nathan Rosen notes in "Chaos and Dostoevskii's Women" that rejection by the virginal aristocrat is equivalent to a sentence of death; the hero can turn now only to suicide or madness.[63]

Whereas Edmée resolves to redeem and educate Bernard when he spares her virtue, Dunia flees from Svidrigailov like a madwoman, and Svidrigailov resorts to suicide out of despair and self-loathing. The primary difference between the two scenes stems from the fact that Dunia's endeavors to rehabilitate Svidrigailov precede this attempted rape. Dunia has a past with Svidrigailov, having worked as a governess in his household, and knows him to be a rogue.

In a café prior to his "appointment," he relates to Raskolnikov that Dunia had been strongly attracted to her employer from the beginning. Her proud chastity, however, had prevented her from expressing her affections romantically. She had engaged instead in a messianic effort to change him—to lift him out of his depravity and to channel his energies into useful outlets. However, she fails to redeem the blackguard. Svidrigailov, nearly fifty years old, bears a much stronger resemblance to the demonic aristocrats of the *roman-feuilleton* tradition than does the seventeen-year-old Bernard, who is still a youth and is easily manipulated by his clever cousin. Unlike Bernard, Svidrigailov feigns his progress and repentance. Using Dunia's zeal to reform him as a pretext to see her, Svidrigailov intends to possess her—by seduction if possible, by force if necessary.

Dunia, then, has just cause to bear a weapon. He has a past of mocking her and of injuring her pride. Moreover, she believes that he has poisoned his wife out of love for her (quite possibly this accounts for Dunia's "morbid chastity"). In having the crisis in the "den of vice" come after the program of rehabilitation, Dostoevskii provides Dunia with contemptuous understanding for her would-be rapist. While the episodes in both novels feature various similarities, one quite understandably leads to death and despair while the other ushers in years of growth, learning, mutual understanding, and redemption.

The influence of *Mauprat* appears again in Dostoevskii's *The Brothers Karamazov*. A German critic, V. Komarovich, convincingly identifies scenes, episodes and characters that Dostoevskii could have borrowed from Sand. According to Komarovich, Mitia Karamazov is modeled after Bernard Mauprat. His continual cursing of "all those Bernards" refers to Sand's hero rather than to Claude Bernard, the model of Western sciencticism, as critics had previously assumed.[64] The German critic further contends that the confrontation between Dmitrii Karamazov and Katerina Ivanovna relates back to *Mauprat*, as well as to *Crime and Punishment* in the theme of the noble beauty at the mercy of the wild debauchée. Like Bernard and Svidrigailov, Dmitrii struggles between succumbing to his carnal desires and magnanimously sparing the virtue of the aristocratic virgin. In contrast to Bernard but like Svidrigailov, Dmitrii has a history with his proud, chaste counterpart which precedes the "den of vice" episode. Dmitrii, a wild young army officer stationed in a provincial town, first encounters the beautiful young *institutka* while she is home on a visit to her father. The daughter of a general, Katerina deliberately snubs Dmitrii and he vows revenge. When the general faces charges of embezzlement, Dmitrii communicates to Katia that he is prepared to provide her with the money needed to spare her father if she will come to his room alone. Like Edmée, Katia is ready to sacrifice herself for her beloved father. Like Dunia, moreover, she knowingly submits herself to the mercy of a reprobate. Many of the motives that precede and complicate the scene, however, are absent from Sand's *Mauprat*. Katia's position is more scandalous than that of Edmée or even Dunia. Katia meets alone with Mitia, expecting to trade her virtue for money.

Dmitrii confides later to his virtuous younger brother, Alësha, that his first impulse had been to rape her. Unlike Bernard in Sand's novel, however, Dmitrii begins to scheme. Taking his entire savings, a five-thousand-ruble note, Dmitrii hands it to Katia with a most respectful bow and opens the door to dismiss her. Dmitrii delights in knowing that he, an impoverished, immoral army officer, has exquisitely insulted a woman with intellect and breeding who stands helplessly before him. Although he considers himself a brute, Dmitrii revels in the inequality of their relationship. He relishes his own baseness and degradation:

> At that moment she was beautiful because she was noble, and I was a cad; she in all the grandeur of her generosity and sacrifice for her father, and I—a bug! And scoundrel as I was, she was altogether at my mercy, body and soul. She was hemmed in. I tell you frankly that thought, that venomous thought, so possessed my heart that I was almost overcome. (*The Brothers Karamazov*, 111–12)

Dmitrii seizes the opportunity to lash back at Katerina for having greeted him with the cool arrogance that the aristocracy reserves only for those infinitely below them. Overcoming his lust, he resolves to behave in a manner which exceeds hers in nobility. Edward Wasiolek explains in *Dostoevskii: The Major Fiction* (1964) that Dmitrii's gesture is "not an act of sacrifice executed in selflessness and taken in gratitude, but . . . a subtle and exquisite insult. It is sacrifice used as insult, and ravishment, by comparison, would have been kind."[65] Mitia and Katia engage in a cruel game of one-upmanship. After this magnanimous gesture, Katia finds herself hopelessly in debt to Dmitrii. For the time being, her only solace consists of loving him through wounded pride in an act of self-laceration.

Katia vows mercilessly to uphold her promise to remain true to Dmitrii, in spite of his infidelity. She has already sought Ivan's full approval and tells Alësha self-righteously that she will become nothing but an instrument for Dmitrii's happiness. And he will see it all his life (*The Brothers Karamazov*, 177)! Alësha courageously confronts the virginal aristocrat's hypocrisy:

> What I see is that you don't love Dmitrii at all . . . and never have, from the beginning. . . . And Dmitrii has never loved you . . . and only respects you. . . . Call Dmitrii. I will bring him—and let him come here and take your hand and take Ivan's and join your hands. For you're torturing Ivan, simply because you love him—and torturing him because you love Dmitrii through "self-laceration"—with an unreal love—because you've persuaded yourself. (*The Brothers Karamazov*, 175)

Edmée and Dunia are much more self-reliant and practical than Katia, who craves Dmitrii's insults. They offer her the perfect occasion to admire her own heroic fidelity in the face of humiliation. When Alësha reveals the truth behind her motives, she denounces him as "a little religious idiot," her face turning white and her lips quivering in anger (*The Brothers Karamazov*, 179). Her reaction reveals not the outrage of the unjustly accused but rather the stinging revelation of truth.

As further proof of Sand's influence on Dostoevskii, Komarovich points to the convincing evidence that Dostoevskii's rough draft of *The Brothers Karamazov* contains passages in French which clearly allude to *Mauprat*.[66] According to the German critic, just as Ivan Karamazov and Smerdiakov are accountable for the murder of which Dmitrii is accused, so Bernard's brutal uncles, Antoine and Jean de Mauprat, are accountable for the murder of which Bernard is unjustly accused. Komarovich's argument, although based upon a microscopic investigation of the two texts, appeared sufficiently ingenious to compel a French reviewer to conclude that in Dostoevskii's work "le pastiche . . . confine au plagiat"[67] (pastiche borders upon plagiarism).

Significantly, in the trials of both Bernard and Dmitrii the most incriminating evidence consists of a letter written to the "beloved," expressing a motive and an intention to kill. In both novels, the virginal aristocrat holds the authority in the courtroom to redeem or to convict the hero. Both Edmée and Katia create a stir among the spectators, who wait anxiously to see how she will behave toward the accused. In both situations, the hero who had earlier spared the virtuous woman from an act of potential debauchery now stands helplessly before her.

Whereas Edmée had already exacted sufficient revenge by making Bernard endure arduous trials to earn her love, Katerina Ivanovna seizes her moment of revenge at the trial. Proving that purity and virginity do not a redemptress make, Katia brings Dmitrii's incriminating letter with her to the courtroom, having clearly premeditated the prospect of ruining him with her testimony. In her first episode on the witness stand, Katia proceeds modestly and resolutely. It appears as though she is willing to ruin herself to save him. But suddenly, Ivan confesses hysterically to the murder and Katia contends with the crisis of dissolving her love triangle. To save Ivan, she ruins Mitia, producing the letter in which he had discussed killing Fëdor. Whereas Edmée spares Bernard with a testimony that bares her genuine love for him, a feeling she had kept secret for seven years, Katia lies and produces false evidence to convict Dmitrii. In Dostoevskii's work, the proud, chaste woman redeems no one. Svidrigailov commits suicide when Dunia rejects him. A humble prostitute, Sonia, saves Raskolnikov. In the end, Mitia's fate is tied to Grushenka rather than to Katia. The highly intelligent, strong Grushenka, who has had to cultivate a keen sense of business and a capacity for hard work in order to purchase her freedom from the merchant Samsonov, lacks completely Katia's proud chastity. She proves instead that she genuinely loves Dmitrii in a self-assured, level-headed manner. A coarse, crafty, hot-blooded creature,

Grushenka shares Dmitrii's largeness of spirit and is prepared at the novel's end to accompany him to Siberia or to escape with him to America. Like Bernard's, Dmitrii's ultimate redemption comes through genuine, passionate love of a kindred spirit.

5

Horace, the Superfluous Rake: Triangulation of Desire

La jalousie et l'envie supposent une triple présence: présence de l'objet, présence du sujet, présence de celui que l'on jalouse ou de celui que l'on envie.[1]

Jealousy and envy imply a triple presence: presence of the object, presence of the subject, and presence of the one we are jealous of or the one we envy.

In René Girard's *Mensonge romantique et vérité romanesque (Deceit, Desire, and the Novel)*, the author explores the notion of the triangulation of desire. In order for a vain subject to desire an object, he must convince himself that this object is already desired by a third party to whom he attaches a certain prestige. This third party (termed *mediator* by Girard) constitutes a rival who carries an element of fascination for the subject. George Sand's *Horace* exemplifies this notion with the love triangle Horace/Marthe/Paul. In spite of his prejudices regarding her lowly social station, Horace initially desires the proprietress of a café due to the presence of numerous suitors around her cashier's counter. Horace assumes the gratifying challenge of supplanting these other admirers to prove his competence among his peers.

Girard reveals further that the vain romanticist persuades himself that he is supremely original when, in fact, he diminishes the importance of the role which "the Other" plays in his desires by subscribing to clichés of the reigning ideology. Girard explains, "Seuls les romanciers révèlent la nature imitative du désir . . . car l'imitation la plus fervente est la plus vigoureuse-ment niée" (Novelists alone reveal the imitative nature of desire . . . because the most fervent imitation is the most vehemently denied).[2]

In the case of Sand's novel and of those Russian novels which feature characters patterned after Horace, romanticism determines the behavior of the vain subjects. Their desires constitute mere mental abstractions. Their joys and agonies remain intangible and spiritual. The primary conflict in these novels features a vain subject as the third, superfluous (and often destructive) member of the love triangle, a member who faces a series of obstacles in his sentimental education. Here, "desire for the end" culminates positively in the successful maturation of the superfluous man who relinquishes his naïve illusions and ultimately conforms. The worst-case scenario ending reveals three disillusioned members of the love triangle, their lives shattered by the intervention of the well-meaning but destructive character who repeatedly aspires to higher ideals on a spiritual plane, but who fails to convert his inspirations into tangible, productive actions.

Horace's difficulty in outgrowing adolescence and in learning to take responsibility for his actions comprises the primary conflict of the novel. This conflict is complicated by the hero's inability to sustain a given identity, underscored by his insistence on his actual brilliance and originality. Later in the novel, Théophile marvels at Horace's apparently complete transformation due to his conscious imitation of the young noblemen with whom he associates. Horace attempts tirelessly to win the approval of his peers. He strives to assert himself as a strong, aggressive, masculine figure by supplanting other would-be suitors, as in Marthe's case. Moreover, once he wins her affections, Horace immediately broadcasts the news of his conquest. Having taken a mistress, Horace relates to Théophile that he wants everyone to know that Marthe is his. His concern with establishing his superiority over friends reveals Horace's susceptibility to peer pressure. He demonstrates his immaturity further in the despotic control that he exercises over Marthe. Théophile relates, "Horace exerçait sur sa maitresse un tel empire que désormais elle nous retira toute sa confiance" (Horace exercised such sovereignty over his mistress that she withdrew her trust in us thereafter) (*Horace*, 157).

In identifying the complex aspects of jealousy, Girard explains that the same people repeatedly suffer from jealousy due to a fascination for their rivals and a tendency to desire that which is inaccessible because it is desired by another. Those who suffer from a "jealous temperament" or an "envious nature," Girard explains, share a propensity to imitate the desires of others.[3]

Horace's jealousy flares up when anyone threatens his exclusive control over his mistress. When Laravinière chastises Marthe for having chosen as her defender a child lacking reason and dignity, he challenges:

"A votre place, Marthe, je ne resterais pas un instant de plus chez lui."
"Emmenez-la donc chez vous, Monsieur!" dit Horace avec un
mépris sanglant, "j'y consens de grand coeur; car je comprends
maintenant ce qui se passe entre elle et vous." (*Horace*, 191)

"If I were you, Marthe, I wouldn't stay another instant with him."
"Take her with you, then, Sir!" said Horace with cutting contempt,
"I consent to it wholeheartedly; for I see now what's going on between
the two of you."

His jealousy of Paul Arsène is compounded by the fact that Horace
does not consider Arsène a worthy opponent.[4] Horace's penchant for employing romantic conquests as a measure of his worth in relation to other
men serves as a basic motivating force behind his behavior with women. In
competition for the favors of Marthe, Horace suffers greatly from the comparison between himself and Arsène.

Horace subscribes to a code of chivalry that precludes his acceptance of
Arsène as a legitimate rival. To fulfill his quest as a romantic hero, Horace
may pursue only a noblewoman. In spite of her affiliation with the working
class, Horace pursues Marthe; he does so on the basis of her noble nature
(and because she is desired by others). However, by accepting the atten-
tions of a lowly born man, Arsène, Marthe loses all right to Horace's esteem
in his own eyes. Later he admits bitterly:

C'était pour moi une injure sanglante la comparaison qu'elle pouvait
faire entre nous deux au fond de son coeur. . . . Je savais bien qu'il
l'aimait, lui, et que son amour était plus digne d'elle que le mien. Mon
orgueil souffrait de l'idée qu'un autre que moi pouvait lui donner le
bonheur que je lui devais; et je crois que, dans mes accès de délire, je
l'aurais tuée plutôt que de la voir sauvée par lui! (*Horace*, 215)

I was painfully injured by the comparison that she was able to make in
her heart of hearts between the two of us. . . . I knew well that he loved
her, and that his love was more deserving of her than my own. My
pride suffered from the idea that someone else could give her the
happiness that I owed her; and I really believe that in my delirious fits,
I would have killed her rather than see her rescued by him!

Horace occupies himself principally with appearances. He calls attention to his own physical attractiveness by constantly commenting on the
deficiencies of others in this respect. His comments on the ugliness and

deformities of others always carry with them an implied comparison to his own perfection. His propensity to evaluate himself with regard to others, to imitate the mannerism of others and to long for the same objects of desire as those of others all fit Girard's notion of the triangulation of desire. His indecisiveness, vanity, and destructive tendencies manifest themselves repeatedly in a cast of superfluous rakes featured in Russian novels patterned after Sand's *Horace*. These include Ivan Goncharov's *A Common Story* (1847), Alexandr Herzen's *Who is to Blame?* (1847), and Ivan Turgenev's *Rudin* (1856).

In *Conformity's Children: An Approach to the Superfluous Man in Literature* (1978), Ellen Chances delineates two types of protagonists belonging to this tradition: a social misfit, exemplified by Eugene Onegin, and a metaphysical rebel, embodied by Pechorin.[5] She explains that these earliest examples of hypersensitive, aimless, alienated Byronic heroes evolved in the mid-1840s through the 1850s into aristocrats rejected by society. With the transition from romanticism to realism, Chances explains, "Herzen and Turgenev created a new type, the liberal reformer, idealistic by nature, but incapable of effecting social change."[6]

These dreamy idealists failed repeatedly to convert ideas successfully into productive action. The Russian authors of these novels attribute this inability to act decisively to a combination of personal weakness (often as a result of having been overly indulged by doting mothers), to a sentimental education steeped too heavily in romanticism, and perhaps most significantly, to political and social restraints on the individual. In the fall of 1836, Pëtr Chaadaev (1793–1856) published a document entitled "First Philosophical Letter." Chaadaev vehemently attacked his country's "empty" past, "intolerable" present and "hopeless" future on the grounds that its geographical and historical position between East and West had isolated it from the cultural heritage of either world. Having failed to develop a "single spiritual idea" that might have established its own national character, Russia "was a country 'untouched by the universal education of mankind'; its national tradition was 'devoid of any powerful teaching'; its inhabitants were 'like children who had never been made to think for themselves,'" in Chaadaev's opinion .[7]

Similarly, in these novels featuring superfluous men, the protagonists are often disillusioned landowners who feel helpless and lost in spite of the privileges afforded by their education and upbringing. Historically, intellectually stimulating Western education had deprived Russian aristocrats and intelligentsia of a sense of belonging in their native land, where over 90 percent of the population was illiterate even at the end of the nineteenth century.[8] Worse, there was the Russian disease. Carole Karp relates in "George Sand and the Russians," the morbid self-paralysis of this disease:

> We Russians have set ourselves no other task in life but the cultivation of our own personalities—and so we get again one monster the more in the world, one more of those worthless creatures in whom habits of self-consciousness distort the very striving for truth.[9]

The woman in this correspondence, Karp reveals, protests that futile, fickle young men destroy the potential of the intelligent young Russian woman. Because there are no male heroes, it becomes incumbent upon the women to be strong, responsible and self-reliant.

The tradition of superfluous men in literature abounds with the strong woman motif. These novels often juxtapose the weak dreamers with self-actualizing women who can act decisively, understand reality, and participate in life in some useful capacity. These women generally are mere foils to their superfluous counterparts, however. The redemption of the hero's ego serves as the real subject of the novel, and these women often appear in a limited episode of the superfluous man's life; they are almost invariably portrayed as they relate to men and not as they relate to each other and to their own work.

The Russian creators of these superfluous men share an ambivalent attitude toward their misfit characters. Chances examines the reverence for conformity in Russian culture, citing the presence of Eastern Orthodoxy as one instance of the passion to conform. The will to belong permeates past and present culture in Russia, "a country reputed to denigrate individuality, to value submission to authority and the sacrifice of individual needs to the good of the collective."[10] The superfluous man fails in some capacity to integrate himself successfully into the collective.

D. I. Pisarev (1840–68) established a hierarchy of these heroes to account for the transformation of the early liberal aristocratic hero into the later young nihilist, Bazarov of Turgenev's *Fathers and Children*. The first group, those with "will without knowledge," includes the early prototypes of Onegin and Pechorin. These clear, capable young men suffer from "spiritual hunger, boredom and disenchantment." The second group, patterned largely after Sand's character Horace, has "knowledge without will"; it features gloomy, frustrated idealists who aspire to great pursuits, but fail consistently to take action to realize their passionate ideals and to convert them into tangible realities. Beltov, Aduyev and Rudin comprise this second group. The evolution completes itself ultimately with Bazarov, the representative of "knowledge and will," who unites thought and deed into "one solid whole."[11] The superfluous man is either a positive figure, a victim of his hopeless environment, or a negative one impeding social progress, depending on whether the critic is pro-liberal or pro-radical. The radical critics, Chernyshevskii and Dobroliubov, denigrated these flabby, weak-willed liberal heroes, insisting that Russia needed men of action rather than inert dreamers.[12]

Dobroliubov identified the common themes uniting the natures of these superfluous heroes: their writing, reading, civil service, domestic life, attitudes toward women, and their tendency toward self-humiliation. The environment in midnineteenth-century Russia rendered them incapable of overcoming their inertia and attacking the political system with full force. These heroes all suffer from the same barren striving for activity, coupled with the painful awareness that while they are capable of a great many things, in fact, they will achieve nothing.[13]

George Sand's writings struck a sympathetic chord with the frustrated Russian intelligentsia. Utopian schemes for the transformation of society, like Saint-Simon's New Christianity and Fourier's *phalanstères*, appealed enormously to young Russian idealists of the 1840s.[14] Echoes of these utopian themes reverberated in Sand's *Horace*. In addressing the unfortunate predicament of these overeducated misfits, Sand asserted that their frustration stemmed from the inappropriateness of their education or experience in the face of contemporary moral, social, and political trends. "C'est un malheur des génération placées entre celles qui ne savent rien et celles qui sauront assez: elles savent trop" (It is a hardship for the generations situated between those who know nothing and those who will know enough; they know too much) (*Horace*, 2). Sand thought that there were only three options for these unfortunate men. They could endow their lives with a measure of meaning through the love of a woman, they could immerse themselves in physical labor, or they could seek refuge in a mystical and transcendental understanding of the universe. Patrick Waddington asserts in *Turgenev and George Sand: An Improbable Entente* that it is easy to see the relevance of this formula to the respective solutions proposed by Russia's literary giants.[15]

Who is to Blame?—Alexandr Herzen

In the early 1830s, German abstract idealism dominated the discussions of Russian intellectuals. Gradually, following the lead of Aleksandr Herzen, "the father of the Russian intelligentsia," the intellectuals turned toward the French radicalism that George Sand promoted in her novels. Aleksandr Herzen, whom Isaiah Berlin has termed the most arresting Russian political writer in the nineteenth century, experimented in the 1840s with the style and subject matter of Sand's novels, as did other *zhorzhzandistki*.[16] Like Belinskii, Herzen first discovered George Sand in reading her mystico-socialist novel *Spiridion*. He read it early in 1839 when it appeared in serial form in the *Revue Indépendante* while he was a political exile in the provincial town of Vladimir. His repeated appeals to a friend in Moscow to forward the issues of the journal containing the final chapters of the novel attest to his earnest excitement.[17]

Of all of Sand's novels, *Horace* appears to have affected Herzen most profoundly. The leading characters in *Horace* and *Who is to Blame?* share a striking resemblance. Like Horace, Beltov displays great liberal ideas, an ability to speak charismatically and influentially, an impressive education, and a dedicated upbringing. Both lack staying power, however, and cause harm unintentionally to those with whom they become closely involved. Like tumultuous hurricane winds, both Horace Dumontet and Vladimir Beltov "hurl themselves upon a peaceful scene, spew forth gusts of destruction, and then abruptly disappear, their trails strewn with the debris of broken lives."[18]

Sand's voice resounds in Herzen's only published novel, *Who is to Blame?* The novel deals with the question of culpability in the love triangle, an issue with which Herzen became all too familiar in his own marital tragedy.[19] Herzen implied that abolishing the institution of marriage would resolve the problem. That Sand's *Horace* influenced Herzen's *Who is to Blame?* manifests itself clearly in Herzen's diary entries during the time he was composing his novel. He noted:

> I'm avidly reading *Horace* by George Sand, a great work, full of artistic and profound significance. . . . Horace is indeed a contemporary personality, a victim more of the times than of the system. He would always have been incapable of strong passions and of deep and lasting convictions. He would always have been petty and egotistical. But this transitional era of conflict between two worlds—which rubbed salt into all wounds, proclaimed all the rights of the individual, and offered unrestrained might and power—opened up to egotism an unprecedented and glorious arena.[20]

In his biography, *Aleksandr Herzen and the Birth of Russian Socialism* (1965), Martin Malia relates that from Sand's work Herzen "derived a reaffirmation of his old faith in the Saint Simonians' New Christianity, the task of which was "to regenerate mankind through a religion no longer otherworldly and mystical, but social and terrestrial."[21]

Sand created Horace as a representative figure of his era, making her intentions clear in the preface and dedication of her book. Similarly, Herzen conceived of his Beltov as a representative figure for the Russia of his time. Herzen noted of his leading character, "If Beltov threw himself from one thing to another it was because the social activity to which he aspired was not permissible. He was like a bee whom [sic] one had forbidden to lay eggs or to deposit honey."[22]

Sand's *Horace* struck Herzen like a bolt of recognition. In the fictional lead character Herzen saw himself and his entire generation of "superfluous men," who were all talk and no accomplishment:

> And besides, are there not many, who, when looking into the depth of their soul, will detect a lot of "Horace" in them? On the one hand, the bragging about non-existent feelings, about suffering for the people, and the expression of longing for strong passions and great deeds and, on the other, the utter failure to achieve anything. The urge to repent, to beg forgiveness, and the next day, to sin anew—all this I have experienced myself. Oh Lord, how man loves to sit behind a desk and play the hero.[23]

Although Herzen denigrates the egotism of Sand's hero, his sympathetic treatment of Beltov in *Who is to Blame?* complicates the question of culpability. Herzen appears to distribute the fault between circumstance, individual character, and the nature of life itself. He affirms the complexity and insolubility of life's fundamental problems, but offers no definitive answer to the question raised by the novel's title. Russian writers and critics would subsequently venture their own solutions to Herzen's troubling question. The radical Chernyshevskii would even go so far as to pose another, more practical, question, one demanding action rather than reflection: What is to be done?

Beltov suffers a triple failure in his intervention into the love triangle with the Krutsiferskiis. Not surprisingly, Soviet criticism of Herzen's novel has tended to attribute Beltov's failure to the conditions of midnineteenth-century Russia. Lenin declared that all of the issues raised by Herzen in *Who is to Blame?* (family upbringing, marriage, the status of women, environmental factors in personality development) pale in comparison to the single main problem: "All social questions are fused in the struggle against serfdom and its remnants."[24] Martin Malia reiterated the party line in determining the assignment of culpability. In Herzen's biography, Malia argues that no one is to blame and that the answer lies in the defects of Russian society. Consequently, the "alienation imposed by 'cursed Russian reality' are to 'blame' for Beltov's triple failure of human promise."[25]

Chaadaev's "First Letter" conveyed the predicament of the individual Russian intellectual who lacks any useful employment for his talents. "It is a trait of human nature," Chaadaev wrote, "that a man gets lost when he can find no means to bind himself to what has come before him and what will follow after him. Lacking the guiding sense of continuous duration, he finds himself lost in the world."[26] The protagonist, Vladimir Beltov, is Herzen's portrait of the "lost soul" about whom Chaadaev had written. In his "First Letter" Chaadaev had defined the essence of that character:

> the flightiness of a life totally lacking in experience and foresight . . . which results simply from the ephemeral existence of an individual detached from the species. Such a life holds dear neither the honor nor the progress of any community of ideas or interests, not even a traditional family outlook or that mass of prescriptions and perspective which compose . . . both public and private life.[27]

Who is to Blame? essentially serves as a documentary tracing the emergence of a social type. Herzen endows each character with a rich background of biographical detail. Beltov, though the main character, enters the novel late and indirectly. A wealthy landowner and intellectual of noble birth, Beltov is first heard of through rumors, gossip and paradoxes. Herzen successfully depicts multidimensional characters through his examination of the complex factors determining personality development. No personage enters the narrative without carrying with him many branches of his family tree, replete with his exposure to fundamental social institutions (aristocracy, bureaucracy, marriage, illegitimacy, serfdom and education). Even Beltov's appearance presents contrasts that heighten the mystery. Herzen's main character is good-natured, but supercilious; a gentleman, but a rake; and melancholy, but passionate. Beltov arouses both intellectual curiosity and emotional anxiety.[28]

Isaiah Berlin has succinctly summarized Beltov's predicament in one of his many essays on the life and works of Aleksandr Herzen:

> [The hero is] too idealistic and too honest to accept the squalor and the lies of conventional society, too weak and too civilized to work

effectively for their destruction, and consequently displaced from his proper function and doomed to poison his own life and the lives of others.[29]

Beltov takes his noble goals to Petersburg where he engages in the civil service and makes his debut in high society. In possession of too great an intelligence, he finds life in the bureaucracy devoid of interest and soon retires. An older co-worker comments of Beltov:

> He isn't aware of the appropriate forms. If it were because he is stupid or inexperienced, it wouldn't be so bad. He could learn them. But it is because he's so intelligent. He makes romance out of business matters, and the main point slips through his fingers. He doesn't care who submitted the communication, or what the proper procedure is, or to whom it should be forwarded. He merely "skims the surface," that's what. Yet if you ask him a question, then for sure he will try to educate us old-timers. (*Who is to Blame?* 164)

His disappointment with the civil service stems from the sobering realization that "only the drudges do any work." With youthful vehemence and a dreamer's irresponsibility, Beltov grows angry at circumstances. He realizes that the drudges work "only because the badgers and mongooses simply can't accomplish anything. All they can contribute to humanity is their strivings and aspirations—often noble, but almost always futile" (*Who is to Blame?* 166). A prolonged period of disillusionment ensues in Beltov's life. He spends the next ten years "doing everything but accomplishing nothing." Following his initial disappointment in the civil service, Beltov tries his hand at medicine, painting, and travel, but the attempts result invariably in boredom. At the end of Part I, Herzen's main character returns to Russia in order to take part in the local elections in the provincial town of N. When Herzen writes that Beltov wants to take part in provincial elections, he probably has in mind a more radical means of engaging political activity. The hallmark of the "superfluous man" stemmed, after all, from his status as a misfit. Severed intellectually from their countrymen and their native land, these Western-educated Russian aristocrats repeatedly attempted to effect some change in the political climate. Officials banned criticism of governmental policies from the pages of newspapers or political journals. As a result, discussion often took form in literature or in literary criticism, accounting in part for the enormous impact of George Sand's writing on the Russian intelligentsia during the 1830s and 1840s.

Unable to secure a position in local politics, Beltov finds solace in the friendship offered him in the Krutsiferskii family. Beltov unintentionally wreaks havoc on the household and finds himself incapable of resolving the situation on his own. Dr. Krupov, who had introduced Beltov to Liubonka and Dmitrii, chastises his young friend as he recites the litany of lives shattered by Beltov's influence:

> They accepted you as if you were their own kin; they offered you warmth. And how did you repay them? You will be pleased to learn that one of these days the husband will either hang himself or drown himself in water or in wine, I still don't know which. The wife will develop consumption, take my word for it. The child will become an orphan and be raised by strangers. (*Who is to Blame?* 280)

Beltov, having admitted to Krupov that he is a useless man and that few diseases are worse than the consciousness of useless energies, charges the doctor that it is simple for him to ask and condemn. Nevertheless, Beltov can offer no explanations for his behavior:

Why not simply ask me how I go on living? I really don't know the answer! Perhaps in order to destroy that family, to ruin the finest woman that I have ever met. . . . Let me answer your questions. Yes, I now feel the need not to justify myself but to speak out. I accept no one as judge; of my actions except myself. . . . I have no desire whatever to challenge you to a duel, if for no other reason than she needs you so desperately (*Who is to Blame?* 233).

The events that occasion Beltov's greatest crisis include his failure to gain elected office, the news of the death of his beloved mentor, Monsieur Joseph, and his acquaintance with the Krutsiferskii family. At the moment of his spiritual nadir when Beltov comes to recognize his superfluity and his consistent surrender to external circumstances, he wins the love and discovers the strength, intelligence, and sympathy of Liubonka Krutsiferskaia. Every day Liuba would observe new aspects of the man "fated to destroy within himself such awful strength of character and such staggering breadth of intellect" (*Who is to Blame?* 233). Herzen plays the devil's advocate in determining his main character's motivation for pursuing the happily married Liuba. Initially, Beltov had thought that he would flirt with her a bit. Having acquired considerable experience in this field and possessing a skillful and dangerously bold tongue, he is no longer frightened off by false modesty. Liuba's strength, simplicity and natural goodness, however, quickly deter Beltov from engaging in any vulgar flirtation. Because Liuba is never *en garde*, Beltov fails to launch a successful assault on her. Instead, an entirely new relationship develops between them, much like the one that had brought Dmitrii together with his wife years earlier. They realize that they understand each other even before they have managed to exchange a single word. The narrator explains: "This kind of affinity can neither be nurtured nor suppressed. It merely demonstrates a fact of parallel development in two individuals, whenever and wherever they meet. If they come to recognize each other, to understand their kinship, then each of them will sacrifice a less important relationship for this higher one, if circumstances so dictate" (*Who is to Blame?* 233). They become kindred spirits, understanding the melancholy and the ferment in the soul of each other. And yet Beltov himself has difficulty discerning whether he is truly in love with the teacher's wife or has simply found a friend, a sympathetic soul.

> Granting Beltov's own desire to tell the truth, even he would have had considerable difficulty answering these questions. Many things drew him to that house. The elections were over, as were all the dinners and balls associated with them. Needless to say, Beltov was not elected to any office. He remained in town only to hear the end of some lawsuit that was being tried in the Civil Court. I leave it to you to imagine the endless tedium of his life in the town of N. had it not been for his acquaintance with the Krutsiferskiis. (*Who is to Blame?* 229)

As with Horace, Beltov's egotism yields destructive results for those with whom he is most closely involved. When he professes his love for her, Liuba's defense of her husband's right to her exclusive affection startles Beltov. "Just imagine," he replies, "that was the one answer that I did not expect, yet it seems as if none other was possible" (249). He then challenges Liuba's objection, asking if she must absolutely reject one attachment for another, as if she had only a limited quantity of love to dispense.

Beltov confides later to his friend, Dr. Krupov, that although he means Dmitrii Krutsiferskii no harm, he believes firmly that the teacher has been remiss in joining his life with that of a woman who possesses such strength of character. Krupov must concede this point, having cautioned Dmitrii about this very danger years earlier. Both of Liuba's loves share the misfit status that marks the superfluous man tradition in literature. Moreover, she serves as a classic strong woman foil to both ineffectual dreamers.

Liubov Alexandrovna serves as Herzen's contribution to the Woman Question. "The oppressiveness of her surroundings, the harsh treatment that she receives, her virtual isolation from meaningful human contact—all result in an extraordinary and seemingly inexplicable development of her soul and her spirit."[30] A powerful portrait of the emerging "new woman," Liubonka derives in part from Pushkin's Tatiana and the heroines of George Sand, and in part from the author's own experience and that of his progressive wife, Natalia Alexandrovna.[31] A compassionate, intelligent, independent person, Liuba discovers (but fails to confront effectively) the contradictions inherent in her position in midnineteenth-century Russia. Typical of the strong woman foil to the superfluous man, Liuba emerges as a noble character, morally superior even to the hero. Sympathizing with the victims of the system, Liuba eventually falls prey to the knowledge and sensibilities she has developed. Although the "new woman" attempts valiantly to emerge, she fails to resolve the moral dilemmas in her path. The end of the novel leaves Liuba devoid of her former physical and spiritual well-being. Having lost both of her loves because each had proved to be an ineffectual dreamer, Liuba sinks into a rapid decline.

Her moral dilemma, with regard to her position in the love triangle, stems from her inability to resign herself to an admission of guilt. By condemning herself, Liubonka would have only to repent to return everyone's life to normalcy. Like the narrator, though, Liuba finds it difficult to determine who is to blame for the tragic emotional impasse. To her diary she confides:

> I am beginning to despise myself. Yes. Worse than anything else, and least comprehensible, is that my conscience is still at peace. I have dealt a terrible blow to a man whose life was devoted to me, whom I love, and all I feel is unhappiness. It seems that it would be easier if I considered myself a culprit. Oh, then I could throw myself at his feet, embrace him, and make amends with my repentance.
>
> Repentance erases all stains from the soul. He is so loving; he could not possibly resist. He would forgive me, and we would suffer together and be happier for it. (*Who is to Blame?* 264)

Through the medium of her diary (much like Vera Pavlovna's dream sequence employed by Chernyshevskii) Herzen documents Liuba's awakening to adulthood. Deeply pensive from an early age, "Liubonka began to feel and understand the sort of thing that many people never learn before they die" (96). Also like Chernyshevskii's more effective "new woman," Vera Pavlovna, Liuba struggles with the heart-wrenching anxiety of feeling great gratitude and friendship for the adoring husband who has delivered her from an abominable home life and yet of feeling hopelessly unfulfilled:

> May 23. Sometimes there occur strange moments when one is troubled by a desire to lead a fuller sort of life. I don't know whether this is a lack of gratitude for one's own fate or simply human nature. But I have been experiencing this desire frequently of late. It is very hard to put into words. I love Dmitrii dearly, but sometimes my soul needs something more, something that I don't find in him. . . . There still exist other needs; the soul yearns for strong, bold thoughts. Why does Dmitrii lack this need to search for truth, to be tormented by an idea? Whenever I turn to him with a burdensome question or with some doubt, he always comforts and consoles me. He wants to soothe me as if I were a little child. But that's not what I want at all. He may soothe himself with those childish beliefs, but I cannot. (*Who is to Blame?* 256–57)

Like Vladimir Beltov, Dmitrii Krutsiferskii has grown up in a world of abstractions. Also a dreamer, albeit of a different kind, the teacher fails as abysmally as Beltov to confront the tasks of practical experience. The young tutor with whom Liuba first falls in love represents the new breed of intellectual called *raznochintskii*. These "men of various origins and classes" belonged neither to the nobility nor the gentry. Herzen emphasizes the humble origins, modest aspirations and limited spiritual horizons of his "commoner," Krutsiferskii.[17] The narrator comments:

> It is very hard to define Dmitrii's character. He possessed a gentle nature, loving in the highest degree, feminine and submissive. He was so simple-hearted and pure that it was impossible not to love him, even though his purity was a result of his inexperience and constantly reminded one of a child's innocence.
>
> It would be difficult to find a person who knew less about the practical side of life. Everything he knew came from books; as a result, his knowledge was unreliable, romantic, and theoretical. (*Who is to Blame?* 229)

Krutsiferskii reacts to disillusionment by avoiding unpleasantness and disappointment. This he accomplishes by subsiding into the comforting world of make-believe, often induced by too much alcohol. His romantic isolation leads to an unhappiness no less pronounced than Beltov's. "Liubonka inveighs against her husband for conducting himself unnaturally: his love is too self-sacrificing, too kind, too humble."[33] Such lofty behavior, the fruit of his idealistic upbringing, further complicates his marriage when Beltov arrives on the scene to generate, albeit unwittingly, certain catastrophe for the couple.

In Sand's novel *Horace*, Paul Arsène shares Dmitrii Krutsiferskii's tendency toward self-effacement. Each is extremely forgiving when the rakes, Horace and Beltov, disrupt the peaceful pursuit of their love interests with Marthe and Liuba respectively. Arsène makes a magnanimous concession to Théophile when he has learned of Horace's conquest:

> Voyez-vous, mon ami, j'ai remporté une grande victoire le jour où j'ai compris que ce qu'on appelle les fautes d'une femme étaient imputables à la société et non à de mauvais penchants. Les mauvais penchants sont rares et Marthe n'en a que de bons. Si elle a choisi Horace au lieu de moi c'est qu'alors je n'était pas digne d'elle et qu' Horace lui a semblé plus digne. Incertain et farouche tout en m'offrant à elle avec dévouement, je ne savais pas lui dire ce qu'elle eût aimé à entendre. (*Horace*, 184)

> You see, my friend, I won a great victory the day I understood that a woman's so-called "faults" were attributable to society rather than to malicious tendencies. These evil inclinations are rare, and Marthe's tendencies are all well-intentioned. If she chose Horace over me, it is because I was not worthy of her, and Horace appeared to her to be more so. Bashful and uncertain as I was in offering myself to her with devotion, I didn't know how to tell her what she would have liked to hear.

Once Marthe has ceased to love the obsessive egotist who perpetually challenges her devotion, she removes the sole obstacle to her love with Arsène. Unlike other novels by George Sand in which one primary conflict would involve Marthe's realization of Paul's qualities, Marthe admires him completely from the beginning and laments that she is (as yet) unable to love him as he deserves. Later, when their relationship solidifies, Arsène often defends Marthe's former lover and gently scolds her for her severity toward Horace:

> Mon amie... parlons sans amertume et sans ressentiment d'un homme plus faible que mauvais, et plus malheureux que coupable. Ton vengeance a été bien sévère et il pourrait arriver que tu en eusses regret par la suite. Horace n'est qu'un enfant, il le sera peut-être encore pendant plusieurs années; mais enfin il deviendra un homme, et il

abjurera peut-être les erreurs de son coeur et de son esprit. Il se repentira du mal qu'il a fait sans le comprendre, et tu seras dans sa vie un remords. (*Horace*, 294–95)

My friend, let us speak without bitterness or resentment of a man who is more weak than bad, and more unhappy than guilty. Your vengeance was very severe, and it could happen that you may regret it later. Horace is but a child, and he shall remain so perhaps for a good many years; but eventually he will become a man, and he may well renounce the errors of his heart and soul. He will feel remorse for the harm he has caused without understanding what he was doing, and you will be a source of regret in his life.

As mentioned, Krutsiferskii displays a remarkable indulgence toward his rival's audacious behavior. When Beltov enters the Krutsiferskii household and gradually wins Liuba's heart, the teacher fails completely to accommodate such extraordinary events. He submits to desperate attempts at prayer and declines rapidly into vulgar drunkenness. All the while, he chastises himself for secretly casting blame on his wife, admitting characteristically that he has almost come to love Beltov himself. Watching his sleeping child one evening, Dmitrii confronts the bitter truth that Liuba loves another. Vacillating between his position as a jealous, punitive husband and that of a self-sacrificing idealist, Dmitrii has a host of generous thoughts:

Am I right to accuse her? Did she really want to fall in love with him? What's more, he . . . I am nearly in love with him myself. . . Let her be happy. Let her recognize my altruistic love. So long as I can see her and know that she exists. I will become a brother to her, a friend! (*Who is to Blame?* 267)

Sand's Horace shares with Herzen's Beltov a doting mother, a promising youth, and eloquence and ambition. Théophile excuses Horace's numerous immature outbursts, attributing them to the charismatic power and self-confidence of his young friend. He forgives Horace on the basis of what he might become in the future. Horace boasts unabashedly to Théophile:

Vous voulez dire des idées? reprit-il avec ce sourire et ce regard qui imposaient par leur conviction triomphante; j'en ai déjà, des idées, et si vous voulez que je vous le dise, je crois que je n'en aurai jamais de meilleures; car nos idées viennent de nos sentiments, et tous mes sentiments, à moi, sont grands! Oui, Monsieur, le ciel m'a fait grand et bon. . . . Les grandes choses m'énivrent jusqu'au délire. Je n'en tire et n'en peux tirer aucune vanité, ce me semble; mais je le dis avec assurance, je me sens de la race des héros! (*Horace*, 16)

"You want to talk about ideas?" he replied with the look and the smile that overawed with their triumphant conviction. "I already have them— ideas—and to tell you the truth, I believe I'll never have any greater. Our ideas, you see, come from our feelings, and all of my own passions are grand. Yes, sir, heaven made me great and passionate. Great things intoxicate me to delirium. I do not and could not derive any sense of vanity from this, it seems to me; but I say it with conviction: I feel a part of the race of heroes.

Madame Dumontet had spared no expense to enable her promising son to pursue his law career in Paris. The limited resources of his provincial parents had required that they sacrifice a great deal to realize Horace's ambitious dreams. Théophile explains that the woman who lacks talent, purpose, and fortune has no other means to exist than to help her own to pursue their dreams. She does so by exercising the last-recourse option of robbing herself and by economizing wherever possible in the family's consumption. These sacrifices render life void of charity, gaiety, variety or hospitality. So convinced is she of her son's brilliant prospects, though, that Madame Dumontet would live on black bread and walk without shoes to serve him (*Horace*, 6-8).

Similarly, Beltov's mother, Sofia, endows her son from an early age with every conceivable advantage to fulfill his extraordinary potential. After her husband's death, Sofia fails to recover from the series of traumas that she had endured prior to marriage. Becoming increasingly pensive and withdrawn, she concentrates all of her morbid sensibility on her son's upbringing, separating him from his peers and isolating him from reality. Her entire existence revolves around her Little Voldemar. "If he slept badly, she didn't sleep at all. If he seemed slightly indisposed, she became ill. In a word, she lived for him, breathed with him, served as his nursemaid, wet nurse, cradle and toy" (*Who is to Blame?* 144).

Beltov reciprocates his love for his mother, although he is less obsessive than she. He writes to her often. His letters, though glum, conceal a great deal from her for the sake of her weak heart and are always full of love. For Sofia, Beltov's letters strengthen, comfort and embody the source of life itself for her. Shedding copious tears on the dear lines, she leafs through the pages of each letter a hundred times over (*Who is to Blame?* 170).

In the realm of filial love, Horace contrasts completely with Beltov. Ungrateful for the sacrifice made by his parents, Horace squanders the money on gambling, hoping to prosper without working. His father's stature in society is modest and Horace's ambition is to escape the restrictions of inadequate income. Although he initially follows his father's plan for him to study law, Horace quickly becomes bored and begins to act according to his own judgment. Achieving respectability through honest effort loses much of its value for Horace, as he attempts repeatedly to accelerate his acquisition of wealth.

Although Beltov does not submit to greed in the same manner as Horace, he nevertheless also fails to realize his potential in the workplace. In Beltov's youth, Sofia had employed the services of an extraordinary Swiss tutor named Monsieur Joseph, a forty-year-old "youth" well educated in the works of Rousseau and romanticism. He introduces Vladimir to abstract ideas, noble ideals and beautiful dreams. After his inappropriate early education, Beltov continues at Moscow University. Graduating full of grand plans and noble goals, he enters the civil service in Petersburg. After Vladimir has served for three-months, an older colleague concludes that Beltov's temperament is not right for the job:

> No, my friend, I can recognize a promising young man right away; when I first saw him I thought, "He seems to be a clever fellow; perhaps he'll have a career here. He's not yet accustomed to the civil service, but he'll manage—he'll get accustomed to it." But now, three months later, he is still fussing about every trifle and losing his temper as if, God forbid, he were trying to save his own father from being murdered. Where will that get him? We've seen that kind of young whippersnapper before: he's not the first, and he won't be the last. They all use words to great advantage: "I will eradicate these evil practices"; but they don't even know which *practices* or why they are *evil.* (*Who is to Blame?* 164)

In a key passage, the narrator explains that the education Beltov had received under Joseph's tutelage and later at the university had failed to prepare him to contend with the surroundings in which he was to earn his livelihood. Beltov's education, filled exclusively with universal concepts, had been deficient in informing him of reality in general and of Russian reality in particular. The author writes with unusually deep conviction that education must be climatological: for every age, as for every country, even more so for every class and perhaps even for every family, there should exist a particular kind of education (*Who is to Blame?* 31).

Vladimir Beltov's problems stem from the fact that his extraordinary gifts cannot thrive within the narrow confines of mediocre midnineteenth-century Russian society. After all, the narrator himself claims that environment rather than psychic makeup keeps children of great promise from generally fulfilling their potential in later life. He reflects:

> Who is not aware of the popular old belief that children who seem all too promising rarely live up to their promise as adults? Why is this? Can it be that a person's life forces are distributed in such limited quantity that if they are expended in youth nothing remains for maturity? It is such a complicated question. I cannot answer it, nor do I even want to try. But I think that one should seek the answer in the atmosphere, environment, influences, and contacts of a particular person rather than in some kind of incongruous personal psychological makeup. (*Who is to Blame?* 166)

This indictment of the environment comes closest to answering the question posed by Herzen's novel. His "lost soul," Beltov, exemplifies the inevitable superfluity of a highly sensitive, educated man attempting in vain to find an appropriate niche for himself in stagnant petrine Russian society. Beltov's involvement in the Krutsiferskii love triangle stems largely from Liuba's intuitive understanding of his tormented soul. Beltov cannot help but discern that in spite of her genuine appreciation of Dmitrii, Liuba longs for a more satisfying soul mate. Dmitrii's incapacity to cope with reality further perpetuates the dissolution of his marriage and obscures any clear-cut assignment of culpability in the dilemma of who is to blame.

A Common Story—Ivan Goncharov

Horace and *A Common Story* fulfilled comparable tasks in their respective countries. Each depicts a generation tragically deceived by the chimerical dreams of romanticism. Horace Dumontet and Aleksandr Aduev both have artistic ambitions and temperaments but lack the requisite talent and will to realize their aspirations. Whereas Aleksandr experiences a truly sentimental education or even purgation, during which he metamorphoses into a mature version of his youthful, idealistic self, Horace retains his self-deceptions until the end, and we are informed in an aside that he eventually resumes his pursuit of law with success. The reader witnesses the transformation process in Goncharov's novel.

In *A Common Story*, as in *Horace*, the primary conflict revolves around the main character's successful maturation. The real obstacle both must overcome is adolescence. Goncharov's comedy about coming of age treats the hero's loss of illusions and the compromises of maturity as they are repeated in the lives of both uncle and nephew. The plot evolves symmetrically in *A Common Story* as both main characters follow the same route, but at different times. Alexandra and Sverre Lyngstad explain that Goncharov's novel has the simple, archetypal quality of a fairy tale. A young man of twenty leaves his placid provincial home to seek his fortune in St. Petersburg (as had his uncle at the same age). The issues of prime importance on which Goncharov focuses include conflicts between old and new, the provinces and the capital, country squire and industrialist-in-the-making—a dialectic reminiscent of the polarization between Westernizers and Slavophiles.[34]

Both Horace and Aleksandr lose in love as the superfluous third wheel in a love triangle. Moreover, each exemplifies the notion of the "triangulation of desire," as defined by René Girard. In *Mensonge romantique et vérité romanesque*, Girard explains that the jealous party affirms that his own desire has preceded the intervention of his rival. He presents the mediator as an intruder who has maliciously interrupted a blissful romance. The jealous one systematically depreciates the qualities of his rival, all the while secretly desiring them. The mediator becomes a subtle, diabolical enemy who thrives on pilfering the most cherished possessions from their rightful owner.[35]

When on that fateful day Aleksandr arrives earlier than usual at the home of his beloved Nadenka, unfamiliar sounds reach him from the house while he is still in the garden. "What is it? Could it be a cello? As he draws near, he makes out the sounds of a man's voice—and what a voice!" The count's intellect, good looks, aristocratic manners and artistic talents increase Aleksandr's feelings of insecurity. Even worse, the count appears consistently wise, deliberate, brilliant and gracious to Aleksandr. The young idealist fails to engage his rival in a conflict because the count never acknowledges Aduev as a threat.

Both the products of romantic educations, Horace and Aleksandr see themselves and others in literary terms. Aduev works indefatigably when in love with Nadia.

The dawn often found him working at some elegy. All the time not spent at the Lyubetskiis was devoted to poetry. He would write a poem and read it to Nadia. She would copy it on a pretty sheet of paper and learn it by heart, and he knew the poet's highest bliss—to hear his works from beloved lips. "You are my Muse," he told her. "Be the vestal virgin of that sacred flame which burns in my breast! If you neglect it, it will be eternally extinguished." (*A Common Story*, 142)

Part II of *A Common Story* serves as an ironic parallel to Aleksandr's love for Nadenka in Part I. Iulia, the second of Aleksandr's Petersburg loves, receives a lengthy history explaining her romantic nature. Her romantic penchant for "sincere effusions" matches Aleksandr's own (she serves as his double) and she soon wearies him. A languid voluptuary of the emotions, Iulia suffers the ills of a faulty education with indiscriminately mixed Western elements. The narrator says of the young widow:

The trouble with her was that her heart was exaggeratedly developed, moulded and prepared by novel-reading not so much for first love, as for that romantic love that is to be found in certain novels but never in life, and which is invariably tragic—simply because it is a practical impossibility. Iulia's mind had never found healthy nourishment in her novel reading, and had not been able to keep up with her heart. She was utterly unable to imagine quiet, simple love with no tempestuous manifestations, with no exaggerated tenderness. (*A Common Story*, 273)

Like Aleksandr, Iulia attempts to model her life after the precedent established by a literary prototype. She memorizes Pushkin's *Evgenii Onegin*, keeping the verses near her pillow at night. She takes Tatiana as her model, mentally repeating to an ideal lover the burning lines of the heroine's letter to her superfluous man. "Her imagination seeks now an Onegin, now a hero from the masters of the new school—pale, mournful, disillusioned" (*A Common Story*, 279).

Similarly, Horace attempts to conform to the role of a romantic hero and tries to reshape Marthe's character to suit the feminine counterpart of that ideal. He demands that she devote herself exclusively to reading and grooming herself. For three months she has to play the role of Marguerite to suit Horace's rendition of *Faust*. She occupies herself according to his fancy, alternately watering the flowers on the window-ledge and brushing her long tresses before a gothic mirror, which Horace has procured at an inflated price. The images of women created by his favorite authors shape

Horace's attitude toward his lover. To preserve his aristocratic pretentions, Horace must eliminate all reminders of Marthe's lowly status prior to their union. Ironically, Horace pursues Marthe, having resolved to overcome the primary barrier in his literary career—his lack of experience in the realm of passion. Desiring her because Marthe has a large and enthusiastic following over which Horace resolves to triumph, he devotes more attention to strategy than to her. Once Marthe leaves Théophile and Eugénie to live with Horace, he chooses to remake her in the image of a romantic heroine, rather than to study Marthe as an individual and to learn to cooperate with her. The role is precarious and changes according to the feminine ideal of the book in hand.[36]

> Horace avait pris, dans les romans où il avait étudié la femme, des idées si vagues et si diverses sur l'espèce en général, qu'il jouait avec Marthe comme un enfant ou comme un chat joue avec un objet inconnu qui l'attire et l'effraie en même temps. (*Horace*, 159)

> From novels in which he had studied women, Horace had developed ideas so vague and so diverse with regard to their nature in general that he played with Marthe as a child or as a cat plays with a strange object that attracts and frightens it at the same time.

Both Horace and Aleksandr, considering themselves naturally gifted, turn to literary pursuits. Aduev's uncle believes Aleksandr should develop his proven ability as a translator and writer in the field of agriculture. Pëtr expresses the view that real work, not mere routine, could arrest the stagnation prevailing all over Russia. He counters the idle, dreamy, affected side of the old morals represented by Aleksandr with a new, sober, practical appreciation of reality. When assessing how to employ Aleksandr's abilities most, profitably, Pëtr asks Aleksandr which areas he considers himself to be most capable in. Citing "divinity, civil, criminal, natural and public law, diplomacy, political economy, philosophy, esthetics and archaeology," Aleksandr falters when his uncle demands to know the merits of his spelling and penmanship (*A Common Story*, 145).

Like Beltov and Horace, Aleksandr finds the very notion of work alien to him. "'What is talent for?" he asks. "The mediocre toiler works. Talent creates with ease and freedom" (*A Common Story*, 145). Aleksandr, too, becomes disillusioned when his talent fails him. He recalls that his articles on agriculture, and even his verses, have gradually improved and attracted the attention of the public only after arduous revisions. The superfluous men all subscribe to the fallacy that talent is inborn and effortless, that only the drudges do any work. They lack a practical work ethic, adopting instead the sentiments espoused by romantic prototypes in literature. Onegin and his like scorn the pettiness of work but lack the wherewithal to commit themselves to anything worthwhile. In "Luchshe pozdno, chem nikogda" (Better late than never), Goncharov declares the theme of his novel to be "the necessity of *work* . . . and of lively activity in the struggle against Russian stagnation." *A Common Story* serves to a significant degree as a programmatic novel. Aleksandr's conversion to the values of his uncle assumes the aspect of a literary conversion. Pëtr refuses to embrace Aleksandr and openly acknowledge his merits until he has secured a career and a fortune. This entails relinquishing his lofty, inflated, and conventionally romantic diction, indicative of a language divorced from material things ("sweet bliss," "sincere effusions," "colossal passions"), in favor of the language of things that characterizes literary realism.[38]

Pëtr effectively dissuades his nephew from pursuing a literary career by agreeing to submit Aleksandr's novel under his own name to an editor friend. The editor realizes that Pëtr is just a front and offers his assessment of the author's character:

> Since you are interested in the author of this novel you would probably like to know my opinion. Here it is. The author must be a young man. He is no fool, but for some obscure reason he is angry with the whole world. He writes so savagely, so bitterly. No doubt a disappointed man. Oh, Lord, when will we get rid of people like that! It's too bad that, owing to a false attitude to life, so much talent perishes among us in empty, sterile dreaming, in vain efforts to accomplish that for which the writer has no vocation. (*A Common Story*, 246)

The editor then condemns the superfluity of these idealistic dreamers, suggesting that only hard, practical work can spare them from this malaise:

> Vanity, dreaminess, the precocious development of emotional tendencies and lack of mental activity, with the inevitable result—idleness—such are the causes of this evil. Science, toil, practical work—only these are capable of bringing our sick, idle young folks to their senses. (*A Common Story*, 247)

Horace, too, tries his hand at writing. His literary ambitions depend on Marthe, whose influence on him continues, long after he seems to have forgotten her. Unlike Théophile, who prods Horace into productivity, Marthe serves as a passive catalyst, impelling others to decisive action because she refuses to assume responsibility for herself.[39] Horace incorporates the subject of his affair with Marthe first into a poem, composed specifically to seduce the Vicomtesse de Chailly, and then into his first novel. This novel enjoys moderate success, although his second novel fails abominably. Horace had exhausted in the first novel the little sum of talent that he had amassed; he had spent there the modest sum of emotion he had experienced (*Horace*, 313). Like Aleksandr, Horace finds his literary ambitions extremely difficult to fulfill. He spends three sleepless nights struggling to produce something brilliant and subsequently laments to Théophile:

> Moi! Je n'ai rien écrit. Pas une ligne de rédaction; c'est une chose plus difficile que je ne croyais de se mettre à barbouiller du papier. Vraiment, c'est rébutant. Les sujets m'obsèdent. Quand je ferme les yeux, je vois une armée, un monde de créations se peindre et s'agiter dans mon cerveau. Quand je rouvre les yeux, tout cela disparait. J'avale des pintes de café, je fume des pipes par douzaines, je me grise dans mon propre enthousiasme, il me semble que je vais éclater comme un volcan. (*Horace*, 87)

> I haven't written anything. Not a single line of composition. It's much more difficult than I had imagined to begin to scrawl on a piece of paper. Really, it's infuriating. I'm obsessed by all sorts of subjects. When I close my eyes, I see an army, a world of creations depicted and in motion in my brain. When I open my eyes, it all disappears. I swallow quarts of coffee, I smoke pipes by the dozen, I get lightheaded by my own enthusiasm, and I feel as though I'm going to erupt like a volcano.

Horace resolves to improve his literary career by living the life of a romantic hero. This entails, of course, experiencing and sustaining heightened emotions. The need for strong stimuli of the senses constitutes a common theme of the romantic period. Eighteenth-century philosophers, rejecting all metaphysical explanations of natural phenomena, placed the burden of proof of any fact on the experience of the senses. The logical extension of this thought was the need to affirm the physical reality of existence by constantly renewed sensations.

These sensations could take many forms, from the plunge into action typified by Byron's joining the Greeks in their war against the Turks, to the consumption of drugs to heighten one's perception of the surrounding environment. All of these actions resulted from the lack of an accepted religious base for existence.[40]

In light of his selfishness and immaturity, Horace appropriately reaches his state of heightened emotion by conjuring his own anger into a state of frenzy, as in the temper tantrum of a spoiled child. Théophile assesses that Horace abuses delirium and despair the way others abuse opium and hard liquor. Laravinière says of Horace's fits, so inconsistent with his adult appearance:

> Il n'a qu'à se sécouer un peu, disait Jean, aussitôt ; la fureur vient comme par enchantement, et vous le croiriez possédé de mille passions et de dix mille diables. Mais ménaces le de le quitter, et vous le verrez se calmer tout à coup comme un enfant que sa bonne ménace de laisser sans chandelle. (*Horace*, 226)

> He has but to exert himself a bit, said Jean, and the fury suddenly appears as if by magic. You would believe him to be possessed by a thousand passions and by ten thousand devils. But order him to stop, and you will see him calm down suddenly like a child whose nanny has threatened to leave him alone in the dark.

This example of emotional immaturity indicates the state of Horace's entire character, one engaged in the slow process of development from adolescence to maturity. Consistently, when Marthe appears to have committed suicide, Horace resolves to "punish" those who have chastised him for the unjust treatment of his mistress. In a manner common to adolescent behavior, Horace fantasizes his own heroic, untimely death, one which will enhance his image in the minds of his harsh critics and, most importantly, will cause them to regret their cruelty when their "victim" has met his tragic end.[41]

Also consistent with this adolescent immaturity is Horace's rebellion against his parents' values. His choice of career and his desire to attain elevated social standing contrasts completely with his modest, provincial upbringing. His republicanism rebels against his father's cautious conservatism; his irresponsible expenditures are juxtaposed to his mother's parsimony (on his behalf). He attempts to emulate the manners of the aristocracy, changing the spelling of his name to Du Montet and claiming that his father is a "conseilleur au parlement."[42] His inability to maintain an assumed identity further illustrates Horace's immaturity and lack of sophistication.

Like Beltov and Horace, Aleksandr enjoys the indulgence of a doting mother who believes unqualifiably in his brilliant future. Their childhood milieu—excessive pampering and emotionalism—has acted as a protective womb. The romantic idealism that each of these "superfluous" men has imbibed at the university further perpetuates his inability to work practically and effectively in the real world.

The Lyngstads develop an illuminating study of "flight and fall" imagery in Goncharov's *Common Story*. A prodigal son, Aleksandr sets out for St. Petersburg to "try his wings." His uncle constantly finds him "soaring" or "being carried away," whether on the "wings" of poetry or love. Goncharov's double-edged style oscillates between pathos and burlesque, a flight to the realm of lofty romanticism juxtaposed with the sobering fall to mundane (and often cruel) reality. Goncharov ridicules the sentimental clichés with which Aleksandr's speech abounds. His bliss with Nadia ends abruptly when her mother tells them to eat their yogurt. Moreover when Nadia asks him, "And do you love me so much?" wiping a tear from her cheek, "Aleksandr move[s] his shoulders imperceptibly in a gesture of inexpressible eloquence. Pëtr Ivanich would have called the expression of his face idiotic . . . but how much bliss there was in this idiotic expression" (*A Common Story*, 135). His preference for lofty language and ideas (characterized by recurring references to "sincere effusions," "cup of happiness," "sacred fire" and to money as "filthy lucre") condemns Aleksandr's experience to descent from his elevated ideals. The imagery of flight and fall that shapes the novel's action is so closely enmeshed in the texture of this common story that it renders even common clichés more ridiculous. Nadia threatens, for example, to "tell Mother" at a moment when their first kiss "transports" Aleksandr. Her threat causes him to "fall from the clouds."[43]

This flight and fall imagery pertains to the ineffectual dreamers, Beltov and Horace, as well. The higher their aspirations, the harder their descents into disillusionment.

Rudin—Ivan Turgenev

Like Sand, Herzen and Goncharov, Turgenev employs in *Rudin* the complications inherent in a love triangle in which a loving, unselfish woman falls prey to the lure of deceptively noble appearances. She is loved by two very different men, with a third standing by as a sort of judge. Sand was certainly not unique in having established this basic dramatic situation. This same love triangle was exploited earlier, for example, by Molière. That which is remarkable, however, is the manner in which these Russian novelists adopted Sand's ideas into a purely Russian context. The similarities pointed out by critics between *Horace* and *Rudin* are quite striking. As I have discussed previously, Turgenev mentioned several times the role that Sand had played in his development. The reference to both George Sand and Charles Dickens is regularly cited by critics as a prefiguring of Turgenev's own development. Russia revered the works of these two European novelists for their capacity to render contemporary social issues vividly. Turgenev's novels later enjoyed comparable acclaim.[44]

Structural parallels abound between *Horace* and *Rudin*. A Russian woman-novelist, Vladimir Karenin, an authority on George Sand, ventured to claim that the character of Rudin was entirely inspired by the French writer's *Horace:*

> Apart from all details of nationality and class which make their mark on Dmitrii Rudin and Horace, we find ourselves face to face with the same person, one and the same type of noble phrasemonger leading others and led himself by his fictitious warmth and his flaming discourse, but incapable of any real action, of any absolute real feeling; an enthusiast "à froid," in reality inferior to men less brilliant than himself . . . [45]

Karenin continues the comparison, citing the significance of cultural affiliation in the behavior of the French *homme inutile* and the Russian *lishchnii chelovek:*

> And if Dmitrii Rudin dies on the barricades of 1848 whereas Horace wisely avoids implication in the affair of Saint-Merry; if Rudin is in general much more likeable, more disinterested and more to be regretted than his prototype, we must seek the cause precisely in the nationality and in the caste that we have already mentioned. . . . Rudin belongs to the Russian nobility, is a dilettante of thought, an independent free man thanks to his position and his fortune. He has at the same time a nature eminently Russian, a little incoherent and broad. Horace, on the contrary, is a French petit bourgeois, a practical man aspiring to find a place for himself and if, at the beginning he is in error, carried away as he is by his exalted ideas, he knows how to take advantage of them at the right time, while preaching them for the most useful ends.[46]

All of Sand's principal characters in *Horace* find Russian counterparts in Turgenev's *Rudin*. Lezhnev observes and comments (often judgmentally) from the sidelines, as does Théophile. And like Théophile, Lezhnev concedes that the superfluous hero does have redeeming qualities, particularly those of charm and enthusiasm. Volyntsev is Rudin's rival in the love triangle with Natalia. Like Paul Arsène, he is honest, simple, and has a good heart. In his novel, Turgenev presents Rudin and Volyntsev in terms that are less black-and-white than Sand's treatment of Horace and Paul. Nevertheless, both novelists endow their superfluous men with dual personalities. Both Horace and Rudin oscillate between assuming a role as an actor and observing through the eyes of the genuine self. Both men speak passionately on almost any subject under the sun, albeit with the thoughts and opinions they have purloined from other people.

Natalia and Marthe share the same ardent, noble soul. Mme. Lipine and Eugénie cautiously protect them from Rudin and Horace, respectively. These women escape the seductive lure of the engaging speakers, preferring men of actions to men of words.[47]

Rudin and Horace both possess the music of eloquence. Their beautiful words act as a smokescreen, however, to conceal a battalion of foibles. Rudin understands intuitively how to elicit an emotional response from his listeners. He engages his audience by strumming upon one of the heart's chords to make it emit a troubled sound and set all the others to quivering. A spectator might not be able to understand precisely the subject of his speech, but Rudin heaves his breast high and all listen to him with profound attention. "He talks in a masterly manner, fascinatingly not quite clearly . . . but this very lack of clarity imparts a certain charm to his speech" (*Rudin*, 57). An accomplished orator, Rudin has a poor ear for language. Though he enjoys his capacity as a captivating speaker—shaking others to their depths and setting them on fire—Rudin often stutters and lacks precision. An impoverished nobleman and a passionate exponent of German romantic philosophy, Rudin is not a "phrasemaker" but rather someone whose excessive inspiration stifles his expressive ability.[48] He works tirelessly and zealously, but like his superfluous counterparts in literature, Dmitrii Rudin fails to abandon the realm of abstract theory and deal effectively with the prosaic realities of life. Lezhnev judges him accordingly, identifying Rudin's single redeeming quality as his status as an individual living cooperatively within a community:

> There is some genius in him, I admit, but as for temperament. . . .
> Therein lies his whole misfortune, that there is no temperament whatever about him. . . . But that is not the point. I wish to speak of that which is good and rare in him. He has enthusiasm; and that, believe

me, for a phlegmatic man, is the most precious quality of all in our day. We have all become intolerably reasonable and languid: we have fallen asleep, we have congealed, and we owe thanks to any man who will, even for an instant, move us and warm us up. (*Rudin*, 191)

Horace also speaks with flamboyance and enthusiasm, rendering his manner more important than the subject he is addressing. On the occasion of their first meeting, Théophile admires Horace's energetic and enthusiastic manner of expressing himself. He recalls: "Ses manières obligeantes, son air ouvert, son regard vif et doux, me gagnèrent à la premiere vue" (His affable ways, his open expression, and his sweet, lively look won me over at first sight) (*Horace*, 10). After their second meeting, Théophile is struck by the flamboyant bluntness with which Horace develops his ideas. His ambition consumes his conversation. He speaks exclusively of his supreme capabilities and the means of attaining his goals. Although Théophile does not agree with Horace on all points, he succumbs to the young man's magnetism and finds that he cannot contradict him. There is an element of truth in what Horace says and he says it with such conviction that until Théophile has left him, he does not feel a compulsion to point out the errors in the younger man's thinking. He finds, though, that upon seeing Horace again, he falls anew under the charm of Horace's words and mannerisms.

Horace and Rudin also share a nature that manifests itself outwardly as passionate and warm, but proves ultimately to be cold and detached. They suffer from a limited capacity for loving others selflessly. Rudin burns to profess his love to Natalia. The desire that propels him consists of the disclosure itself rather than the consummation of their passion. For Horace, desire takes shape in the egotistical thrill of supplanting rivals and in gaining emotional experience with which to promote his literary career. The narrator reveals of Rudin:

> Rudin—clever, penetrating Rudin—was not in a position to say with certainty whether he really loved Natalia, whether he were suffering, whether he would suffer on parting with her. Why, without pretending to be a Lovelace,—one must render him that justice—had he led astray a poor young girl? Why was he waiting for her with secret trepidation? To this there is but one answer: No one is so easily carried away as the unimpassioned people. (*Rudin*, 146)

When Rudin does reveal his love for her, Natalia surprises him by vowing to be his. After her departure, Rudin emerges from the arbor, smiling, the moon brightly illuminating his face. "I am happy. Yes, I am happy," he repeats, as though desiring to convince himself (*Rudin*, 131). When Natalia's mother opposes her daughter's union with Rudin, however, the superfluous hero easily dismisses his responsibility to contend with this obstacle. He finds it insurmountable and submits entirely to Daria Mikhailovna's will, in spite of the fact that Natalia fervently resolves to unite her life with his. His incapacity to love proves to be a self-fulfilling prophecy. Prior to his protestation of love to Natalia, Rudin had assessed himself with resignation:

> My hopes, my dreams, and my own personal happiness have nothing in common. Love." (at this word he shrugged his shoulders.)—"love is not for me. I . . . am not worthy of it. The woman who loves has a right to demand everything from a man, and I can no longer give everything. Moreover, pleasing is an affair of youth; I am too old. How should I turn other people's heads? God grant that I may keep my own on my shoulders! (*Rudin*, 121)

Rudin later reveals to Natalia in a letter that the responsibility has frightened him. He acknowledges that the very first obstacle has completely scattered him to the winds. He destines himself to remain the same incomplete creature he has been hitherto. He continues with what will prove to be an even more tragic self-fulfilling prophecy:

> What I lack is, in all probability, that without which it is as impossible to move the hearts of man, as it is to subdue the hearts of women; and sovereignty over minds alone is both uncertain and useless. Strange, almost comic is my fate: I surrender the whole of myself, eagerly, completely—and cannot surrender myself. I shall end by sacrificing myself for some nonsense or other, in which I shall not even believe . . . (*Rudin*, 173)

When Rudin does die on the Paris barricades in 1848, he proves to be a misfit even in death. The French insurgents incorrectly identify him as a Pole rather than a Russian. Rudin and Horace both prove to be perpetual monetary parasites, revealing their childish irresponsibility and their self-serving dependence on others. When Horace brags about his gambling winnings, Théophile's incredulity that his friend appears to have completely forgotten his debt to him silences the narrator. He is so confounded by Horace's arrogance that he lacks the wherewithal to demand repayment.

Lezhnev, who has access to Rudin's less-than-noble past, is enraged to learn that the newcomer has extracted five hundred rubles from Daria Mikhailovna and two hundred from Volyntsev immediately after his arrival. He reports condescendingly of Rudin's past:

> He received his education in Moscow, first at the expense of some uncle or other, and later on, when he was grown and got his feathers, at the expense of some wealthy pretty prince with whom he had sniffed up some sort of understanding . . . well, pardon me, I will not do it again! (*Rudin*, 86)

When Lezhnev later forgives Rudin, he reassesses his earlier evaluation of him. "He is not an actor, as I termed him," Lezhnev reveals. "He is not a deceiver, nor a rogue; he lives at other people's expense, not like an intriguer, but like a child" (*Rudin*, 191). Horace shares this childish dependence on others both monetarily and emotionally. Like Rudin, he lacks the passion necessary to love unselfishly and to sustain a lasting relationship. Théophile reflects:

> Horace n'était point né passionné. Sa personnalité avait pris de telles dimensions dans son cerveau, qu'aucune tentation n'était digne de lui. Il lui eût fallu rencontrer des êtres sublimes pour éveiller son enthousiasme; et, en attendant, il se préférait, avec quelque raison, à tous les êtres vulgaires avec lesquels il pouvait établir des rapports. (*Horace*, 91)

> Horace was not born the least bit passionate. His personality had taken on such dimensions in his mind, that no temptation was worthy of him. It would have been necessary for him to encounter sublime beings to evoke his enthusiasm. And in the meantime, he preferred himself, with some reason, to all of the vulgar beings with whom he was able to establish relationships.

Although Horace is capable of great devotion to himself, he encounters considerable difficulty in genuinely appreciating others. Théophile explains that Horace is not a cold egotist, as Jean Laravinière believes him to be. Rather, Horace's nature proves to be simultaneously cold and passionate. Although he is, in fact, egotistical, Horace also has a need for friendship, caring, and sympathy. This need is so powerful, in fact, that Horace submits to childish demands to the point of jealous domination in order to fulfill it. Whereas a true egotist lives alone, Théophile argues, Horace fails to survive a quarter of an hour without company (*Horace*, 234). The fact that Horace and Rudin both have an incapacity to love is not surprising in light of the sweeping condemnation made by Théophile of the majority of his sex:

> Horace n'était ni aussi respectable ni aussi méchant qu'elles [Marthe et Eugénie] se l'imaginaient. Le triomphe le rendait volontiers insolent; il avait cela de commun avec tant d'autres, que si on voulait condamner rigoureusement ce travers, il faudrait mépriser et maudire la majeure partie de notre sexe. Mais son coeur n'était ni froid ni dépravé. Il aimait certainement beaucoup; seulement, l'éducation morale de l'amour lui ayant manqué, ainsi qu'à tous les hommes, comme il n'était pas du petit nombre de ceux dont le dévouement naturel fait exception, il aimait seulement en vue de son propre bonheur, et, si je puis m'exprimer ainsi, pour l'amour de lui-même. (*Horace*, 149)

> Horace was neither as respectable nor as mean as Marthe and Eugénie believed him to be. Triumph made him insolent; he had that in common with so many others that were we to condemn this eccentricity rigorously, we would have to scorn and censure the majority of our sex. But his heart was neither cold nor depraved. He certainly liked a lot of things; but lacking a moral education in love, along with all other men, since he was not among the very few whose natural devotion is the exception, Horace loved only to suit his own happiness, and if I may say so, for love of himself.

Lezhnev and Théophile share the status of judgmental bystander. In contrast to the destructive natures of Rudin and Horace, these characters exemplify safe, conformist behavior and provide a narrative conscience and voice of reason in assessing the notorious impact of their superfluous counterparts. Both stand outside the love triangle looking on. Occasionally this narrative tool ventures into the realm of voyeurism and diminishes the tale's verisimilitude. Karenin objects to Théophile's presence in such discussions as those concerning the advisability of Marthe's becoming his mistress and the responsibilities inherent in respecting her honor. Of his own mistress, Eugénie, Théophile somewhat didactically informs Horace by right of the special privileges of friendship, that she is his companion, his sister—his wife, if you will. But he cautions that he did not lift the veil of secrecy covering their love until he had been assured by reflection and experience of the solidity of their mutual affection. Théophile points out to Horace that he hadn't presented Eugénie to his friends after the first night

of elation, telling them, "This is my mistress, respect her because of me."
Instead, he had hidden his happiness until he could tell them with confi-
dence and loyalty, "Voici ma femme, elle est respectable par elle-même"
(This is my wife. She is respectable in her own right) (*Horace*, 150).

Théophile's involvement in the action of the novel consists of his
standing by to observe Horace committing his various atrocities, later chastising his friend for his childish behavior, and attempting to reform Horace's
character. Their opinions on love and work differ completely. Horace aspires to a great, tragic passion with a woman of noble birth. Théophile, on
the other hand, lives happily with a seamstress and feels relieved to have
been saved from passion, from mistakes and from suffering by an affection
full of sweetness and truth.[49] Moreover, Théophile pursues medical school
with quiet diligence, having been influenced by his father's mortal illness.
He endeavors to attain the degree of sang-froid necessary in order to be
helpful and useful to others, without sacrificing the sentiments of pity and
human sympathy. In contrast, Horace pursues law as a means of attaining
power and personal glory. Profoundly bored with law studies, Horace resolves to fulfill his goals by cultivating his "natural gift" as a literary giant.
When that proves too arduous, Horace, still maintaining the same ultimate
goals of prestige and renown, decides to fulfill his aristocratic potential by
securing a wealthy (and desirable) mistress of noble birth.

As Rudin's boon companion from university days, Lezhnev has access
to his less-than-noble past. Not as indulgent with the behavior of his superfluous friend as Théophile, Lezhnev vehemently opposes Rudin's later
intrusion into his circle of friends. Within close range of Rudin, Lezhnev
launches a verbal assault on his former colleague, intended to expel him
from the Lasunskii nest. He confides to Aleksandra Pavlovna:

> "Not very well informed . . . he is fond of living at the expense of
> others, he is playing a part, and so forth . . . all that is in the common
> order of things. But the ugly thing about it is that he is as cold as ice."
> "He, that fiery spirit, cold!"
> "Yes, cold as ice, and he knows it and pretends to be fiery. The bad
> part of it is," continued Lezhnev, gradually becoming animated, "that
> he is playing a dangerous game, —not dangerous for himself, of course,
> he would not stake a kopek or a hair on a card himself, but others stake
> their souls." (*Rudin*, 98)

Through his own exemplary behavior, Lezhnev indicates Rudin's comparative incapacity to conform successfully to social protocol. After univer-

sity days, Lezhnev outgrows the past, but Rudin, like Beltov, neglects to recognize that the world of idealism is a realm reserved for books. These superfluous heroes, by leading their lives according to abstract theory, fail to establish a productive place for themselves in the prosaic world of tangible realities. When Natalia challenges Rudin to translate his theoretical statements into concrete terms that relate to their feelings toward each other, she completely disorients him. In contrast, Lezhnev makes consistently sober observations. He connects with life and with others around him. Rudin cannot. His ideas, or more accurately, the ideas that Rudin purloins from others, always attract people to him. Rudin assumes the identity of another and ultimately fails to make it his own. The tragedy of Turgenev's tale derives from the harsh finality of the collective judgment that condemns a morally weak man who is not who he appears to be. Indeed, the movement of Turgenev's novel, from Rudin's first public success when he arrives unexpectedly at Lasunskaia's to his public exile into the world beyond the manor house, emphasizes this theme of insurmountable group condemnation. Sensitized by Lezhnev's caution that Rudin is not the man he claims to be, all of the other characters pursue the secret of Rudin's personality so fervently that all other concerns virtually vanish. The novel's title appropriately names both the main character and the primary preoccupation of all the other characters.[50]

Stung by his failure at Avdiukhin Pond, Rudin writes to both Natalia and his rival Volyntsev in a departure from his usual style. Feeling compelled to explain his motives, Rudin admits to them his errors, seeking only a measure of understanding from those he has hurt. Instead, everyone dismisses the letters as the strategy of an insincere man who is trying to salvage his pride. Lezhnev harshly judges Rudin's integrity:

> He is going away. . . . Well! May his path be as smooth as a table-cloth! But here's the curious part of it: he regarded it as *his duty*, to write you this letter, and he presented himself to you, from a sense of duty. . . . It is duty at every step with these gentlemen. (*Rudin*, 161)

Rudin recognizes that he can harbor no hope to redeem himself and must move on. "He knows now, by experience, how society people do not even cast aside, but simply drop a man, who has become unnecessary to them: like a glove, after a ball, like the wrapper from confections, like a ticket in a society lottery, which has not drawn a prize" (*Rudin*, 169).

Similarly, Horace suffers public scorn because of his demonstrated inability to maintain an acquired identity. The schoolgirl's parents discover his motives; the wealthy widow learns of his tendency toward indiscretion; his editor rejects him; he loses at gambling; he is unmasked during a critical social supper; and, although he wins at gambling while staying at Louis de Meran's country house, Horace nearly loses the esteem of his newfound friends when he orders a new wardrobe in inadmissibly poor taste.[51] Horace's character alternates constantly between opposing images throughout the novel. Théophile assesses Horace as a liberal, idealistic, generous young man. Horace's conversation, his treatment of his friends (and especially lovers), and his desire to imitate his noble acquaintances (such as the Marquis de Vèrne) betray a contradictory aspect of the main character. As always, Théophile lends insight into the shortcomings of Horace's character:

> L'esprit d'Horace n'était certes pas stérile; il avait raison de se plaindre du trop d'activité de ses pensées et de la multitude de ses visions.... Il ne savait pas travailler; plus tard, j'appris qu'il ne savait pas souffrir. (*Horace*, 88)

> Horace's spirit was certainly not sterile. He had reason to complain of the excessive activity of his thoughts and of the multitude of his visions.... He didn't know how to work; later, I learned that he didn't know how to suffer.

Like Théophile, Lezhnev does extend a measure of sympathy to Rudin eventually. But even though Lezhnev voluntarily reverses his original verdict of Rudin, the result is of dubious value. Only when Rudin has sought refuge in distant parts does Lezhnev appreciate him. Drinking to his health, he praises those qualities that distinguish Rudin as a unique individual, qualities which he had formerly decried as vices and affectations. No longer an intruder on Lezhnev's turf, Rudin eventually wins Lezhnev's forgiveness. Significantly, his change of heart occurs immediately following Lezhnev's dismissal of all of Rudin's practical efforts during the interval since his break with Natalia: his work on a canal, his work as an agronomist, and his work as a teacher. Lezhnev's change of opinion derives from a surge of sympathy and the security that Rudin can no longer wield influence over anyone with whom Lezhnev is acquainted. Lezhnev reflects magnanimously:

> Why do Rudins make their appearance among us? But let us be grateful to him for what good there is in him. That is easier than it is to be unjust to him. It is not our business to punish him and it is not necessary; he has punished himself far more harshly than he has deserved.

... And God grant, that unhappiness has expelled all evil from him, and left in him only what is fine! (*Rudin*, 194)

Rudin and Horace both ultimately fail because they suffer from a lack of will, an invidious ability to absorb all events into a bewildering system of their own construction. These superfluous heroes fail to reconcile abstract ideals with purposeful activity. Chernyshevskii examines Rudin in a historical perspective, comparing Turgenev's hero to his predecessor, Beltov: "One [Beltov] is contemplative by nature, ineffective, perhaps because the time has not yet come for men to act. The other [Rudin] works, works ceaselessly, but almost fruitlessly."[52] Rudin lacks prospects for meaningful change due to the bewildering nature of the society in which he lives, and compounds his limitations with his purposeless flamboyance.

Rudin and Horace both fail to act at critical moments. Whereas Horace's attack on society implies a desire for action, he appears to be interested primarily in action for its own sake and for his sake. His unwillingness to accept responsibility for his child with Marthe constitutes his first and most significant failure. Horace argues that because he lacks financial security, he is in no position to serve as protector to a woman. He asks Théophile how he can be expected to marry when he hasn't been able to take care of his own life properly. "Cela n'a pas de sens commun! Je suis mineur, et mes parents ne me permettront jamais..." (There's no common sense in that! I'm a minor and my parents will never allow me...) (*Horace*, 124–27).

Ironically, although Horace challenges his parents' authority in every aspect of his life otherwise, he retreats to the security they offer when challenged with adult responsibilities. Moreover, when Horace believes the insurrection is imminent, he seeks refuge from Théophile, asking his advice. The narrator offers Horace an honorable excuse to break his commitment. Horace, unable to face the inevitable ridicule such a change in attitude would elicit from Laravinière, leaves Paris claiming that his mother has fallen ill. Once again he retreats to the parental security so cherished by a child (if only as an excuse). Lacking a firm belief in the worth of the insurrection, Horace submits to his instinct for self-preservation.[53]

More important than the structural parallels between Sand's *Horace* and Turgenev's *Rudin* is the pervasive manner in which the French novelist influenced this and other Russian writers. The great Russian writers who absorbed Sand's novels, whether directly (*Polinka Saks*) or through the mediation of others (*The Reef*), never entirely overcame the influence she exerted on them in their formative periods, as Dostoevskii acknowledged in *Diary of a Writer*. Sand remained part of their literary imagination throughout their lives. In *Rudin*, the disturbing visitor who arrives on the stage of the country house was modeled after the Bakunin of his Berlin years, the years before 1848. Although Rudin is not the extremist whom Herzen described as a Columbus without an America or even a ship, Rudin does share Bakunin's eloquence, his spell over the young, his perpetual borrowing, his meddling with minds and hearts, and his incapacity to commit himself wholeheartedly.[54] Rudin's indebtedness to *Horace* therefore illustrates wonderfully Turgenev's method. Modeled after that of Bakunin, the protagonist's philosophy derives from the Stankevich circle. Natalia descends from Pushkin's Tatiana. Moreover, Turgenev wrote *Rudin* years after having read *Horace* and greatly preferred Sand's pastorals to her romances.[55] So pervasive was Sand's influence that Turgenev unintentionally incorporated many of her ideas. Halpérine-Kaminski wrote of her influence upon the Russian realist that it is not in the details of characters and inventions that one should look for Sand's influence upon Turgenev. It transcends the structural parallels. One finds it in the sensitivity toward the meek and the victims of society, the taste for rustic settings, the minute attention to description, and the vivid believability of the characters.[56]

6

The Woman Question:
What is to be Done?

> To write, or read, or think, or to inquire, would cloud our beauty, and
> exhaust our time, and interrupt the conquests of our prime, whilst
> the dull manage of a servile house is held by some our utmost art and
> use.
>
> —Lady Winchilsea

The Woman Question emerged at a crucial turning point in history. The half-century following the humiliating defeat of the Crimean War proved to be an era of historical self-evaluation. The contributions of female medical personnel during the war vindicated those who had argued that women could employ their capacities in worthwhile social endeavors. Pirogov published a ground-breaking essay in 1856 following his return from the Crimean War, in which he had supervised a detachment of volunteer nurses. He proved highly instrumental in making women's education one of the most widely discussed issues of his day. In "Questions of Life," Pirogov focused on the purpose of life, the nature of education, and its relation to society. He sharply criticized the education which attempted to turn the upper-class woman "into a doll, putting her on display before a class of idlers and having her perform like some marionette."[1] Pirogov stressed instead preparation for a fixed career rather than the development of women's "innate" capacity.

The concept of higher education won acceptance very early in Russia. The shortage of secondary schools hampered its implementation, however. In 1757, I. Shuvalov and Lomonosov drew up the project for the first Russian university (in Moscow). The Senate granted them permission to have the physics lectures delivered in French (due to a lack of Russian lecturers). Moreover, they obtained permission to open these lectures to women. In 1823, ten women were among the thirty students who attended a course on "physico-chemistry and mineralogy"—a small number but a striking percentage. Following the accession of Nicholas I, however, official attitudes to education for women remained in a state of perpetual transition.[2]

The emancipation of the serfs encouraged women to pursue their own emancipation. The increasing pressures for the spread of education resulted in a rapidly growing demand for trained teachers, largely at the primary level. This lent added impetus to the development of secondary education for women. By 1911, primary school teaching had already become a predominantly female field.[3] Decrees of 1858 and 1860 established the principle of secondary education for girls of all classes. In practice, however, only a small number actually benefited. The development of higher education for women entailed creating separate women's courses rather than integrating those already existing. Although many young women began attending university and medical school lectures as observers, a decree of 1863 officially halted admission to women for over a decade. Renewed deferments of educational reform stymied attempts to reopen universities and medical schools to women. Large numbers of them went abroad to pursue their educations. The universities of Zürich and Paris drew the majority of these women. Of the 152 women students at the Sorbonne in 1889, two-thirds were Russian.[4] In Zürich, women could enroll on an equal basis with men. By 1873, out of 300 students, 104 were women.[5]

During the reign of Alexander II, advocates of the Woman Question fell into three schools of thought: the Feminist Response, the Nihilist Response and the Radical Response. Of the three, feminism enunciated first a philosophy of initiating action. In tsarist Russia, educated women of leisure became the first feminists. They enjoyed the time to reflect upon their problems, as well as the means and skills necessary to engage in action.[6]

Anna Filosofova, Nadezhda Stasova and Maria Trubnikova founded the feminist movement in Russia. All daughters of prominent families, these three founders were concerned about the extremely limited role for women in the tsardom.[7] Initially, feminists seemed to have no clearer purpose than to meet in salons to discuss literature, adultery, work and education. The ties among feminists grew closer as networks arose in the 1860s. Most of these noblewomen distinguished themselves as social workers striving to rescue slaves, drunks, destitute women, and prostitutes. In contrast to their nihilist and radical counterparts, feminists searched for solutions within the existing framework of Russian society. Conducting charity work for the poor and providing spiritual and material support to prostitutes and other unfortunate women gave an attractive "feminine" appearance to their notions about women's emancipation. Taking their cue from Clara Balfour and other English feminists, these women developed a faculty of self-help; they were women helping other women.

In the early 1860s Russian society employed the label *progressive* to refer to both feminists and nihilists. It is difficult to distinguish between the two during this era, since they tended to participate in the same activities. It can be said that whereas feminists tended toward philanthropic and apolitical goals, nihilists and radicals founded their platforms on anthropological and political considerations.

More ascetic and dramatic than her feminist compatriots, the *nigilistka* believed that it was better to *be* good than to *do* good. Unlike the philanthropic nature of feminism and the social collective aspects of radicalism, nihilism proved to be profoundly individualistic. This term, initially coined by Turgenev to describe the "nihilist" character Bazarov in *Fathers and Children*, is difficult to define. The term bears a clear association with negation, but nihilists rejected the status quo not merely on this basis, but in an endeavor to restructure their individual lives and society as a whole according to new and more rational objectives. All of the ills of the discredited era would consequently have to be annihilated. Bazarov negated the "higher values" held sacred by society. On that plane he proclaimed to see *nihil*, standing in opposition to idealist dreamers.

Impatient with the slow pace and "superfluity" of feminism, many women nihilists *(nigilistki)* adopted a free-spirited individualistic orientation, at odds with the imperatives of organized activity, whether feminist or radical. The *nigilistka* rejected the subservience imposed by men. Moreover, she wanted her male comrades to value her as a fellow worker. The nihilist woman, therefore, sought to diminish her physical attractiveness by wearing a straight, plain dark woolen dress, by cutting her hair short or hiding it under a cap, and by donning glasses with smoked lenses. In rejecting chivalric attention from men, the *nigilistka* seemed to be saying to them, "Value us . . . as equals with whom you can speak simply and plainly."[8] Her comrades would travel to the other side of the city to help the *nigilistka* with her studies but would refrain from standing when she entered a room. Direct often to the point of rudeness, the *nigilistka* refused to abide by ordinary etiquette and social conventions. During the 1860s, the term *nigilistka* had become a household word in Russia. The term was used to refer to an entire generation of young people, in the way that *beatnik* or *hippie* described the rebellious generation of the 1960s in America. Her portrayal in literature generally tends to be a caricature, as in this 1864 description in the reactionary paper *Vest'* (*The News*):

... nihilist women are usually very plain, exceedingly ungracious; ... they dress with no taste and in impossibly filthy fashion, rarely wash their hands, never clean their nails, often wear glasses, always cut their hair short and sometimes even shave it off ... they despise art, use the familiar form of the pronoun *you* with young men, light their cigarettes not from a candle but from other men who smoke, are uninhibited in their choice of expressions, live either alone or in phalansteries, and talk most of all about the exploitation of labor, the silliness of marriage and the family, and about anatomy.[9]

The *nigilistki* tended either to maintain sexual unions out of wedlock or to remain chaste altogether. Sand's notion of "freedom of the heart" did not appeal to them as much as did her outlandish individuality. To the young nihilists who came to the fore in Russia in the 1860s, George Sand had appeared as the right person (a liberated, self-actualizing person) in the right place (Paris) at the right time (1848). She proved to be the "New Woman" of their dreams.[10]

Although many nihilists of the 1860s were drawn to radical causes, they had an aversion to group affiliation. Radical women shared with feminists a tremendous capacity for self-sacrifice. They pursued their studies with vigor, aware that their education could make them useful to others. Russian women encountered radical circles through friends, families, and lovers in the large cities of Europe, particularly in Paris and Zürich. They abandoned the personal liberation espoused by nihilism and dedicated themselves to complete social reform. Radical women came to the conclusion that only a revolution capable of abolishing all exploitation would enable them to live as equals with men. Their cause was indissolubly linked to that of the working class.[11] Most of the radical publications of the period that women helped to distribute offered no mention of the Woman Question. They called for a federative form of government but failed to discuss marriage, education, or employment for women. They discussed the difficulties of child rearing only to suggest that children be raised collectively. Even social democracy, in which Marxist theory singled out women as particularly oppressed, suppressed emphasis on sexual conflict in the interest of the large revolution.[12]

Russian radicalism differed from Western European radical movements in the prominent role played by its women members and in their ability to work well with their male comrades. Unlike the women of the peasantry and the proletariat, the educated radical women of Russia shared a common language and purpose with their male counterparts. They engaged in a struggle for social change that they believed would be beneficial to all. Moreover, the tradition of self-sacrifice and moral fervor characteristic of their noble mothers enabled the radical daughters to intensify the rigor and asceticism of their political groups. Their daughters, in turn, transmitted radicalism to *their* own daughters. Lenin said that the Bolsheviks could hardly have initiated the revolution without the participation of women. Had two prior generations of female radicals (1860–1917) not fought ardently alongside their male comrades, the Bolsheviks could hardly have won. August Bebel's *Women and Socialism* (1879) urged women to march in harness with male comrades to render revolution a viable possibility. Bebel merely added the term *proletariat* to indicate how and why that revolution must come to pass.

In the spring of 1874, the great crusade "to the people" began on a large scale. The crusade entailed moving out among the peasants in order to share their toil and hardship. The intelligentsia longed to purge itself of its guilt. The women's commitment proved particularly powerful. Many sought replacements for their own abandoned families and beloved serfs among their egalitarian groups and the peasants they helped. Many of these women experienced difficulty returning to "normal life." They sought refuge in their family's home or married. Attempts to institute collective dwellings had failed, and women remained financially dependent on family resources. Perhaps this accounts for the progressive engagement (or desperation) of these radical women. Many began by pursuing education abroad and exposing themselves to the politically active émigré colonies. They then committed themselves wholeheartedly to the cause that ultimately undermined their own. Finally, many engaged in illegal activities for the cause and converted to terrorism. At the risk of both personal freedom and intellectual progress, the radical terrorists came to regard their previous objectives as too limited. Their courage, principles, and propensity toward self-sacrifice won the admiration of their comrades, contemporaries, and the police. Their zeal proved excessive, however, and their commitment to terrorism claimed innocent lives without ameliorating social conditions. They abandoned these terrorist activities subsequent to the assassination of Alexander II.

Women who assumed the radical response to the Woman Question sacrificed feminism for populism and revolution. In the 1870s George Sand remained a venerated ancestor, especially among the populists. According to articles culled from *Fatherland Notes*, the journal which served as the major organ of Russian populism in the 1870s, populists used Sand's utopian socialism: "We have grown up under the influence of men formed in part by her."[13]

As indicated by the numerous borrowings from Sand's novels, nineteenth-century Russian authors shaped opinions and stimulated action with their literary depictions of heroines and their plights. However, although the male literary giants appear to have attempted to reflect the courage and complexity of Russian women by celebrating the virtues of their literary heroines, these artists were, in fact, much more interested in the implications of the hidden "male" theme of their works. Great male authors such as Turgenev, Herzen, Goncharov, Ostrovskii, Tolstoi, and Dostoevskii share the following aspects in their treatment of the Woman Question: 1) Their superfluous (or underground) hero manages to attract a spirited young woman. 2) Because females are allegedly more emotional and males more oriented toward ideas, the hero has these ideas put to the test when he falls in love and fails to sustain them and integrate them into a future family life. 3) These superfluous men ultimately flee the scene, unable to reciprocate in love. They commonly engage in attempts to embellish their own qualities and achievements through airs of superiority or by belittling themselves before the stronger woman counterpart. 4) Finally, the heroine, left alone, proves to be all the wiser and superior, whole and perfect in herself. Although it appears as though these novelists have treated the heroine as if she were the equal of her male counterpart in literary development, a careful study of these works reveals that the author considerably short-changes her in the number of passages which demonstrate her in action. Often, the heroine serves merely as an episode in the man's life. His unhappy love affair demonstrates to the reader how the hero came to be even more disillusioned. The story of how the woman came to be the way she is proves to be much less dramatic. She simply lived at home and received an education suitable to promote her prospects for marriage.[14] With the possible exceptions of the characters of Dostoevskii, Ostrovskii and Goncharov, Russian literary heroines generally derived from the nobility, whereas Western European writers tended to depict middle-class women.

Beginning in the 1860s, the Russian novel became a weapon for social reform in the hands of progressive members of the intelligentsia. Russian literature greatly strengthened the women's movement. During the 1860s, virtually no authors portrayed heroines who secured a life of fulfillment in marriage and motherhood, a leading motif in Tolstoi's works. Written for women consumers of fiction and significantly influenced by George

Sandism, Russian novels examined the difficulties and joys of men and women in love and marriage.[15] Besides establishing a model of personal liberation for young Russian women, the novel redefined male roles. They represented equality, self-respect and self-denial as norms for male behavior. They denigrated jealousy as a proprietary emotion that had no place in the new morality. Authors established new forms of association between men and women in an endeavor to create a new society.

Pushkin served as a pioneer in Russian feminism through his works. In *Roslavlev* (1836) he wrote: "There is no doubt that Russian women are more cultivated, read more and think more than men, who occupy themselves with God knows what."[16] In *Evgenii Onegin* (1833), Pushkin depicted a strong, romantic, intelligent heroine; she served as the prototype for women characters in the idealistic novels of Goncharov, Turgenev, Nekrasov, Tolstoi, Chekhov and others. The product of a rural upbringing and petty nobility mentality, Tatiana grows up nurtured by dreams and romance. The ideal heroine of the nineteenth-century literary giants tended to be a girl like Tatiana, a girl on the eve of womanhood (generally around seventeen years of age). As she falls in love, the heroine's inner beauty blossoms into glorious physical attractiveness.

This male fascination with the beautiful young heroine and his desire to win her over is strikingly reflected in the myth of virginity. Simone de Beauvoir writes in *The Second Sex* (1949):

> Now feared by the male, now desired or even demanded, the virgin would seem to represent the most consummate form of the feminine mystery; she is therefore its most disturbing and at the same time its most fascinating aspect.[17]

Initially rejected by her suitor, Tatiana receives a blow which shatters her fragile dream of a perfect love. Choosing the traditional alternative, Tatiana enters a loveless marriage but remains true to her husband even when confronted by Onegin's protestations of love years later. Tatiana divines Evgenii's true character only through a perusal of his library. Noting which passages Evgenii has marked, Tatiana "step by step . . . at last begins to see . . more clearly than in face and feature: A strangely bleak and reckless creature."[18] The naïve girl becomes a woman for whom "happiness had been so close, but whose lot had been cast for good."[19] Significantly, Tatiana's disenchantment enables her to embark upon an important process of self-evaluation. Pushkin's heroine exemplifies the potential forces of the Russian woman. She becomes the ideal foil to her counterpart, the superfluous man.

Next to Chernyshevskii, Dobroliubov exerted the most influence in literary and social criticism during the 1860s. His reviews were pretexts for social commentary, rather than aesthetic or structural analysis. His work continued to mark an impression on Russian literary criticism for years to come. Dobroliubov paid particular attention to the manner in which artists portrayed Russian women in literature. His reviews, which helped to shape the opinions of a large part of the reading public, trace every species of depravity among the different social classes to the distortions of the patriarchal family unit.

As reflected by the strong woman archetype in nineteenth-century Russian literature, the impact of love lifts these women high above vicious society life and endows them with a strong sense of self-assurance. They traditionally transcend the bounds of narrow feminism and assert themselves both as useful members of the new society and as man's better half. These Russian novelists demonstrate extremely good intentions in their praise of women's strengths; however, they elevate women to a "terrible perfection,"[20] a dubious honor indeed.

In *What is to be Done?* for example, Vera Pavlovna manages a sewing cooperative, studies to become a doctor, spends evenings at the theater and the opera, indulges her sweet tooth over leisurely cups of tea and pastries, enjoys long, hot baths, and entertains friends and associates. All the while, the dishes, beds, laundry and child care appear to take care of themselves. Domestic drudgery never hinders this elevation of women to a realm of beauty, intellect and moral superiority. Socialist society expected women to assume the responsibilities not only of a full-time job comparable to that of her male counterpart (albeit a job which men in the Soviet Union would generally not condescend to take), but of maintaining complete care of her household and children, as well. With the advent of socialism, the bourgeois Vera Pavlovnas and their maids would become a thing of the past. The woman of the twentieth century in Russia would have to prove perfect indeed in order to cope with the extreme burden of "social equality."[21]

Christine Delphy argues convincingly in *Close to Home: A Materialist Analysis of Women's Oppression* that the situation of the married woman who has a job clearly reveals the legal appropriation of her labor power. Economic exchange can no longer account for the servitude of the housewife. Because she earns her "keep" by working outside the house, her domestic "duties" can no longer justify the fact that she is not remunerated for housework. Delphy concludes that women are clearly performing domestic work for nothing.[22] The Communist party asserted that "an equal distribution of difficulties and fatigue in a household is a *limited concept* of equality."[23]

Like his predecessor Pushkin, Turgenev proclaimed the superiority of the strong-minded woman over the weak, superfluous man and influenced the psychology of the Russian revolutionary youth more than any of his contemporaries. Goncharov, too, depicted strong, pioneering Russian women. These literary heroines revealed to the reading public the extent to which an educated Russian woman could develop into an independent, socially conscious and realistic person during the 1860s. The literary critic G. Korik contended that the women characters of Goncharov and Turgenev enabled the reader to follow the step-by-step development of Russian ideals among the intelligentsia. Another critic, P. Pluksh, thought Goncharov's Olga and Chernyshevskii's Vera most clearly reflected the positive impact of women's emancipation.

The two most renowned Russian novelists of this period treated the Woman Question in a more traditional manner, however. Tolstoi believed motherhood to be a woman's exalted calling and considered women's emancipation to be a confused conception of life that caused her to go astray. To become a mother she needed no courses. She had only to read the Bible with her eyes, ears, and especially with her heart, and the Bible did not mention anything about independent activities for women outside her family circle.[24] A bourgeois writer cited by Bebel sums up this ideal:

> Man longs not only for one whose heart beats for him alone, but whose hand laves his brow, who radiates peace, order, tranquility, and who exercises a quiet control over him and over the things he finds when he gets home each day; he wants someone to exhale over everything the indefinable perfume of woman, the vivifying warmth of life at home.[25]

Tolstoi's Dolly, Kitty, Natasha, Sonia and Pasha correspond to his conception of the ideal woman, obedient to God and to her husband, and the devoted mother of a large brood of children. As Simone de Beauvoir explains in *The Second Sex*, the marriage rites deprive the "good wife" of her magic weapons of illusiveness and virginity and subordinate her both economically and socially to her husband. Man takes pride in his "better half" as he does in his home and his wealth. Through his most precious treasure, his "good wife," man displays his power before the world.[26]

Tolstoi treated with severity the women characters who failed to conform to these criteria. Strongly disapproving of Sand's doctrine of freedom of the heart, Tolstoi depicted its ramifications in *Anna Karenina*. He demonstrated that a woman who longed for love outside of marriage would gain nothing from the experience except guilt and disillusionment. Unable to cope with the psychological and sociological consequences of adulterous love, Tolstoi's Anna, like Ostrovskii's Katerina, commits suicide. Though the novel bears Anna's name, the "good wife" Dolly and the "virgin" and subsequent "good wife" Kitty serve as the positive heroines.

In contrast to Tolstoi's women characters, Dostoevskii's women appear to become true heroines only after their fall from virtue. Their activity manifests itself generally in a desire for revenge, as with Nastasia Filippovna in *The Idiot* and Katerina Ivanovna in *The Brothers Karamazov*. Dostoevskii's heroines find in love the pure and noble strength with which to transcend their social and spiritual limitations. According to the eminent politician T. G. Masaryk, Dostoevskii tends to feature women characters who are essentially weak and passive due to their social origin. Their parents' home had denied them an education and had subjected them to patriarchal absolutism. Choosing prostitution as an economic and social escape proves to be their only means of securing independence. Dostoevskii's works reflect the destitution of prostitution and the poor wretches who spend their lives in its inescapable abyss.[27]

Significantly, Dostoevskii avoids stereotypes about male and female psychology. Most of his women characters prove to be just as tormented, sadistic, cruel, loving, devoted, or idealistic as their male counterparts. The circumstances they encounter, as opposed to a priori absolutes, determine their behavior.

Ironically, the creator of this pathological, degenerate world considered Pushkin's pure Tatiana the ideal of Russian womanhood.[28] Dostoevskii believed that the Woman Question could find a solution in terms of Christian love of mankind. In his own work, however, Dostoevskii never portrayed a happy marriage or a strong heroine comparable to Tatiana. He preferred to focus his work on criminal psychology, mental illness, poverty, and emotional crises.

Several Russian male authors of the nineteenth century described credibly the physical and emotional phenomena particular to women. Tolstoi and Chekhov conveyed with great skill the feelings associated with such intimate female states as pregnancy and miscarriage.[29] The fact remains, however, that many of these male proponents of the Woman Question,

particularly Turgenev and Chekhov, tended to portray the truly emancipated Russian woman as a dirty, loud-mouthed, chain-smoking bluestocking and, moreover, as a character quite unnecessary to the plot.[30]

Ironically, we owe our knowledge of the Russian woman's struggle for
emancipation to the works of male authors. Women, endowed with the
"terrible perfection" previously discussed, were encouraged to be modest
consumers rather than brazen, audacious producers of literature. The women
novelists who did attempt to address the Woman Question were considered to be much less capable of discussing the issue than were their well-
educated, artistically sophisticated male counterparts. Shelnugov and other
literary critics contended that women writers had not made a thorough
study of the women's cause and lacked the capacity to represent their
evolution in a true perspective.[31]

Christine Delphy argues convincingly that although masculine parti-
sans of women's liberation hold honorable objectives, these "friends" actually place the women's cause in jeopardy. Delphy contends that these
friends have the following in common:

1. They want to substitute themselves for women;
2. They actually speak instead of women;
3. They approve of women's liberation, and even of the participation of
women in this project, so long as liberation and women follow and certainly
do not precede them.
4. They want to impose on women their conception of women's liberation, which includes the participation of men, and they want to impose
their participation so as to control the movement and its direction: the
direction of women's liberation.[32]

The enemies of women's liberation attack from the front and candidly
acknowledge their objective: to maintain their superior position in the
social hierarchy and by analogy to keep women in their place. The "friends"
of women's liberation, however, maintain their place in a more subtle way.
In Vera Pavlovna's words, they "reign under a mask of servility"[33] and
infiltrate the ranks of women's resistance. Delphy reasons that, whereas
the enemies remain outside the feminist ranks, which matters little to
them since they still have the rest of society, the friends "envisage nothing
less than maintaining their power even within the small bastion of resistance to that power."[34]

Although most women who dared to compete with male novelists of nineteenth-century Russia attempted to emulate George Sand in their fictional accounts of conjugal conflict, none created a comparable impact with their writings. The George Sands and George Eliots of Russia were men.

Their families and acquaintances strongly dissuaded women from pursuing literary endeavors. General Korvin-Krikovskii berated his daughter Anna for having sold a short story for publication, charging, "First you sell your story, next you'll sell yourself."[35] Critics generally considered women writers to be bluestockings and claimed that they no longer belonged to the female sex.[36] Uneducated provincials and other traditionalists regarded these women as enemies, fearing that they satirized fellow citizens in their works.

Maria Vernadskaia composed the first major writing by a woman that directly addressed the Woman Question. In an economic treatise, Vernadskaia urged women to become financially independent. "Mesdames," she exhorted her readers, "cease to be children. Try to stand on your own two feet."[37]

Nadezhda D. Khovshchinskaia, who published under the pseudonym V. Krestovskii, and Nadezhda Suslova both portrayed the *nigilistka* as a strong and determined woman living according to her principles. These women writers attempted to promote social progress, depicting the nihilist woman as a "new person" whose independence indicated the possibility of a more just and national society. Their impact remained limited, however, due to public opinion regarding women writers.

Because of the public scorn confronting women writers, they repeatedly denied having any literary ambitions (even though they did so through the printed word) and said they wrote only at the urging of others.

Women writers in nineteenth-century Russia sought forms of expression which were not so completely dominated by men: poetry and autobiography. Barbara Heldt writes in *Terrible Perfection* that many of these works have not been discussed since their year of publication. Moreover, the few that have received some degree of renown have often gained their notoriety because of their historical contents. Women protagonists in these works occupy themselves by leading independent lives as people, often free from married life and occasionally ostracized from society life. Women writers did not consider themselves to be the victimized slaves of passion often depicted by male authors. In fact, the writing of genders differs greatly in that, while men feel compelled to write about Woman, women rarely write about men as sexual beings and never idealize them as Man.[38]

Women writers commonly introduce another factor rarely featured in the Russian novel, the theme of the generally self-inflicted isolation of the independent woman. In fact, we might postulate isolation from mainstream notions of womanhood as a prerequisite for most Russian female autobiographies. Perhaps the most unconventional autobiographer, Nadezhda Durova (1783–1866), bobbed her hair, assumed male garb (much like George Sand) and endured the rigors of military life during the Napoleonic wars. The artificiality of her mother's life repulsed Durova. Boyish in looks and temperament from birth, Durova had been thrown from a moving carriage during infancy by her mother and later rescued by hussars who returned her to her father. The writer attributes this incident to her passion for independence and for military life.[39] Her own feminine education in childhood appears to have convinced the writer (who used to refer to herself as "he") that females should refuse the decorative domesticity that society would have them embrace.

Norine Voss writes in "Saying the Unsayable: An Introduction to Women's Autobiography" that the rich canon of autobiography constitutes the literary genre in which women have excelled the most for the least amount of recognition for their achievements. Starting with an understandable interest in the better-known men's autobiographies, critics have focused attention on the works of a handful of great white males, among them Augustine, Rousseau, Franklin, Goethe, Mill and Adams. These works have defined the genre and set the aesthetic standards. Deviating from the conventional masculine norm, women's autobiographies have been barred from the patriarchal canon.[40]

Joanna Russ in her monograph "How to Suppress Women's Writing" has identified and studied the various phallocentric strategies critics have used to discourage women's writing. They have denied authorship, applying double standards for authors and "authoresses." Critics have deliberately assigned women writers to the wrong category, perpetuated the myth of the isolated achievement and blatantly excluded women from the literary canon. George Sand herself fell prey to these tactics. Critics have attacked Sand often for displaying typical faults of gynographs: writing excessively, rapidly and with little regard to style. Baudelaire argued that women who write generally know nothing of art or logic, and cited George Sand as an example of a great and illustrious (woman) writer who failed to escape these tendencies, in spite of her superiority. She tossed her masterpieces in the mail, according to Baudelaire, as one would do with letters.[41]

Isabelle Naginski points out in *George Sand: Writing for her Life* (1991),

that Sand placed herself in the literary canon, while simultaneously maintaining her distance from it. She believed that to be heard, a woman writer
must exempt herself from the "female ghetto of the imagination"[42] to
which her male colleagues would relegate her. By employing male narra-
tors in many of her novels, Sand adopts an androgynous style that engages
her male readers with a conspiratorial wink, only to expose society's contempt for that which is most sacred about women and to attempt in her own
way to lift women out of their abjection. Naginski argues that while Sand
did adopt a male pseudonym, she defamiliarized the name by spelling it
differently from the traditional French *Georges*. Sand neither limited herself to lighter women's writing (the feminine ghetto), nor did she buy into
phallocentrism by abandoning her gender. George Sand was a remarkable
artist in her capacity to maintain a double-gendered, androgynous vision.
In rejecting the confines of either model of writing, Sand "became a creature of a strange sex, neither male nor female. A George without an 's.'"[43]
Mary Ellmann argues wittily in *Thinking About Women* that there must always be two literatures, like two public toilets: one for men and one for
women.[44] George Sand dared to be an exception to the rule.

Several Russian male novelists depicted their female protagonists writing or reading self-reflective journal entries. Herzen indicates Liubonka's
quiet, contemplative nature and the manner in which her parents' cruelty
compels her to turn inward and write about her reflections. Chernyshevskii's
heroine comes to the painful realization that she feels gratitude rather than
love for Lopukhov as she is forced to read the pages of her mental diary in
the third dream. Russian women as "others" existed apart from society, but
they had to learn to act upon society. Turgenev's heroines in *On the Eve* and
Rudin employ the freedom of their circumstances to cultivate their moral
sensibility. Both Elena and Natalia enjoy a great deal of time free from
parental supervision. They watch and reflect, tending to deal passively
with their surroundings, which offer few opportunities for significant action. When they do act (and both make important practical decisions), they
do so with the force of a carefully nurtured, contemplative personality.[45]

Talented Russian women writers sought a voice in the literary genre of
poetry, as well. Anna Bunina (1774–1829) was the first woman poet to
support herself by her writing. Poor and self educated, Bunina composed her
first poems at thirteen. Proving that a literary woman could preserve herself
publicly only through modesty, Bunina entitled her first book of poetry *The
Inexperienced Muse*. She gratefully accepted the patronage of her male peers.
Although Bunina did not attempt to imitate the works of her male counter-

parts, she freely assimilated elements of works which appealed to her and suited her own personal seriousness and wit.[46]

Perhaps the most extensive treatment of the female condition appears in the novel *A Double Life*, by nineteenth-century Russia's most gifted female poet, Karolina Pavlova (1807–1903). Barbara Heldt's study of Pavlova led her to discover the Russian writer's extraordinary biography (replete with slanders by most male contemporaries), private letters (full of despair, a bold show of valor and the perseverance that enabled her to write excellent poetry), and this novel that Heldt translated into English.[47] Pavlova's novel employs images of the self that, at first reading, tend to disguise the fact that a woman is present at all. It recounts the story of Cecily, a future disillusioned wife, prior to her marriage. The woman as "other" again dares to assert herself only in denying her presence. Her novel, a mixture of prose and poetry, points specifically, and with a peculiarly female irony, to the shallowness of men.[48]

Have the attempts to resolve the Woman Question in Russia been successful? The question in the title of Chernyshevskii's revolutionary novel *What is to be Done?* was answered by the Bolshevik insurrection. The Soviet government constantly articulated that women should be equal to men. But are today's Russian woman better off than their predecessors? In spite of endless assertions of a Soviet policy of equality, Russian women had to contend with male-dominated spheres that remained beyond their grasp. Coveted positions in the Communist party, the military, the KGB, the foreign service, the various professions, and the Writer's Union, remained essentially male hierarchies.[49] We have yet to see if the new Commonwealth of Independent States will better the status of women in Russia and the republics, after problems of starvation, alcoholism, poverty, and political unrest are tended to.

What Chernyshevskii overlooked with regard to women is that the "right" to work has saddled the contemporary Russian woman with double the responsibility of her predecessor. Both government policy and private attitudes place responsibility for the home and children with women, so she is a full-time worker, as well as a full-time housekeeper. Moreover, social standards still require her to keep herself physically appealing. Olga Michailova, secretary of the Central Committee of the Communist Youth Organization, articulated in a 1944 interview an attitude all too prevalent today:

> Soviet women should try to make themselves as attractive as nature and good taste permit. Girls are to be told to behave properly and walk

like girls, and for this reason they will probably wear very narrow skirts which will compel a graceful carriage.[50]

In order to judge better the efficacy of resolutions to the Woman Question, scholars must—like Barbara Heldt and Beatrice Stillman, who translated Sofia Kovalevskaia's *Memoirs* (1978)—rediscover the female voices that have fallen into undeserved obscurity. Bunina, Dashkova, Zhadovskaia, Rostopchina, Kokhanovskaia, Tur, Gan and Khvoshchinskaia have been slighted within their own country and ignored outside of Russia because they have never been translated.[51] Although Russian archives maintain a rich collection of women writings that are either unpublished or were published obscurely, Soviet bibliographies do not specify the gender of authors. Consequently, scholars can discover materials often only in the course of pursuing other critical reading.[52] These works warrant rescue from oblivion, translation, and critical study because of their enormous contribution to a fuller understanding of the forgotten female voice—a voice that male "friends" of the women's liberation assumed in her stead. Moreover, we would learn more clearly how the daughters of mothers who had devoured Sand's novels sought to address the issue of what was to be done in the aftermath of George Sandism.

Notes

Chapter 1. Introduction

1. Henry James, *French Poets and Novelists* (London, 1878), 162.

2. Wolfgang Iser, *The Act of Reading: A Theory of Aesthetic Response* (Baltimore and London: Johns Hopkins University Press, 1978), 27.

3. A term coined in a text by Barbara Heldt, *Terrible Perfection: Women and Russian Literature* (Bloomington and Indianapolis: Indiana University Press, 1987).

4. Steven G. Kellman, *Loving Reading: Erotics of the Text* (New York: Archon Books, 1985), 4.

5. D. S. Mirsky, *History of Russian Literature* (New York: Random House/Vintage Books, 1958), 178.

6. Ibid.

7. Wladimir Weidlé, *Russia: Absent and Present*, trans. A. Gordon Smith (New York: John Day, 1952), 158.

8. Milan Kundera, *Immortality* (New York: HarperCollins, 1992), 198.

9. Weidlé, *Russia*, 161.

10. Ibid., 165.

Chapter 2. Women and Fiction: Who is to Blame?

1. Richard Stites, *The Women's Liberation Movement in Russia: Feminism, Nihilism and Bolshevism 1860–1930* (Princeton: Princeton University Press, 1978), 6–7.

2. Barbara Alpern Engel, *Mothers and Daughters: Women of the Intelligentsia in Nineteenth-Century Russia* (Cambridge: Cambridge University Press, 1983), 8.

3. Ibid.

4. Ibid., 10.

5. Stites, *Women's Liberation Movements*, 7.

7. Leo Tolstoy, *Anna Karenina*, trans. Joel Carmichael (New York: Bantam Books, 1960), 648.

8. Engel, *Mothers and Daughters*, 10.

9. Stites, *Women's Liberation Movements*, 10.

10. Aurore Dupin Dudevant employed the pen name George Sand after having been scolded by her mother-in-law for pursuing a writing career. She cautioned Aurore not to soil the family name. George Sand coauthored her first book, *Rose et Blanche*, with Jules Sandeau. She used the pen name Georges Sand initially with the publication of her first novel, *Indiana* (1832). By the time she published *Lélia* (1833), the author had abandoned the traditional French spelling by dropping the *s* from *Georges*. She defamiliarized (and one might argue, castrated) the name, rendering it neither feminine nor fully masculine, but different, foreign, "Other."

11. Carole Karp, "George Sand and the Russians," *George Sand Papers Conference Proceedings, 1978* (New York: AMS Press, 1978), 151 .

12. Letter to Natalya Nikolaevna Pushkina, 29 September 1835. Quoted in B. V. Thomashevsky, *Pushkin u Frantsiya* (Pushkin and France) (Leningrad: Sov. Pisatel, 1960), 168.

13. Felizia Seyd, *Romantic Rebel: The Life and Times of George Sand* (New York: Viking Press, 1940), 270.

14. Fyodor Dostoevsky, *Diary of a Writer*, trans. Boris Brasol (New York: Octagon Books, 1973), 368.

15. Ibid., 340.

16. Lesley Singer Hermann, "George Sand and the Nineteenth-Century Russian Novel: The Quest for a Heroine," diss., Columbia University, 1979, 26.

17. Wanda Bannour, "L'Influence de George Sand en Russie," in *George Sand: Collected Essays,* ed. Janis Glasgow (Troy, N.Y.: Whitston, 1985), 102.

18. D. V. Grigorovich, "Literaturnya Vospominaniia" (Literary memoirs), in *Polnoe Sobranie Sochinenii* (Complete edition), 12:270.

19. D. S. Mirsky, *History of Russian Literature* (New York: Random House/Vintage Books, 1958), 161.

20. Dostoevsky, *Diary*, 343

21. I. Aizenshtock, "Frantuzskie pisateli v otsenkakh-tsarskoi tsenzury" (Tsarist censorship edition of French writers), in *Literaturnoe Nasledstvo* 33–34 (1939): 807–16.

22. Hermann, "George Sand," 17.

23. Karp, "George Sand and the Russians," 152.

24. Renato Poggioli, *The Phoenix and the Spider* (Cambridge: Harvard University Press, 1957), 6.

25. Ibid.

26. Carole Karp, "George Sand and Turgenev: A Literary Relationship," *Studies in the Literary Imagination* 12, no. 2 (1979): 73–81.

27. Vladimir Karénine, *George Sand, sa vie et ses oeuvres* (George Sand: Her life and works), 4 vols. (Paris,1899–1926), 2:115.

28. Dostoevsky, *Diary*, 342.

29. Karp, "George Sand's Reception in Russia, 1832–1881," diss., University of Michigan, 1976, 157. The *Entsiklopedicheski Slovar* (Dictionary encyclopedia) features a separate entry entitled "The Woman Question," which informs us that this heated controversy "was raised under the direct influence of George Sand."

30. Stites, *Women's Liberation Movement*, 38.

31. Ibid., 39.

32. Ibid.

33. Gail Warshofsky Lapidus, *Women in Soviet Society: Equality, Development and*

Social Change (Berkeley, Los Angeles, and London: University of California Press, 1979), 29. For a more detailed treatment, see R. Stites, "M. L. Mikhailov and the Emergence of the Woman Question," *Canadian Slavic Studies* (Summer 1969), 178–99.

34. Stites, *Women's Liberation Movement,* 40.

35. Hermann, "George Sand," 25.

36. George Sand, *Indiana,* ed. Béatrice Didier (Paris: Folio, 1984), 50.

37. Ibid.

38. Stites, *Women's Liberation Movement,* 24.

39. Hermann, "George Sand," 30.

40. Ibid, 32–33.

Chapter 3. Jacques, the Enlightened Husband: Narrative Desire

1. Peter Brooks, *Reading for the Plot: Design and Intention in Narrative* (New York: Vintage Books, 1985), 37.

2. Ibid.

3. Ibid.

4. Wolfgang Iser, *The Act of Reading: A Theory of Aesthetic Response* (Baltimore and London: Johns Hopkins University Press, 1978), 35.

5. Janis Glasgow, "The Use of Doubles in George Sand's *Jacques,*" in *George Sand Papers: Conference Proceedings*, ed. Natalie Datlof et al. (New York, 1982), 35.

6. Arnold Weinstein, *The Fiction of Relationship* (Princeton: Princeton University Press, 1988), 124.

7. Iser, *Act of Reading,* 193.

8. Ibid., 54.

9. Carole Karp, "George Sand and the Russians," in *George Sand Papers: Conference Proceedings, 1978* (New York: AMS Press, l978), 184.

10. Cited in ibid., 180–81.

11. Introduction to Lesley Singer Hermann, "George Sand and the Nineteenth-Century Russian Novel: The Quest for a Heroine," diss., Columbia University, 1979.

12. Cited in S. A. Vengerov, "Druzhinin," in vol. 5 of *Kritikobiograficheskii slovar russkikh pisatelei i uchenykh* (Critical biographical dictionary of Russian writers and scientists) (1897), 393.

13. Cited in Hermann, "George Sand," 43.

14. Ibid., 45.

15. Ibid., 46.

16. Ibid.

17. Ibid., 47.

18. E. Vodovozova, *Na zare zhizni* (At the dawn of life) (Moscow, 1964), 477.

19. Hermann, "George Sand," 52.

20. Victor Ripp, *Turgenev's Russia: From "Notes of a Hunter" to "Fathers and Sons"* (Ithaca and London: Cornell University Press, 1980),

21. Hermann, "George Sand," 39.

22. V. S. Pritchett, *The Gentle Barbarian. The Life and Work of Turgenev* (New York: Random House, 1977), 45–46.

23. Hermann, "George Sand," 181.

24. Ibid., 52.

25. Carole Karp, "George Sand and Turgenev: A Literary Relationship," *Studies in the Literary Imagination* 12, no. 2 (1979): 77.

26. E. Halpérine-Kaminski, *Ivan Tourguénev: Lettres à Mme Viardot* (Paris, 1907), 40.

27. Cited in Karp, "George Sand and Turgenev," 77.

28. Richard Kappler, "Turgenev and George Sand." *Washington State University Research Studies* 34, no. 1 (March 1966): 42.

29. Karp, "George Sand and Turgenev," 79.

30. Ibid., 81.

31. Cited in ibid., 80–81.

32. Kappler, "Turgenev and George Sand," 43

33. Nikolai Chernyshevsky, *What is to be Done?* trans. N. Dole and S. S. Skidelsky (Ann Arbor: Ardis, 1986). See the introduction by Kathryn Fever, xii.

34. Victor Ripp, *Turgenev's Russia,* 38.

35. Lesley Singer Hermann, "George Sand," 4.

36. William F. Woehrlin, *Chernyshevskii: The Man and the Journalist* (Cambridge: Harvard University Press, 1971), 79.

37. N. G. O. Pereira, *The Thought and Teachings of N. G. Černyševskii* (The Hague and Paris: Mouton, 1975), 79.

38. Hermann, "George Sand," 49.

39. Fever, introduction to *What is to be Done?* by Chernyshevsky, xx–xxi.

40. Ibid., xx.

41. Renée Winegarten, *The Double Life of George Sand: Woman and Writer* (New York: Basic Books, 1978), 147.

42. Janis Glasgow, "The Use of Doubles in George Sand's *Jacques,*" in *George Sand Papers: Conference Proceedings,* ed. Natalie Datlof et al. (New York, 1982), 32–33.

43. Ibid., 33.

44. Hermann, "George Sand," 124.

45. Fever, introduction to *What is to be Done?* by Chernyshevsky, xv.

46. Ibid., xxii.

47. Richard Stites, *The Women's Liberation Movement in Russia: Feminism, Nihilism and Bolshevism 1860–1930* (Princeton: Princeton University Press, 1978), 89.

48. Barbara Alpern Engel, *Mothers and Daughters: Women of the Intelligentsia in Nineteenth-Century Russia* (Cambridge: Cambridge University Press, 1963), 74.

49. E. Lampert, *Sons Against Fathers: Studies in Russian Radicalism and Revolution* (Oxford: Clarendon Press, 1965), 172.

Chapter 4. Edmée, the New Woman: Desire for Androgyny

1. Felizia Seyd, *Romantic Rebel: The Life and Times of George Sand* (New York: Viking Press, 1940), 203.

2. Lesley Singer Hermann, "'Woman as Hero' in Turgenev, Goncharov and George Sand's *Mauprat,*" *Ulbandus Review* 2, no. 1 (Fall 1979): 128–38.

3. Dennis O'Brien, "George Sand and Feminism, " in *The George Sand Papers: Conference Proceedings*, ed. Natalie Datlof et al. (New York, 1982), 82.

4. Carolyn G. Heilbrun, *Toward a Recognition of Androgyny* (New York: Alfred A. Knopf, 1973), 51.

5. Ibid., 91.

6. Ibid., ix–x.

7. Ibid., 91–92.

8. Ibid., 22.

9. Lesley Singer Hermann, "George Sand and the Nineteenth-Century Russian Novel: The Quest for a Heroine," diss., Columbia University, 1979), 140.

10. Gail Warshofsky Lapidus, *Women in Soviet Society: Equality, Development and Social Change* (Berkeley, Los Angeles, and London: University of California Press, 1979), 29. For a more detailed treatment, see R. Stites, "M. L. Mikhailov and the Emergence of the Woman Question," *Canadian Slavic Studies* 3 (Summer 1969): 178–99.

11. Peter Brooks, *Reading for the Plot: Design and Intention in Narrative* (New York: Vintage Books, 1985), 38.

12. Ibid., 52.

13. Emily Toth, "The Independent Woman and 'Free' Love," *Massachusetts Review* 16 (1975): 653.

14. Naomi Schor, "Female Fetishism: The Case of George Sand," in *The Female Body in Western Culture: Contemporary Perspectives*, ed. Susan Rubin Suleiman (Cambridge and London: Harvard University Press, 1986), 369.

15. Kathryn J. Crecelius, *Family Romances: George Sand's Early Novels* (Bloomington and Indianapolis: Indiana University Press, 1987), 156.

16. Ibid., 154.

17. Ibid., 157.

18. Toth, "Independent Woman," 652–53.

19. Crecelius, *Family Romances*, 151.

20. Ibid.

21. Nancy Rogers, "George Sand: Social Protest in Her Early Works," in *The George Sand Papers: Conference Proceedings*, ed. Natalie Datlof et al. (New York, 1982), 72–73.

22. Alexandra Lyngstad and Sverre Lyngstad, *Ivan Goncharov* (New York: Twayne, 1971), 93.

23. Ibid., 94

24. Ibid., 84.

25. Lesley Singer Hermann, "'Woman as Hero' in Turgenev, Goncharov and George Sand's *Mauprat*," *Ulbandus Review* 2, no. 1 (Fall 1979): 132.

26. Ibid., 135.

27. Ibid., 132.

28. Cited in Hermann, "Woman as Hero," 128.

29. Lesley Singer Hermann, "George Sand and the Nineteenth-Century Russian Novel: The Quest for a Heroine," diss., Columbia University, 1979), 146.

30. V. S. Pritchett, *The Gentle Barbarian: The Life and Work of Turgenev* (New York: Random House, 1977), 132.

31. Ibid., 133.

32. Ibid., 132–33.

33. Ibid., 133.

34. Hermann, "Woman as Hero," 132

35. April Fitzlyon, "I. S. Turgenev and the 'Woman Question'," *New Zealand Slavonic Journal*, 1983, 167.

36. Ibid.

37. Ibid.

38. Cited in ibid., 168.

39. Ibid.

40. Ibid., 170.

41. Victor Ripp, *Turgenev's Russia: From "Notes of a Hunter" to "Fathers and Sons"* (Ithaca and London: Cornell University Press, 1980), 173.

42. Lesley Singer Hermann, "George Sand," 146.

43. Carolyn G. Heilbrun, *Toward a Recognition of Androgyny*, 91.

44. Hermann, "George Sand," 146.

45. Ripp, *Turgenev's Russia*, 169–70.

46. Ibid., 172.

47. Ibid., 173.

48. Ibid., 180.

49. Hermann, "George Sand," 149.

50. Carole Karp, "George Sand and the Russians," in *George Sand Papers: Conference Proceedings, 1978* (New York: AMS, 1978), 152.

51. F. M. Dostoevsky, *The Diary of a Writer* (Salt Lake City: Peregrine Smith, 1985), 348.

52. Ibid.

53. Joseph Barry, trans. and ed. *George Sand: In Her Own Words* (Garden City, N.Y.: Anchor Books, 1979), 8.

54. Hermann, "Woman as Hero," 129.

55. Karp, "George Sand's Reception in Russia, 1832–1881," diss., University of Michigan, 1976, 145.

56. Cited in ibid., 167.

57. See Isabelle Naginski, "The Serenity of Influence: The Literary Relationship of George Sand and Dostoevsky," in *George Sand: Collected Essays,* ed. Janis Glasgow (Troy, New York: Whitston, 1985).

58. Cited in Karp, "George Sand's Reception," 144–45.

59. Cited in Hermann, "George Sand" 55.

60. Naginski, "Serenity of Influence," 110.

61. A. L. Bem, *O Dostoevskom* (About Dostoevsky) (Prague, 1933), 2:7–24. Dostoevsky refers specifically in his own writings to the following George Sand works. Critics presume that he read several other works as well.

La Marquise (1832)	*L'Uscoque* (1839)	*Les Dames Vertes* (1859)
Leone Leoni (1834)	*Jeanne* (1844)	*Confessions d'une fille* (1865)
André (1835)	*Teverino* (1845)	*Césarine Dietrich* (1871)

Les Maîtres Mosaïstes (1837)	*Le Meunier d'Angibault* (1845)	*Journal d'un voyageur pendant la guerre* (1871)
Mauprat (1837)	*Lucrezia Floriani* (1846)	*Flamarande* (1875)
La Dernière Aldini (1838)	*L'Homme de Neige* (1859)	*Les Deux Frères* (1875)

He translated most of *La Dernière Aldini* only to discover, to his great disappointment, that a translation had already been done. (Source: Isabelle Naginski, "Two Opponents of the Anthill.")

62. Hermann, "George Sand," 155.

63. Nathan Rosen, "Chaos and Dostoevsky's Women," *Kenyon Review* 20 (Spring 1958): 276.

64. Cited in Karp, "George Sand's Reception," 141–42. See: V. Komarovich, "Dostoevsky und George Sand'," in *Die Brüder Karamazoff: Neue Untersuchungen und Materialen* (München: Piper Verlag, 1929).

65. Edward Wasiolek, *Dostoevsky: The Major Fiction* (Cambridge: MIT, 1964), 141.

66. Karp, "George Sand's Reception," 141.

67. Cited in ibid., 140–41.

Chapter 5. Horace, the Superfluous Rake: Triangulation of Desire

1. René Girard, *Mensonge romantique et vérité romanesque* (Paris: Bernard Grasset, 1961), 23.

2. Ibid., 22.

3. Ibid., 28.

4. Sand explains in her preface to the novel that no individual had served as a model for Horace. Rather, this character type, which was familiar to everyone at the time, derived in her work from a compilation of ten to twelve examples. Numerous acquaintances and public figures continued to charge her with having used them as models, so prevalent was this type. The notice of 1852 to *Horace* attests to this reaction: "Il faut croire qu'Horace représente un type moderne très fidèle et très répandu, car ce livre m'a fait une douzaine d'ennemis bien conditionnés" (One would have to believe that Horace represents a very real and widespread character type, since this book has made me a dozen well-conditioned enemies) (*Horace*, 1).

5. Ellen B. Chances, *Conformity's Children: An Approach to the Superfluous Man in Russian Literature* (Columbus, Ohio: Slavica, 1978), 21.

6. Ibid., 18.

7. Peter Yakovlevich Chaadayev, *"Philosophical Letters" and "Apology of a Madman,"* trans. M. B. Zeldin (Knoxville, Tenn., 1969), 31–51.

8. Chances, *Conformity's Children*, 20–21.

9. Cited in Carole Karp, "George Sand and the Russians," in *George Sand Conference*

Proceedings, 1978 (New York: AMS, 1978), 90. Arnold Weinstein relates in *The Fiction of Relationship* (1985) an anecdote of John Updike's adventures with a Soviet writer while in Russia: "The story makes fun of one trait common to several East European nationalities: the impression people give that while they admit unashamedly that in many respects their nation does not amount to much, they insist with pride that in suffering they are supreme" (p. 126).

10. Chances, *Conformity's Children*, 14.

11. Cited in the introduction by Michael R. Katz to *Who is to Blame? A Novel in Two Parts*, by Alexander Herzen, trans. Michael R. Katz (Ithaca and London: Cornell University Press, 1984), 37.

12. Chances, *Conformity's Children*, 23.

13. Katz, introduction to *Who is to Blame?* by Alexander Herzen, 37.

14. Carole Karp, "George Sand in the Estimate of the Russians," in *George Sand Papers: Conference Proceedings, 1976* (New York: AMS, 1976), 181.

15. Patrick Waddington, *Turgenev and George Sand: An Improbable Entente* (Totowa, N.J.: Barnes and Noble, 1981), 44–45.

16. Lesley Singer Hermann, "George Sand and the Nineteenth-Century Russian Novel: The Quest for a Heroine" diss., Columbia University, 1979, 34.

17. Karp, "George Sand and the Russians," 154–55.

18. Chances, *Conformity's Children*, 50.

19. For a discussion of Herzen's personal love-triangle relationships, refer to chapter 2.

20. Cited in Karp, "George Sand in the Estimate of the Russians," 184–85.

21. Hermann, "George Sand," 37.

22. Karp, "George Sand in the Estimate of the Russians," 184.

23. Ibid., 185.

24. V. A. Putintsev, *Gertsen-pisatel* (Herzen, the writer)(Moscow, 1963), 70.

25. Alexander Herzen, *Who is to Blame? A Novel in Two Parts*, introduced, translated, and annotated by Michael R. Katz (Ithaca and London: Cornell University Press, 1984), 39.

26. Ibid., 22-23.

27. Ibid, 30.

28. Ibid.

29. Ibid., 32.

30. Ibid., 27.

31. Ibid., 28.

32. Ibid

33. Chances, *Conformity's Children*, 60-61.

34. Alexandra Lyngstad and Sverre Lyngstad, *Ivan Goncharov* (New York: Twayne, 1971), 41.

35. René Girard, *Mensonge romantique et vérité romanesque* (Paris: Bernard Grasset, 1961), 27–28.

36. Harriet Kay Stow, "Narrative and Thematic Structures in George Sand's *Horace*," diss., University of Wisconsin, 1979, 135.

37. Ivan Goncharov, *Polnoe sobranie sochinenii i pisem* (Complete edition of writings and correspondence), ed. M. Lemke (Petrograd, 1919–25), 8:73.

38. Milton Ehre, *Oblomov and His Creator: The Life and Art of Ivan Goncharov* (Princeton:

Princeton University Press, 1973), 118–19.

39. Stow, "Narrative," 171.

40. Ibid., 150.

41. Ibid., 155 and 167.

42. Ibid., 128–30

43. Lyngstad, *Ivan Goncharov*, 48–49.

44. Victor Ripp, *Turgenev's Russia: From "Notes of a Hunter" to "Fathers and Sons"* (Ithaca and London: Cornell University Press, 1980), 84.

45. Cited in Richard G. Kappler, "Turgenev and George Sand," Research Studies (Pullman, Wash.) 34 (1966): 42.

46. Ibid

47. Patrick Waddington, *Turgenev and George Sand*, 45.

48. Harriet Kay Stow "Narrative," 26–27.

49. Ibid., 94.

50. Ripp, *Turgenev's Russia*, 128–29.

51. Ibid., 132.

52. Ibid., 92.

53. Ibid., 156.

54. V. S. Pritchett, *The Gentle Barbarian: The Life and Work of Turgenev* (New York: Random House, 1977), 93.

55. Waddington, *Turgenev and George Sand*, 45.

56. Carole Sue Karp, "George Sand's Reception in Russia, 1832–81," diss., University of Michigan, 1976, 125.

Chapter 6. The Woman Question: What is to be Done?

1. Richard Stites, *The Women's Liberation Movement in Russia: Feminism, Nihilism and Bolshevism 1860–1930* (Princeton: Princeton University Press, 1978), 32.

2. April Fitzlyon, "I. S. Turgenev and the 'Woman Question'," *New Zealand Slavonic Journal*, 1983, 162.

3. Gail Warshofsky Lapidus, *Women in Soviet Society: Equality, Development and Social Change* (Berkeley, Los Angeles, and London: University of California Press, 1979), 31.

4. Ibid., 30.

5. Barbara Alpern Engel, *Mothers and Daughters: Women of the Intelligentsia in Nineteenth-Century Russia* (Cambridge: Cambridge University Press, 1983), 127.

6. This contrasts somewhat with early feminists in France and England, who addressed problems regarding economic and working conditions for women of the proletariat such as miners and textile workers. However, as in Russia, the female masses at the lowest rung of the social hierarchy played almost no role in the women's movement until the turn of the century. Activists consisted of leisure-class members.

7. Tova Yedlin, ed., *Women in Eastern Europe and the Soviet Union* (New York: Praeger, 1980), 22.

8. Stites, *Women's Liberation*, 104.

9. Norine Voss, "Saying the Unsayable: An Introduction to Women's Autobiogra-

phy," in *Gender Studies: New Directions in Feminist Criticism,* ed. Judith Spector (Bowling Green, Ohio: Bowling Green State University Popular Press, 1986), 158.

10. Carole Karp, "George Sand's Reception in Russia, 1832–1881," diss., University of Michigan, 1976, 47.

11. Engel, *Mothers and Daughters,* 102.

12. This was not the case, however, with the women's movement in Western Europe. In France, for instance, where women's groups had labored to get women into the First International as equals with a representative voice (notably the so-called *ovalistes* of Lyon), their struggle became subservient as men filled their ranks and claimed that "workers' rights came first." See Hilden, *Working Women and Socialist Politics: France 1880–1914* (Oxford, 1986).

13. Lesley Singer Hermann. "George Sand and the Nineteenth-Century Russian Novel: The Quest for a Heroine," diss., Columbia University, 1979, 50–51.

14. Barbara Heldt, *Terrible Perfection: Women and Russian Literature* (Bloomington and Indianapolis: Indiana University Press, 1987), 13.

15. Caroline Maegd-Soep, *The Emancipation of Women in Russian Literature and Society* (Ghent, Belgium: Ghent State University, 1978), 335.

16. Ibid., 123.

17. Simone de Beauvoir, *The Second Sex: The Classic Manifesto of the Liberated Woman,* trans. H. M. Parshley (New York: Vintage, 1960), 172.

18. Alexander Pushkin, *Eugene Onegin,* trans. Walter Arndt (New York: E. P. Dutton, 1963), 175.

19. Ibid., 220.

20. Barbara Heldt elaborates on this concept in her text. See note 14.

21. Although a high preponderance of women doctors exists in contemporary Russia and the republics, these women receive relatively low wages and lack high professional esteem. Aspiring Russians continue to covet powerful bureaucratic positions. The vast majority of these belong to that portion of the population that still assumes the decision-making power, the men.

22. Christine Delphy, *Close to Home: A Materialist Analysis of Women's Oppression,* translated and edited by Diana Leonarde (Amherst: University of Massachusetts Press, 1984).

23. Ibid., 74.

24. Maegd-Soep, *Emancipation of Women,* 146

25. De Beauvoir, *The Second Sex,* 200.

26. Ibid., 198.

27. Maegd-Soep, *Emancipation of Women,* 142–43.

28. Ibid., 143.

29. Heldt, *Terrible Perfection,* 24.

30. Ibid., 25.

31. Maegd-Soep, *Emancipation of Women,* 100.

32. Delphy, *Close to Home,* 108.

33. Nikolai Chernyshevsky, *What is to be Done?* trans. N. Dole and S. S. Skidelsky (Ann Arbor, Mich.: Ardis, 1986), 120.

34. Delphy, *Close to Home,* 108.

35. Engel, *Mothers and Daughters,* 70.

36. These accusations prevailed elsewhere from the seventeenth century on.

37. Engel, *Mothers and Daughters*, 53.

38. Heldt, *Terrible Perfection*, 68.

39. Ibid., 82–83.

40. Voss, "Saying the Unsayable," 218

41. Isabelle Hoog Naginski, *George Sand: Writing for Her Life* (New Brunswick, N.J.: Rutgers University Press, 1991), 22.

42. Ibid., 27.

43. Edwina Jackie Cruise, "The Ideal Woman in Tolstoi's *Resurrection*," *Canadian Slavic Studies* 2, no. 2 (Summer 1977): 113.

44. Mary Ellmann, *Thinking About Women* (New York: Harcourt, Brace and World, 1968), 33.

45. Fitzlyon, "I. S. Turgenev," 172.

46. Heldt, *Terrible Perfection*, 108–10.

47. Barbara Heldt, "Women Studies in Russian Literature: Opportunities for Research and Publication," in *Women in Print I: Opportunities for Women's Studies Research in Language and Literature*, ed. Joan E. Hartman and Ellen Messer (New York: MLA, 1982), 150–51.

48. Heldt, *Terrible Perfection*, 110.

49. Ibid., 144.

50. De Beauvoir, *The Second Sex*, 143.

51. Heldt, "Women Studies in Russian Literature," 150.

52. Ibid., 151.

Select Bibliography

Primary Sources

Avdeev, Mikhail. "Podvodnyi Kamen'." *Sovremennik* 10 (1860): 415–502; 11 (1860): 103–88.

Chernyshevsky, N. G. *Chto Delat'?* Moscow: Gosudarstvennoye Izdatyelstvo Khudo-zhestvennoy Literatury, 1960.

———. *What is to be Done?* Translated by N. Dole and S. S. Skidelsky. Introduction by Kathryn Fever. Ann Arbor, Mich.: Ardis, 1986.

Dostoevsky, Fyodor. *The Brothers Karamazov.* Translated by Constance Garnett. New York: New American Library, 1980.

———. *Crime and Punishment.* Translated by Sidney Monas. New York: Dell, 1968.

———. *Diary of a Writer.* Translated by Boris Brasol. New York: Octagon Books, 1973.

———. *Dnevnik pisatelya.* Paris: YMCA.

———. *The Gambler, with Polina Suslova's Diary.* Translated by Victor Terras. Chicago: University of Chicago Press, 1972.

———. *The Idiot.* Translated by Constance Garnett. New York: Dell, 1959.

———. *Polnoe sobranie sochinenii v tridtsati tomakh.* Leningrad: Izdatyelstvo Nauka, 1972.

Druzhinin, Aleksandr Vasil'evich. *Polinka Saks.* Moscow: Gosudarstvennoye Izdatyelstvo Khuzhestvennoy Literatury, 1955.

Gan, Elena [Zinaida R-va, pseud.]. "Ideal." *Biblioteka dlya chteniya* 21 (1837): 115–80.

———. "Nomerovannaya lozha." In *Sbornik luchshikh pisatelei.* Kiev, 1911.

———. *Polnoe sobranie sochinenii.* St. Petersburg, 1905.

Goncharov, Ivan. *Oblomov.* Translated by Natalie A. Duddington. Introduction by Nikolay Andreyev. New York: Macmillan, 1929.

———. *O literature.* Moscow, 1962.

———. *Polnoe sobranie sochinenii i pisem.* Edited by M. Lemke. 22 vols. Petrograd, 1919–25.

———. *The Same Old Story.* Moscow: Foreign Language Publishing House, 1959.

———. *Sobranie sochinenii v tridtsati tomakh.* 30 vols. Moscow: Izdatyelstvo Akademiya Nauk, 1954–65.

Herzen, Aleksandr. *Who is to Blame? A Novel in Two Parts.* Translated by Michael R. Katz. Ithaca, N.Y.: Cornell University Press, 1984.

Nestroev, A. [Petr Kudiavtsev, pseud.]. "Bez Razsveta." *Sovremennik* 1 (1847): 95–156.

—— [N. Stanitsky, pseud.]. "Bezobraznyi Muzh." *Sovremennik* 8 (1848): 131–58.

Panaeva, Avdotya. *Vospominaniya.* Introduction by Kornei Chukovsky. Moscow, 1956.

Pavlova, Karolina. *A Double Life.* Translated by Barbara Heldt Monter. Ann Arbor, Mich.: Ardis, 1978.

Pisemsky, Alexei. *Boyarshchina.* Moscow: Izd. Pravda, 1959.

——. *One Thousand Souls.* Translated by the Foreign Language Publishing House. Moscow: Foreign Language Publishing House, n.d.

——. *Polnoe sobranie sochinenii.* St. Petersburg: Izdat. A. F. Marks, 1911.

Pleshcheev, Aleksei. *Izbrannye stikhotvoreniia i proza.* Moscow: Gosudarstvennoye Izdatyelstvo Khudozhestvennoy Literatury, 1960.

——. *Polnoe sobranie stikhotvorenii.* Edited by M. Poliakov. Moscow-Leningrad: Sovietskii Pisatel, 1964.

——. *Zhiteiskie povesti i rasskazy.* St. Petersburg: I. L. Tuzova, 1880.

——. *Polnoe sobranie sochinenii.* 10 vols. Moscow: Izd. Akademii Nauk, 1966.

Pushkin, Alexander. *Eugene Onegin: A Novel in Verse.* Translated by Walter Arndt. New York: E. P. Dutton, 1963.

——. *Sobranie sochinenii v trekh tomakh.* 3 vols. Moscow: Izdatyelstvo Khudozhestvennoy Literatury, 1964.

Rousseau, Jean-Jacques. *Émile.* Paris: Garnier, n.d.

——. *Julie, ou la Nouvelle Héloïse.* Paris: Garnier, 1960.

R-va, Zinaida. *See* Gan, Elena.

Sand, George. *Horace.* Paris: Livre Club Diderot, 1969.

——. *Indiana.* Edited by Béatrice Didier. Paris: Folio, 1984.

——. *Jacques.* Paris: Perrotin, 1842.

——. *Mauprat.* Paris: Garnier-Flammarion, 1969.

——. *Oeuvres Complètes.* Paris: Calmann-Levy, 1825-1926.

Tolstoy, Leo. *Anna Karenina.* Translated by Joel Carmichael. New York: Bantam Books, 1960.

——. "Family Happiness" and "The Kreutzer Sonata" in *The Death of Ivan Ilych and Other Stories.* Translated by Aylmer Maude and J. D. Huff. New York: New American Library, 1960.

——. *Sobranie sochinenii v dvadtsati tomakh.* 20 vols. Moscow: Izdatyelstvo Khudozhestvennoy Literatury, 1960–65.

Tur, Evgeniya (Countess Salias de Turnemir). "Oshibka." *Sovremennik* 17, no. 10 (1849).

Turgenev, Ivan. *Fathers and Sons.* Translated by Constance Garnett. New York: Walter Black, 1942.

——. *The Novels and Stories of Ivan Turgenieff.* Vol 3: *Rudin* and vol. 13: "Jakoff Pasynkoff." New York: Charles Scribner's Sons, 1904.

————. *On the Eve.* Translated by Stepan Apresyan. Moscow: Foreign Language Publishing House, 1958.

————. *Polnoe sobranie sochinenii i pisem.*

————. *Sketches from a Hunter's Album.* Translated by Richard Freeborn. Harmondsworth: Penguin, 1967.

Secondary Sources

Adams, Barbara B. "Sisters under Their Skins: The Women in the Lives of Raskolnikov and Razumov." *Conradiana* 6 (1974): 113–24.

Annenkov, Pavel V. *The Extraordinary Decade.* Edited by Arthur P. Mendel. Translated by Irwin Titunik. Ann Arbor, Mich.: University of Michigan Press, 1968.

Arnold, J. V. "George Sand's *Mauprat* and Emily Brontë's *Wuthering Heights.*" *Revue de Littérature Comparée* 46 (1972): 209–18.

Bailbé, Joseph-Marc. "Jacques ou l'illusion romanesque." *Cahiers de l'Association Internationale des Études Françaises* (Paris) 28 (1976): 315–30.

Bakhtin, Mikhail. *Problems of Dostoevsky's Poetics.* Translated by R. W. Rotsel. Ann Arbor, Mich.: Ardis, 1973.

Bannour, Wanda. "L'Influence de George Sand en Russie." In *George Sand: Collected Essays,* edited by Janis Glasgow. Troy, N.Y.: Whitston, 1985.

Barine, Arvède. "George Sand et la Russie." *Journal des Débats,* 4 October 1899, 39.

Barnes, Julian. *Flaubert's Parrot.* New York: McGraw-Hill, 1984.

Barrett, Michele, ed. *Virginia Woolf: Women and Writing.* London: Harcourt, Brace, Jovanovich, 1979.

Barry, Joseph, ed. *George Sand: In Her Own Words.* Garden City, N.Y.: Anchor, 1979.

————. *Infamous Woman: The Life of George Sand.* Garden City, N.Y.: Doubleday, 1977.

Bayley, John. *Pushkin.* Cambridge: Cambridge University, Press, 1971.

————. *Tolstoy and the Novel.* New York: Viking, 1966.

Beauvoir, Simone de. *The Second Sex.* Translated by H. M. Parshley. Harmondsworth: Penguin, 1974. New York: Vintage, 1974.

Bebel, August. *Women and Socialism.* New York: Socialist Literature Company, 1910.

Becker, Howard S. *Outsiders: Studies in the Sociology of Deviance.* New York: Free Press of Glencoe, 1963.

Belinsky, V. G. *Polnoe sobranie sochinenii.* 13 vols. Moscow: Izd. Akademii Nauk, 1953–59.

————. *Selected Philosophical Works.* Translated by Foreign Language Publishing House. Moscow: Foreign Language Publishing House, 1948.

Belknap, Robert L. "The Origins of Alyosha Karamazov." In *American Contributions to the Sixth International Congress of Slavists* (Prague, 1968). Vol. 2 of *Literary Contributions.* Edited by William Harkins. The Hague: Mouton, 1968.

————. *The Structure of the Brothers Karamazov*. The Hague: Mouton, 1967.

Bem, A. L., ed. *O Dostoevskom*. 3 vols. Prague, 1929–36.

Benson, Ruth Crego. *Women in Tolstoy. The Ideal and the Erotic*. Urbana: University of Illinois Press, 1973.

Berdyaev, Nicholas. *The Russian Idea*. Translated by R. H. French. Boston: Beacon Press, 1962.

Berlin, Isaiah. "Fathers and Children. Turgenev and the Liberal Predicament." *The New York Review of Books*, 18 October 1973, November 1973, 15 November 1973.

————. "A Marvelous Decade." *Encounter*, June 1955, November 1955, December 1955, May 1956.

Bidelman, Patrick Kay. *Pariahs Stand Up! The Founding of the Liberal Feminist Movement in France, 1858–1889*. London: Greenwood Press, 1982.

Billington, James H. *Mikhailovsky and Russian Populism*. Oxford: Clarendon Press, 1958.

————. *The Icon and the Axe. An Interpretive History of Russian Culture*. New York: Alfred A. Knopf, 1966.

Bloom, Harold. *The Anxiety of Influence: A Theory of Poetry*. New York: Oxford University Press, 1973.

Blount, Paul G. *George Sand and the Victorian World*. Athens: University of Georgia Press, 1979.

Bogdanovich, Tatiana. *Liubov liudei shestidesiatykh godov*. Leningrad: "Akademia," 1929.

Bordeaux, Henri. "La vie et l'influence de George Sand." *Le Correspondant* 215 (1904): 805–29.

Bossis, Mireille. "L'Homme-Dieu ou l'idole brisée dans les romans de George Sand." In *George Sand*, edited by Simone Vièrne, 179–87. Paris: CDU/SEDES, 1983.

Bowman, Herbert E. *Vissarion Belinskii, 1811–48. A Study in the Origins of Social Criticism in Russia*. Cambridge: Harvard University Press, 1954.

Boyd, Alexander F. *Aspects of the Russian Novel*. London: Chatto and Windus, 1972.

Brake, Mike, ed. *Human Sexual Relations: Towards a Redefinition of Sexual Politics*. New York: Pantheon, 1982.

Brincken, Alexandra von. "George Sand et Dostoiévsky. Contribution au problème des emprunts littéraires." *Revue de littérature comparée* 13 (1933): 623–29.

Broido, Vera. *Apostles into Terrorists: Women and the Revolutionary Movement in Russia of Alexander II*. New York: Viking 1977.

Brooks, Peter. *The Melodramatic Imagination*. New Haven: Yale University Press, 1976.

————. *Reading for the Plot: Design and Intention in Narrative*. New York: Vintage, 1985.

Cadot, Michel. *La Russie dans la vie intellectuelle française 1839–1856*. Paris: Fayard, 1967.

Carr, Edward H. *Dostoevsky*. London: Unwin Books, 1962.

————. *The Romantic Exiles*. London: Victor Gollancz, 1913.

Chaadayev, Peter Yakovevich. *"Philosophical Letters" and "Apology of a Madman."* Translated by M. B. Zeldin. Knoxville, Tenn., 1969.

Chances, Ellen B. *Conformity's Children: An Approach to the Superfluous Man in Russian Literature*. Columbus, Ohio: Slavica, 1978.

Chantavoine, Henri. "George Sand en Russie." *Le Correspondant* 196 (1899): 174–88.

Chernyshev, K. *Lishnye lyudi i zhenskie tipy v romanakh i povestyakh I. S. Turgeneva.* St. Petersburg, 1896.

Chernyshevsky, N. G. *Polnoe sobranie sochinenii.* 15 vols. Moscow, 1939–53.

———. *Selected Philosophical Essays.* Translated by Foreign Language Publishing House. Moscow: Foreign Language Publishing House, 1953.

———. *What is to be Done?* Translated by N. Dole and S. S. Skidelsky. Introduction by Kathryn Fever. Ann Arbor, Mich.: Ardis, 1986.

———. "Zhizn' Zhorzh Zand." *Sovremennik,* nos. 1, 2, 3, 7 (1855); nos. 4–8 (1856).

Corbet, Charles. *L'Opinion française face à l'Inconnue Russe, (1799–1894).* Paris: Marcel Didier, 1967.

Courrier, Nicole Bodin, Thierry. Introduction to *Horace* by George Sand. Paris: L'Aurore, 1982.

Crecelius, Kathryn J. *Family Romances: George Sand's Early Novels.* Bloomington and Indianapolis: Indiana University Press, 1987.

Cruise, Edwina Jannie. "The Ideal Woman in Tolstoi's *Resurrection.*" *Canadian Slavic Studies* 2, no. 2 (Summer, 1977): 281–86.

Curle, Richard. *Characters of Dostoevsky: Studies from Four Novels.* London: Heinemann, 1950.

Delaveau, Henri. "Le roman satirique en Russie." *Revue des Deux Mondes,* 14 (15 January 1860): 425–53.

De Mages, André. "George Sand en Russie." *La Nouvelle Revue Française* 12 (1899): 766–78.

Delphy, Christine. *Close to Home: A Materialist Analysis of Women's Oppression.* Translated and edited by Diana Leonard. Amherst: University of Massachusetts Press, 1984.

Dement'ev, A. G. *Ocherki po istorii russkoi zhurnalistki 1840–1850.* Moscow and Leningrad: Gosudarstvennoy Izdatyelstvo Khudozhestvennoy Literatury, 1951.

Deschamps, Gaston. "George Sand et les Russes." *Le Temps,* 16 July, 1899.

Dobrolyubov, N. A. *Sobranie sochinenii v devyati tomakh.* 9 vols. Moscow and Leningrad, 1961–64.

Dolinin, A. S. "Dostoevskii i Suslova." In *Dostoevskii: Stat'i i Materialy.* Edited by A. S. Dolinin, 2:153–85.

———, ed. *F. M. Dostoevsky v vospominaniyakh sovremennikov.* 2 vols. Moscow, 1964.

Doumic, René. *George Sand: Some Aspects of her Life and Work.* New York and London: Knickerbocker Press, 1910.

Druzhinin, A. V. *Sobranie sochinenii.* St. Petersburg: Imperatorskoi Akademii Nauk, 1865.

Dunham, Vera Sandomirsky. "The Strong-Woman Motif." In *The Transformation of Russian Society.* Edited by Cyril E. Black. Cambridge: Harvard University Press, 1960.

Duveau, George. "George Sand, témoin lucide du drame social." *Bulletin de la Faculté des Lettres de Strasbourg* 22 (May–June, 1954): 351–55.

Edmondson, Linda Harriet. *Feminism in Russia, 1900–1.* Stanford, Calif.: Stanford University Press, 1984.

Ehre, Milton. *Oblomov and his Creator: The Life and Art of Ivan Goncharov.* Princeton: Princeton University Press, 1973.

Eikhenbaum, Boris. *The Young Tolstoi.* Translated by Gary Kern. Ann Arbor, Mich.: Ardis, 1972.

Ellmann, Mary. *Thinking About Women.* New York: Harcourt, Brace, and World, 1968.

Elnet, Elaine. *Historic Origins and Social Development of Family Life in Russia.* New York: Columbia University Press, 1926.

Engel, Barbara Alpern. *Mothers and Daughters: Women of the Intelligentsia in Nineteenth-Century Russia.* Cambridge: Cambridge University Press, 1963.

Evans, David Owen. *Le socialisme romantique: Pierre Leroux et ses contemporains.* Paris, 1948.

Evnina, H. "George Sand et la critique russe." *Europe,* nos. 102–3 (1954): 157–70.

Faguet, Émile. *Dix-Neuvième siècle: Études littéraires.* Paris: Lécène, Oudin et Cie., 1887.

Fanger, Donald. *Dostoevsky and Romantic Realism: A Study of Dostoevsky in Relation to Balzac, Dickens and Gogol.* Cambridge: Harvard University Press, 1965.

Fasting, Sigurd. "Dostoevsky and George Sand." *Russian Literature* 4 (July 1976): 309–22.

Fitzlyon, April. "I. S. Turgenev and the 'Woman Question'." *New Zealand Slavonic Journal,* 1983.

Frank, Joseph. *Dostoevsky: The Seeds of Revolt, 1821–1849.* Princeton: Princeton University Press, 1976.

Freeborn, Richard. *The Rise of the Russian Novel. Studies in the Russian Novel from "Eugene Onegin" to "War and Peace."* Cambridge: Cambridge University Press, 1973.

———. *Turgenev: The Novelist's Novelist.* London: Oxford University Press, 1960.

Frye, Prosser Hall. "George Sand and her French Style." *Studies of the University of Nebraska* 3 (1903): 199–221.

Gedymin, L. P. "Istoricheskii roman Zhorzh Sand." *Trudy Universiteta Druzhby Narodov* 4 (1964); 200–220.

"George Sand Colloquium." *Nineteenth-Century French Studies* 4 (Summer, 1976).

Gide, André. *Dostoevsky.* Paris: Plon, 1923.

Gifford, Henry. *The Hero of His Time: A Theme in Russian Literature.* London: Edward Arnold, 1950.

Girard, René. *Deceit, Desire and the Novel: Self and Other in Literary Structure.* Translated by Yvonne Freccero. Baltimore: Johns Hopkins University Press, 1976.

———. *Mensonge romantique et vérité romanesque.* Paris: Bernard Grasset, 1961.

Giraud, Raymond Dorner. *The Unheroic Hero in the Novels of Stendhal, Balzac, and Flaubert.* New Brunswick, N.J.: Rutgers University Press, 1957.

Glasgow, Janis. "The Use of Doubles in George Sand's *Jacques.*" In *George Sand Papers: Conference Proceedings,* edited by Natalie Datlof et al. New York, 1982.

Goscilo, Helena, trans. and ed. *Russian and Polish Women's Fiction.* Knoxville: University of Tennessee Press, 1985.

Granjard, Henri. "George Sand en Russie." *Europe*, nos. 102–3 (1954): 144–57.

———. *Ivan Tourguénev et les courants politiques et sociaux de son temps.* Paris, 1954.

Green, Frederick. *French Novelists from the Revolution to Proust.* New York: Frederick Ungar, 1964.

Greene, Gayle. "Women, Character and Society in Tolstoy's *Anna Karenina.*" *Frontiers: Journal of Women Studies* 2, no. 1 (1978): 106–25.

Grossman, Leonid. *Dostoevsky: His Life and Works.* Translated by Mary Mackler. Indianapolis: Bobbs-Merrill, 1975.

Gubler, Donworth V. "Dostoevsky's Women." *Proceedings of the Pacific Northwest Conference on Foreign Languages* 29, no. 1 (1978): 130–35.

Halpérine-Kaminski, E. *Ivan Tourguéneff, d'après sa correspondance avec ses amis français.* Paris, 1901.

———. *Ivan Tourguénev: Lettres à Mme. Viardot.* Paris, 1907.

Haumant, Émile. *La culture française en Russie (1700–1900).* Paris: Hachette, 1913.

———. *Ivan Tourguénieff, la vie et l'oeuvre.* Paris: Armand Colin, 1906.

Heilbrun, Carolyn G. *Toward a Recognition of Androgyny.* New York: Alfred A. Knopf, 1973.

Heldt, Barbara. *Terrible Perfection: Women and Russian Literature.* Bloomington and Indianapolis: Indiana University Press, 1987.

———. "Women Studies in Russian Literature: Opportunities for Research and Publication." In *Women in Print I: Opportunities for Women's Studies Research in Language and Literature*, edited by Joan E. Hartman and Ellen Messer-Davidow. New York: MLA, 1982.

Hermann, Lesley Singer. "George Sand and the Nineteenth-Century Russian Novel: The Quest for a Heroine." Diss., Columbia University, 1979.

———. "'Woman as Hero' in Turgenev, Goncharov and George Sand's *Mauprat.*" *Ulbandus Review* 2, no. 1 (Fall 1979): 128–38.

Herzen, A. I. *My Past and Thoughts.* Translated by Constance Garnett. London: Chatto and Windus, 1968.

———. *Sobranie sochinenii v 30-ti tomakh.* Moscow: Akademiia Nauk, 1954–61.

Hilden, Patricia. *Working Women and Socialist Politics: France 1880-1914.* Oxford University Press, 1986.

Hoock-Demarle, Marie-Claire. "The Nineteenth-Century: Insights of Contemporary Women Writers." In *Woman as Mediatrix: Essays on Nineteenth-Century European Women Writers*, edited by Avriel A. Goldberger. New York: Greenwood Press, 1982.

Hoog, Armand. "Who Invented the 'Mal du Siècle?'" *Yale French Studies* 13 (1965): 42–51.

Hook, Sidney. *The Hero in History. A Study in Limitation and Possibility.* Boston: Beacon Press, 1943.

Howe, Marie Jenney. *George Sand: The Search for Love.* New York: John Day, 1927.

Hunt, H. L. *Le socialisme et le romantisme en France.* Oxford: Clarendon Press, 1935.

Iggers, Georg Gerson. *The Cult of Authority. The Political Philosophy of the Saint-Simonians. A Chapter in the Intellectual History of Totalitarianism.* The Hague: Martinus Nijhoff, 1958.

Iser, Wolfgang. *The Act of Reading: A Theory of Aesthetic Response*. Baltimore and London: Johns Hopkins University Press, 1978.

———. *The Implied Reader: Patterns of Communication in Prose Fiction from Bunyan to Beckett*. Baltimore and London: The Johns Hopkins University Press, 1974.

Iskra. (Cartoon and articles about George Sand.) *Khudozhestvennaya Literatura* (1861): 138–40; 10 (1861): 141.

James, Henry. *French Poets and Novelists*. London, 1878.

———. *Notes on Novelists*. New York: Charles Scribner's Sons, 1914.

Joran, Theodore. "Le féminisme de George Sand." *Reforme sociale* 6 (1926): 607–27.

Jost, François. "Le Roman Épistolaire." In *Essais de Littérature Comparée*. Fribourg: Éditions Universitaires, 1968.

Jurgrau, Thelma. "George Sand and Education: The Mythic Pattern in Three Works." In *West Virginia George Sand Conference Papers*, edited by Armand E. Singer et al. Morgantown: Dept. of Foreign Languages, West Virginia University, 1981.

Kamuf, Peggy. *Fictions of Feminine Desire: Disclosures of Héloïse*. Lincoln: University of Nebraska Press, 1982.

Kappler, Richard G. "Turgenev and George Sand." *Washington State University Research Studies* 34, no. 1 (March 1966): 37–45.

Karénine, Vladimir. *George Sand, sa vie et ses oeuvres*. 4 vols. Paris, 1899–1926.

———."Turgenev i Zhorzh Sand." In *Turgenevskii Sbornik*, edited by A. F. Koni, 87–130. St. Petersburg, 1921.

Karp, Carole. "George Sand in the Estimate of the Russians." In *George Sand Papers: Conference Proceedings, 1976*. New York: AMS, 1976.

———. "George Sand and the Russians." In *George Sand Papers: Conference Proceedings, 1978*. New York: AMS, 1978.

———. "George Sand and Turgenev: A Literary Relationship." *Studies in the Literary Imagination* 12, no. 2 (1979): 73–81.

———. "George Sand's Reception in Russia, 1832–1881." Diss., Univ. of Michigan, 1976.

Kauffman, Linda. *Discourses of Desire: Gender, Genre and Epistolary Fictions*. Ithaca, N.Y.: Cornell University Press, 1986.

Kellman, Steven G. *Loving Reading: Erotics of the Text*. New York: Archon, 1985.

Kennan, George F. *The Marquis de Custine and his Russia in 1839*. Princeton: Princeton University Press, 1971.

Kiiko, E. I. "Geroinia zhorzhsandovskogo tipa v povesti Turgeneva Perepiska." *Russkaia Literatura* 4 (1984): 130–35.

———. "Dostoevskii i Zhorzh Sand." *Acta Litteraria Academiae Scientiarum Hungaricae* 24, nos. 1–2 (1982): 65–85.

Killen, Alice. *Le roman 'terrifiant' ou 'roman noir' de Walpole à Anne Radcliffe et son influence sur la littérature française jusqu'en 1840*. Paris, 1915.

Kiremidjian, David. "*Crime and Punishment:* Matricide and the Woman Question." *American Imago* 33 (1976).

Komarovich, V. "Dostoevsky and George Sand." In *Die Brüder Karamazoff: Neue Untersuchungen und Materialen*. München: Piper Verlag, 1929.

Kostiamin, S. *Turgenevskiia zhenshchiny; kriticheskii etiud'*. Vitebsk: Gubernskaia Tip., 1896.

Krasnoshchekova, Elena Aleksandrovna. *"Oblomov" I A Goncharova*. Moscow, 1970.

Kravtsov, N. "Zhorzh Zand v Rossii." *Khudozhestvennaya Literatura* 8 (1931): 12–16.

Kuhn, Alfred. "Dobroliubov's Critique of *Oblomov:* Polemics and Psychology." *Slavic Review* 30, no. 1 (1971): 93–109.

Labry, Raoul. *Alexandre Ivanovič Herzen*. Paris: Bossard, 1928.

Lacassagne, J. P. "Le Révélateur dans les romans de George Sand: Un Personnage nouveau et une nouvelle relation au lecteur." *Travaux de linguistique et de littérature* 23, no. 2 (1985): 80–91.

Lampert, E. *Sons Against Fathers: Studies in Russian Radicalism and Revolution*. Oxford: Clarendon Press, 1965.

Lapidus, Gail Wardofsky. *Women in Soviet Society: Equality, Development and Social Change*. Berkeley, Los Angeles, and London: University of California Press, 1979.

Lavrin, Janko. *Dostoevsky and His Creation. A Psycho-Critical Study*. London: W. Collins, 1920.

Lecointre, Simone. "George Sand: Le Discours amoureux, deux aspects d'une écriture poétique." In *Colloque de Cérisy: George Sand,* edited by Simone Vièrne, 41–54. Paris: CDU/SEDES, 1983.

Ledkovsky, Marina. "Avdotya Panaeva: Her Salon and her Life." *Russian Literature Triquarterly* 9 (Spring 1974): 423–32.

———. *The Other Turgenev: From Romanticism to Symbolism*. Wurzburg: Jal-Verlag, 1973.

Leger, Louis. *La Russie intellectuelle*. Paris: Maisonneuve, 1914.

Levin, Harry. *The Gates of Horn: A Study of Five French Realists*. New York: Oxford University Press, 1966.

Levinson, André. "Auteur des *Frères Karamazoff*. Dostoevsky et George Sand." *Les Nouvelles Littéraires*, 13 July 1929, 8.

Lourie, Ossip. *La psychologie des romanciers russes du XIX siècle*. Paris: Felix Alcan, 1905.

Lyngstad, Alexandra, and Sverre Lyngstad. *Ivan Goncharov*. New York: Twayne, 1971.

Maegd-Soep, Carolina. *The Emancipation of Women in Russian Literature and Society*. Ghent, Belgium: Ghent State University, 1978.

Mages, André de. "George Sand en Russie." *La Nouvelle Revue Française* 12 (1899): 766–78.

Maigron, Louis. *Le romantisme et les moeurs*. Paris, 1910.

Maksimov, V. E. *'Sovremennik' v 40–50 gg. ot Belinskogo do Chernyshevskogo*. Leningrad, 1934.

———. *"Sovremennik" pri Chernyshevskom i Dobrolyubove*. Leningrad: Gosydarstvennoye Izdatyelstvo Khudozhestvennoy Literatury, 1936.

Malia, Martin. *Alexander Herzen and the Birth of Russian Socialism*. New York: Grosset & Dunlap, 1965.

Mallet, Francine. *George Sand*. Paris: Grasset, 1976.

Mamonova, Tatyana, ed. *Women and Russia: Feminist Writings from the Soviet Union*. Boston: Beacon Press, 1984.

Marix-Spire, Thérèse, ed. *Lettres inédites de George Sand et de Pauline Viardot (1839–1849)*. Paris: Nouvelles Éditions Latines, 1959

Marx, Karl, Frederick Engels, V. Lenin, and J. Stalin. *The Woman Question*. New York: International Publishers, 1951.

Masaryk, Thomas. *The Spirit of Russia*. New York: Macmillan, 1919 .

Mathewson, Rufus W., Jr. *The Positive Hero in Russian Literature*. 2d edition. Stanford, Calif.: Stanford University Press, 1975.

Matlaw, Ralph, ed. *Belinsky, Chernyshevsky and Dobrolyubov: Selected Criticism*. New York: Dutton, 1962.

Mazon, André. *Un maître du roman russe, Ivan Gontcharov*. Paris: Honoré Champion, 1914.

Menche de Loisne. *Influence de la littérature française de 1830 à 1850 sur l'esprit public et les moeurs*. Paris: Jacques Lecoffre et Cie., 1910.

Michelet, Jules. *L'Amour. La Femme*. In *Oeuvres complètes de J. Michelet*. Paris: Flammarion, n.d.

Mikhailov, M. L. *Zhenshchiny ikh vospitanie i znachenie v sem' e iobshchestve*. St. Petersburg: Kartavova, 1903.

Miller, Martin A. *The Russian Revolutionary Émigrés 1825–70*. Baltimore and London: Johns Hopkins University Press, 1986.

Miller, Wright. *Russians as People*. New York: Dutton, 1960.

Mirsky, D. S. *History of Russian Literature*. New York: Random House/Vintage Books, 1958.

Mouchulsky, Konstantine V. *Dostoevsky: His Life and Work*. Translated by Michael A. Minihan. Princeton: Princeton University Press, 1967.

Moers, Ellen. *Literary Women*. New York: Doubleday, 1976.

Monter, Barbara Heldt. *A Double Life, by Karolina Pavlova*. Ann Arbor, Mich.: Ardis, 1978.

———. "Rassvet (1859–62) and the Woman Question." *Slavic Review: American Quarterly of Soviet and East European Studies* 36 (1977): 76–85.

Moret, Marc Marcel. *Le sentiment réligieux chez George Sand*. Paris: M. Vigne, 1936.

Moselly, Émile. *George Sand*. Paris, 1911.

Moser, Charles. *Pisemsky, A Provincial Realist*. Cambridge: Harvard University Press, 1969.

Moses, Claire Goldberg. *French Feminism in the Nineteenth-Century*. Albany: State University of New York Press, 1984.

Naginski, Isabelle Hoog. *George Sand: Writing for Her Life*. New Brunswick and London: Rutgers University Press, 1991.

———. "A Nigilistka and a Communard: Two Voices of the Nineteenth-Century Russian Intelligentsia." In *Woman as Mediatrix: Essays on Nineteenth-Century European Women Writers*, edited by Avriel A. Goldberger. New York: Greenwood Press, 1987.

―――. "The Serenity of Influence: The Literary Relationship of George Sand and Dostoevsky." In *George Sand: Collected Essays*, ed. Janis Glasgow. Troy, N.Y.: Whitston, 1985.

Nettement, Alfred. *Études critiques sur le feuilleton-roman.* Paris, 1845.

O'Brien, Dennis. "George Sand and Feminism." In *The George Sand Papers: Conference Proceedings*, edited by Natalie Datlof et al. New York, 1982.

Orr, Elaine Neil. *Tillie Olsen and a Feminist Spiritual Vision.* Jackson and London: University Press of Mississippi, 1987.

Pereira, N. G. O. *The Thought and Teachings of N. G. Černyševskij.* The Hague and Paris: Mouton, 1975.

Peterson, Dale E. "From Russia with Love: Turgenev's Maidens and Howell's Heroines." *Canadian Slavonic Papers* 26, no. 1 (1984): 24–34.

Piksanov, N. K., ed. *Letopis' zhizni Belinskogo.* Moscow: Rossiiskaia Akad. Khudozh, Nauk., 1924.

Pisemskii, Aleksei F. *Pis'ma.* Moscow and Leningrad: Izdat. Akademii Nauk, 1936.

Planche, Gustave. "*Indiana*" and "*Valentine.*" *Revue des Deux Mondes* 8 (1832): 687–702.

Poggioli, Renato. *The Phoenix and the Spider.* Cambridge: Harvard University Press, 1957.

Pouzyma, Ivan. "George Sand et Dostoïevski. La Parente Littéraire des *Frères Karamazoff* et de *Spiridion.*" *Études* 1 (1930): 345–60.

Praz, Mario. *The Romantic Agony.* Translated by Angus Davidson. 2d ed. New York: Oxford University Press, 1970.

Pritchett, V.S. *The Gentle Barbarian: The Life and Work of Turgenev.* New York: Random House, 1977.

Pushkin, A. S. *Eugene Onegin.* In *The Poems, Prose and Plays of Alexander Pushkin*, translated by Babette Deutsch and edited by Avrahm Yarmolinsky. New York: Random House, 1936.

Putintsev, V.A. *Gertsen-pisatel.* Moscow, 1963.

Randall, Francis B. *N. G. Chernyshevskii.* New York: Twayne, 1967.

Rea, Annabelle. "Maternity and Marriage: Sand's Use of Fairy Tale and Myth." Paper presented at George Sand Special Section, MLA Convention. Chicago, December 1977.

Ripp, Victor. *Turgenev's Russia: From "Notes of a Hunter" to "Fathers and Sons."* Ithaca and London: Cornell University Press, 1980.

―――. "The Structure of Sincerity: Turgenev's Novels in the Context of the Cultural Movement, 1855–1862." Diss., Columbia University, 1973.

Rogers, Nancy. "George Sand and Germaine de Staël: The Novel as Subversion." In *West Virginia George Sand Conference Papers*, edited by Armand E. Singer et al. Morgantown: Dept. of Foreign Languages, West Virginia University, 1981.

―――. "George Sand: Social Protest in Her Early Works." In *The George Sand Papers: Conference Proceedings*, edited by Natalie Datlof et al. New York, 1982.

Rosen, Nathan. "Chaos and Dostoyevsky's Women." *Kenyon Review* 20 (Spring 1958): 257–77.

———. "Why Dmitrii Karamazov Did Not Kill His Father." *Canadian Slavic Studies*, Summer, 1972, 209–24.

Rosenberg, Ralph. "George Sand in Germany, 1832–1848: The Attitude toward her as a Woman and as a Novelist." Ph.D. diss., University of Wisconsin, 1933.

Rousset, Jean. *Forme et signification: Essais sur les structures littéraires de Corneille à Claudel.* Paris: J. Corti, 1962.

Sacken, Jeanée P. "George Sand, Kate Chopin, Margaret Atwood, and the Redefinition of Self." *Postscript* 2 (1985): 19–28.

Sainte-Beuve, Charles Augustin. Review of *Indiana*. *Le National* 5 (October 1832).

Saintsbury, George. "George Sand." In *A History of the French Novel (To the Close of the 19th Century)*, 2:176–207. London: Macmillan, 1919.

Sand, George. *Correspondance*. Edited by Georges Lubin. Paris: Garnier, 1964– .

———. *Correspondance entre George Sand et Gustave Flaubert*. Paris: Calmann-Levy, n.d.

———. *Oeuvres autobiographiques*. 2 vols. Paris: Gallimard, 1970.

Sanine, Kyra. *Les 'Annales de la Patrie' et la diffusion de la pensée française en Russie (1868–1884)*. Paris: Institut d'Études Slaves de l'Université de Paris, 1955.

Schor, Naomi. "Female Fetishism: The Case of George Sand." In *The Female Body in Western Culture: Contemporary Perspectives*, edited by Susan Rubin Suleiman. Cambridge: Harvard University Press, 1986.

———. "The Portrait of a Gentleman: Representing Men in (French) Women's Writing." *Representations* 20 (Fall 1987): 113–33.

Seduro, Vladimir. *Dostoevsky in Russian Literary Criticism, 1846–1956*. New York: Columbia University Press, 1957.

Seillière, Ernest. *George Sand, Mystique de la passion, de la politique et de l'art*. Paris, 1920.

Selivanova, Nina Nikolaevna. *Russia's Women*. New York: E. P. Dutton, 1923.

Setschkareff, Wsevolod. *Ivan Goncharov: His Life and His Works*. Wurzburg: Jal-Verlag, 1974.

Seyd, Felizia. *Romantic Rebel: The Life and Times of George Sand*. New York: Viking, 1940.

Showalter, Elaine. *A Literature of Their Own. British Women Novelists from Brontë to Lessing*. Princeton: Princeton University Press, 1977.

Sicard, Claude. "En Marge d'une note de *Mauprat*." *Revue d'Histoire Littéraire de la France* 69 (1969): 276–79.

———. "La Genèse de *Mauprat*." *Revue d'Histoire Littéraire de la France* 68 (1968): 782–97.

Simmons, Ernest J. *Dostoevski: The Making of a Novelist*. London, 1950.

Simons, John D. "The Nature of Suffering in Schiller and Dostoevsky." *Comparative Literature* 19 (1967): 160–73.

Skaftymov, Aleksandr. "Chernyshevskii i Zhorzh Zand." *Nravstvennye iskaniia russkikh pisatelei*. Moscow: Gosydarstvennoye Izdatyelstvo Khudozhestvennoy Literatury, 1972.

Skalkovskii, K. A. "Zhorzh Zand." *Razsvet*, 11 (1861): 355–80.

———. *O zhenshchinakh, mysli staryia i novyia*. St. Petersburg: Suvorin, 1896.

Smyrniw, Walter. "Turgenev's Emancipated Women." *Modern Language Review* 80, no. 1 (1985): 97–105.

Steiner, George. *Tolstoy or Dostoevsky: An Essay in the Old Criticism.* New York: Random House, 1959.

Stites, Richard. "M. L. Mikhailov and the Emergence of the Woman Question." *Canadian Slavic Studies*, Summer 1969, 178–99.

———. *The Women's Liberation Movement in Russia: Feminism, Nihilism and Bolshevism 1860–1930.* Princeton: Princeton University Press.

Stow, Harriet Kay. "Narrative and Thematic Structure in George Sand's *Horace.*" Diss., University of Wisconsin, 1979.

Strakhov, Nikolai. "Mill, zhenskii vopros." *Borba s zapadom v nashei literature.* St. Petersburg: Dogrodver, 1882.

Suleiman, Susan R., and Inge Crosman, eds. *The Reader in the Text: Essays on Audience and Interpretation.* Princeton: Princeton University Press, 1980.

Sumtsov, M. "Vliianie Zhorzh Zand na Turgeneva." *Knizhki Nedeli* 1 (1897): 5–12.

Tannev, Tony. *Adultery in the Novel: Contract and Transgression.* Baltimore: Johns Hopkins University Press, 1979.

Terras, Victor. *Belinskii and Russian Literary Criticism. The Heritage of Organic Aesthetics.* Madison: University of Wisconsin Press, 1974.

———. *The Young Dostoevsky (1846–1849). A Critical Study.* The Hague: Mouton, 1969.

Thackeray, W. M. "Madame Sand and the New Apocalypse." In *The Paris Sketchbook,* 233–60. New York: Fred De Fan, n.d., 233-60.

Thibert, Marguerite. *Le féminisme dans le socialisme français de 1830 à 1850.* Paris, 1926.

Thomashevsky, B. V. *Pushkin i Frantsiya.* Leningrad: Sov. Pisatel, 1960.

Thomson, Patricia. *George Sand and the Victorians.* New York: Columbia University Press, 1977.

Tompkins, Stuart Ramsay. *The Russian Intelligentsia: Makers of the Revolutionary State.* Norman: University of Oklahoma Press, 1957.

Toth, Emily. "The Independent Woman and 'Free' Love." *Massachusetts Review* 16 (1975): 647–64.

Trapeznikova, "G. Sand, redaktor i sotrudnik 'Revue indépendante'." Diss., Kazan, 1966.

Tsebrikova, Marie. "Dva romantizma vo Frantsii." *Severnyi Vestnik* 11, 12 (1883).

———. "Zhorzh Sand." *Otechestvennye Zapiski* 6 (1877): 439–72.

Tur, Evgeniya. "Zhenshchina i lyubov po ponyatiyam G. Mishle." *Russkii Vestnik* 21, no. 6 (1859): 461–500.

———. "Zhizh Zhorzh Sanda." *Russkii Vestnik* 3 (1856): 72–93, 693–715; 4 (1856): 667–708.

Turgenev, Ivan. *Literary Reminiscences and Autobiographical Fragments.* Translated by David Magarshack. New York: Farrar, Straus & Cudahy, 1958.

Ullman, Stephen. *Style in the French Novel.* Cambridge, 1957.

Veinberg, Pëtr. "Pamiati Zhorzh Zand." *Russkoe Bogastvo* 6 (1904): 177–92.

————. "Zhorzh Zand. Glava iz istorii novogo romana. Ocherk I." *Severnyi Vestnik* 8 (1894): 67–83; 9 (1894): 98–121.

Vengerov, S. A. "Druzhinin." *Kritiko-biograficheskii Slovar russkikh pisatelei i uchenykh* 5 (1897): 394–99.

Venkstern, Natalia A. *Zhorzh Sand.* Moscow: Zhurnalgazetnoe Ob'ed., 1933.

Viard, Jacques. "Socialistes chrétiens: George Sand, Dostoiévski et Péguy." *Études* 341 (1974): 389–413.

Vincent, Louise. *George Sand et l'amour.* Paris: Champion, 1917.

Vodovozova, E. *Na zare zhizni.* Moscow, 1964.

Voss, Norine. "Saying the Unsayable: An Introduction to Women's Autobiography." In *Gender Studies: New Directions in Feminist Criticism,* edited by Judith Spector. Bowling Green, Ohio: Bowling Green State University Popular Press, 1986.

Waddington, Patrick. *Turgenev and George Sand. An Improbable Entente.* Totowa, N.J.: Barnes & Noble, 1981.

Wall, Nancy. "The Persuasive Style of the Young George Sand." Diss., George Washington University, 1974.

————. "Psychosexual Identity and the Erotic Imagination in the Early Novels of George Sand." Paper presented at the George Sand Special Section, MLA Convention. New York, December 1976.

Wasiolek, Edward. *Dostoevsky: The Major Fiction.* Cambridge: M.I.T. Press, 1964.

Weidlé, Wladimir. *Russia: Absent and Present.* Translated by A. Gordon Smith. New York: John Day, 1952.

Weinstein, Arnold. *The Fiction of Relationship.* Princeton: Princeton University Press, 1988.

Wellek, René. *Dostoevsky. A Collection of Critical Essays.* Englewood Cliffs, N.J. Prentice-Hall, 1962.

Wiener, Leo. *An Interpretation of the Russian People.* New York: McBride, Nast & Company, 1915.

Winegarten, Renée. *The Double Life of George Sand: Woman and Writer.* New York: Basic Books, 1978.

Woehrlin, William. *Chernyshevskii: The Man and the Journalist.* Cambridge: Harvard University Press, 1971.

Wollstonecraft, Mary. *A Vindication of the Rights of Woman.* New York, 1833.

Yarmolinksy, Avrahm. *Turgenev: The Man, His Art and His Age.* New York: Orion, 1959.

Yedlin, Tova, ed. *Women in Eastern Europe and the Soviet Union.* New York: Praeger, 1980.

Zenkovsky, Vasilii V. *History of Russian Philosophy.* Translated by George L. Kline. New York: Columbia University Press, 1953.

————. *Russian Thinkers and Europe.* Translated by Galia S. Bodde. Ann Arbor, Mich.: J. W. Edwards, 1953.

Zernov, Nicolas. *Three Russian Prophets: Khomiakov, Dostoevsky, Soloviev.* London: S. C. M. Press, 1944.

Index

Adams, Henry Brooks, 142
Alexander II, 131, 134
America, 13, 60–61, 68, 70, 71
anatomy, 133
androgyny, 64–66, 68, 72–73, 143
Annenkov, Ivan, 22
aristocracy, 20, 77, 88, 90–91, 96–97, 102, 112, 114, 117, 125
Augustine, Saint, 142
Avdeev, Mikhail, 40, 128; *The Reef,* 40, 128

Bakunin, Mikhail, 23, 38, 129
Balfour, Clara, 132
Balzac, Honoré de, 13, 16–17, 24
Baudelaire, Charles, 142
Bazarov. *See* Turgenev
Beauvoir, Simone de: *The Second Sex,* 136, 138
Bebel, August: *Women and Socialism,* 134, 138
Belinskii, Vissarion, 22–23, 38, 55, 64, 86, 99
Bem, A. L., 86, 151n. 61
Berlin, Isaiah, 99, 101
Bernard, Claude, 89
Biblioteka dlya chteniya, 27, 40
birth control, 19–20
Bloom, Harold, 86
bluestocking, 140–41
Bogdanovich, Tatiana: *Love Among the People of the '60s,* 50
Bokovs, 43
Bolsheviks, 134, 144

Botkin, Sergei, 22
bourgeois, 38, 62, 119, 137–38
Brooks, Peter: *Reading for the Plot,* 15, 29, 14n. l, 15n. 11
Bulgarin, Faddei, 24
Bunina, Anna, 143, 145; *The Inexperienced Muse,* 143
Byron, George Gordon, Lord, 96, 116

Calvino, Italo, 13
canon, 142
Chaadaev, Pëtr, 96; "First Philosophical Letter," 96, 101
Chances, Ellen: *Conformity's Children: An Approach to the Superfluous Man in Literature,* 96–97
Chekhov, Anton, 25, 79, 136, 139–40
Chernyshevskii, Nikolai, 25, 48, 55, 98, 100, 128, 137–38, 144; *What is to be Done?,* 26, 48–63, 82, 105, 137, 140, 144
Chopin, Frederic, 24
Code of Russian Laws, 19
Commonwealth of Independent States, 144, 155n. 21
communism, 138, 144
conservatism, 24, 117
Consuelo, 43
Corke, Hilary, 35
Crimean War, 18, 130
crusade, 134

Dashkova, 145
Daudet, Alphonse, 78

171

Delphi, Christine: *Close to Home: A Materialist Analysis of Women's Oppression,* 137–38, 140

Dernière Aldini, La, 22, 151–52 n. 51

Dickens, Charles, 16, 55, 119

Dobroliubov, N. A., 77–79, 98, 137

Dostoevskii, Fëdor, 16, 22, 25, 83–92, 135, 139, 151–52 n. 61; Anna, 85; *The Brothers Karamazov,* 83–84, 89–92, 139; *Crime and Punishment,* 83–84, 87–89; *Diary of a Writer,* 84, 87, 128; *The Idiot,* 139; "The Landlady," 85; *Netochka Nezvanova,* 85

Druzhinin, Aleksandr, 22, 39, 40; *Polinka Saks,* 25, 38–42, 128

Dudevant, Aurore Dupin (pseud. George Sand), 147 n. 10

Dudevant, Casimir, 62–64, 67, 72, 74

Durova, Nadezhda, 142

education, 20, 62–63, 67, 72, 74, 84, 96, 98–99, 101–2, 110–13, 130–31, 133, 135, 139, 142

Eliot, George (Mary Ann Evans), 28, 141

Ellmann, Mary: *Thinking About Women,* 143

Fatherland Notes, 48, 134

Faust. See Goethe

feminism, 62 63, 65–66, 131–132, 134, 137, 140, 156 n. 6

Figaro, Le, 45

Filosofova, Anna, 131

Flaubert, Gustave, 43

Fourier, Charles, 23, 53, 98; "phalanstères," 98

François le Champi, 44

Franklin, Benjamin, 142

French Revolution, 66

Freud, Sigmund 29

Galatea, 73

Gan, Elena, Baroness (Zinaida R-va), 27, 28, 145; *The Ideal,* 27

gentry, 19–21, 27, 106

George Sandism ("Zhorzhzandism"), 14, 21, 24, 25, 28, 38, 99, 136, 145

German idealists, 38, 98

Girard, René: *Mensonge romantique et vérite romanesque,* 16, 93–94, 112

Glasgow, Janis, 59

Goethe, Johann Wolfgang von, 22, 142; *Faust,* 113

Gogol, Nicolai V.: *Dead Souls,* 20

Goncharov, Ivan, 16, 77, 135–36, 138; "Better Late than Never," 115; *A Common Story,* 96–97, 111–18; *Oblomov,* 40, 73–78, 82–83

Goncourts, 78

Gothic, 83, 113

Grech, N. I., 24

gynographs, 142

Halpérine-Kaminski, 45, 129

Heilbrun, Carolyn: *Toward a Recognition of Androgyny,* 15

Heldt, Barbara, 141, 144 – 45, 155 n. 20; *Terrible Perfection,* 137, 140 – 41, 146 n. 3

Hercourt, Eugénie d', 27

Herwegh, George, 43

Herzen, Aleksandr, 16, 22, 25, 48, 129, 135, 143, 153 n. 19; Natalia, 43, 105; *Who is to Blame?,* 39, 82, 96–97, 98–111, 128, 143

hippie, 132

Histoire de ma vie, L', 28

Hoffmann, E. T. A., 22

Horace, 13, 16, 28, 43–44, 48, 93–129, 152 n.4

Hugo, Victor, 16

Ibsen, Henrik, 66

Idealism, 98, 111–12, 115, 118, 126–27

Iglehart, Hallie, 64

Indiana, 24, 27, 28, 84

"institutka," 39, 42, 89

intelligentsia, 18–19, 22, 24, 49, 55, 96, 98–99, 102, 134–35

Iser, Wolfgang: *The Act of Reading,* 15, 29, 32–38

Iskra, 40

Jacques, 13, 24, 28, 29–63

James, Henry, 13, 17
Joan of Arc, 23
Journal des Débats, 44

KGB, 144
Kamuf, Peggy: *Fictions of Feminine Desire*, 31
Karenin, Vladimir, 25, 119, 124
Karp, Carole: "George Sand and the Russians," 97
Kellman, Steven G.: *Loving Reading: Erotics of the Text*, 15
Khomiakov, Alexei, 24
Khvoshchinskaia, Nadezhda D. (Vladimir Krestovskii), 28, 145
Kokhanovskaia, 145
Komarovich, V., 89
Korik, G., 138
Kovalevskaia, Sofia: *Memoirs*, 145
Krestovskii, Vladimir. *See* Khovshchinskaia, Nadezhda D.
Kropotkin, P. A., Prince, 79
Kuleshov, F. I., 86
Kundera, Milan: *Immortality*, 16

labor, 19, 98, 133, 138, 155n. 12, 155n. 21
Lecointre, Simone, 69
Lélia, 24, 28, 44
Lenin, Vladimir Ilych, 66, 100, 134
Lermontov, Mikhail: *A Hero of Our Time*, Pechorin, 96–97
Leroux, Pierre: *L'encyclopédie nouvelle*, 22, 41
Lomonosov, Mikhail, 130
Lucrézia Floriani, 24, 151–52n. 61
Lyngstad, Alexandra and Sverre, 112, 118

Machiavellian, 24
"mal du siècle," 39
Malia, Martin, 101; *Aleksandr Herzen and the Birth of Russian Socialism*, 99
marriage, 13, 19–21, 24–28, 30–31, 36–39, 42, 49–54, 56, 58–59, 61, 65, 71, 99–101, 107, 109, 133, 135–36, 138–39

Marx, Karl, 133
Masaryk, T. G., 139
Mauprat, 13, 24, 26, 28, 40, 44–45, 64–92, 151–52n. 61
men of the forties, 38, 44
Michelet, Jules, 26
Mikhailov, Mikhail L., 26, 43, 66, 79
Mill, John Stuart, 142
Mirskii, D. S., Prince: *History of Russian Literature*, 23
misogyny, 19. *See also* Michelet; Proudhon
Muscovite, The, 28
Musset, Alfred de: *Les caprices de Marianne*, 59
mystico–socialism, 99

Naginski, Isabelle, 86, 143; *George Sand: Writing for Her Life*, 142–43
Napoléon Bonaparte, 46, 142
Nekrasov, Nikolai, 43, 136
New Christianity. *See* Saint-Simon
New Times (Novoe Vremia), 45
New Woman, 64–92, 105, 133
News, The (Vest'), 132
Nicholas I, 131
nihilist, 62, 131–33, 141
Notes of a Hunter, 44–45

Ogarevs, 43
Onegin. *See* Pushkin
Ostrovskii, Alexander, 135

Panaev, Ivan, 22, 43
Pascal, Blaise, 13
Pavlova, Karolina: *A Double Life*, 144
peasantry, 19, 21, 44–45, 133–34
Pechorin. *See* Lermontov
Perovskaia, Sophie, 79
Peter the Great, 20
Pirogov, N. I., 27; "Questions of Life," 130
Pisarev, D. I., 27, 77, 97
Pisemskii, Alexei, 40
phalansteries, 132. *See also* Fourier
phallocentrism, 143
Philarète, 17

Pluksh, P., 138
Populist movement, 21, 134
Pritchett, V. S., 78
progressive, 54–55, 58–59, 62, 105, 132,
    134–35
proletariat, 133–34
prostitution, 26, 131, 139
Proudhon, P. J., 26
Pushkin, Alexander, 21, 22, 136, 138–39,
    147n. 12; *Eugene Onegin*, 96–97, 113,
    115, 136; Tatiana, 105, 113, 129, 136,
    139; *Roslavlev*, 136
Pygmalion, 73
Pyramus (and Thisbe), 69

R-va, Zinaida. *See* Gan, Baroness Elena
Radcliffe, Ann, 16
radical: French, 99; Russian, 62, 77–78,
    100, 102, 131–34; Western Euro-
    pean, 133
"raznochinets," 62, 106
Realism, 16, 23, 96, 115
republicanism, 68, 117
Revue indépendante, La, 91
"roman-feuilleton," 84, 88
"romans champêtres," 44
Romanticism, 30, 50, 93, 96, 110–11,
    114–16, 118
Rosen, Nathan: "Chaos and
    Dostoevskii's Women," 88
Rostopchina, Countess Evdokia, 28, 145;
    The Duel, 28; *The Happy Woman*, 28
Rousseau, Jean-Jacques, 16, 110, 142
Rousset, Jean: *Forme et Signification*, 30
Russ, Joanna: "How to Suppress
    Women's Writing," 142
Russian Orthodoxy, 20, 86, 97
Russian Revolution, 66, 138
Russo-Turkish war, 79

Saint-Simon, Claude Henri, comte, 23,
    48, 98, 100; New Christianity, 98,
    100
Sand, George (references to in Russian
    fiction), 55, 61
Schiller, J. C. F. von, 22, 65, 86
Schor, Naomi, 70

Schreiner, Olive, 29
Scott, Walter, 16, 22
Sechenov, 43
serfdom, 19, 21, 101, 131, 134
Seylaz, Jean Luc, 31
Shelnugov, 140
Shelnugova, L. P., 43, 79
Shuvalov, I., 130
Skaftymov, A., 49
Slavophiles, 86, 112
social democracy, 133
socialism, 22, 25–26, 48, 55, 63–66, 86,
    99, 134, 137
Soviet, 48, 86, 100, 137, 144–45
Spiridion, 22, 85, 99
Stankevich circle, 129
Starchevskii, 39–40
Stavosa, Anna, 131
Steno, 44
Stillman, Beatrice, 145
Strakhov, Nikolai, 24
suicide, 35–37, 39, 55, 60–61, 83, 88, 91,
    117, 139
Sumtsov, M., 44
superfluous man, 16, 46, 73, 93–129, 135,
    137–38
Suslova, Nadezhda, 141
Suvarin, Alexei, 45

Tanner, Tony: *Adultery in the Novel:
    Contract and Transgression*, 14
terrorism, 79, 134
Time, 40
Tolstoi, Leo, 24, 25, 79, 135–36, 138–39;
    Anna Karenina, 20, 138–39
Trubnikova, Maria, 131
tsardom, 19, 21, 23, 55, 131
Tur, Evgenia, 21, 28, 145; *The Mistake*, 28
Turgenev, Ivan, 16, 25, 40, 42–48, 77–
    83, 118–29, 132, 135–36, 138, 140,
    143; *Fathers and Children* and Bazarov,
    97, 132; "Iakov Pasynkov," 42–48;
    On the Eve, 40, 44, 77–83, 143; *Smoke*,
    25; *Rudin*, 82, 96–97, 118–29, 143

utilitarian, 50, 54
utopia (socialist), 24, 55, 64–65, 98, 134

Valentine, 24
Venice, 59, 77, 81
Vernadskaia, Maria, 141
Viardot, Pauline, 21, 43–44
Vodozova, E., 41; *At the Dawn of Life*, 41
Voss, Norine: "Saying the Unsayable: An Introduction to Women's Autobiography," 142
Vrevskaia, Iulia Petrovna, Baroness, 79

Waddington, Patrick: *Turgenev and George Sand: An Improbable Entente*, 98
Weidlé, Vladimir: *Russia: Absent and Present*, 16, 146n. 7, 146n. 9, 146n. 10

Weil, Simone, 64
Weinstein, Arnold: *Fiction of Relationship*, 14
Western Scientism, 89
Westernizers, 86, 112
Woolf, Virginia: *A Room of One's Own*, 18
"Woman Question" *(Zhenskii vopros)*, 14, 18–21, 26–28, 79, 104, 130–31, 133–35, 138–41, 144, 147n. 29, 152n. 12
Writer's Union, 144

Zazulich, Vera, 79
Zhadovskaia, 145
"Zhorzhzandism." *See* George Sandism